THE
NEUROPSYCHOLOGY
OF LANGUAGE

THE NEUROPSYCHOLOGY OF LANGUAGE

Essays in Honor of Eric Lenneberg

Edited by

R. W. Rieber

John Jay College, C.U.N.Y.
and
Columbia University College of Physicians and Surgeons
New York, New York

PLENUM PRESS · NEW YORK AND LONDON

Library of Congress Cataloging in Publication Data

Main entry under title:

The Neuropsychology of language.

Includes bibliographies and index.
1. Languages – Psychology – Addresses, essays, lectures. 2. Speech, Disorders of – Addresses, essays, lectures. 3. Lenneberg, Eric H. I. Lenneberg, Eric H. II. Rieber, Robert W. [DNLM: 1. Psycholinguistics. 2. Language disorders. 3. Speech disorders. WL340 N494]
BF455.N47   612'.78   76-44370
ISBN 0-306-30972-6

© 1976 Plenum Press, New York
A Division of Plenum Publishing Corporation
227 West 17th Street, New York, N.Y. 10011

Printed in the United States of America

CONTRIBUTORS

Robert S. April, Department of Neurology, New York Medical College, Center for Chronic Disease, Roosevelt Island, New York

Felix Barroso, Department of Psychiatry, SUNY at Downstate Medical Center, Brooklyn, New York

Eric R. Brown, New York University, New York, New York

Jason W. Brown, New York University Medical Center, New York, New York

Noam Chomsky, Massachusetts Institute of Technology, Cambridge, Massachusetts

Barbara Harris, Allen Memorial Institute, Montreal, Canada

Marcel Kinsbourne, Hospital for Sick Children, Toronto, Canada

Helen J. Neville, Department of Neurosciences, A-012, University of California at San Diego, La Jolla, California

R. W. Rieber, John Jay College, CUNY, New York, New York; and Columbia University, College of Physicians and Surgeons, New York, New York

Ola A. Selnes, Department of Psychology, University of Rochester, Rochester, New York

Neil Smith, John Jay College, CUNY, New York, New York

Robert W. Thatcher, Brain Research Labs, New York Medical College, New York, New York

Harry A. Whitaker, Department of Psychology, University of Rochester, Rochester, New York

PREFACE

The essays in this volume have been gathered together to honor Eric H. Lenneberg. Together they represent the broad range of topics in which he took some interest. For one of the distinguishing features of Eric Lenneberg's theoretical work was its synthesizing quality. He was interested in all of the scientific domains that might touch on the study of the mind and brain, and he carefully prepared himself in each of the pertinent disciplines. Beginning with his M.A. degree in linguistics from the University of Chicago in 1951, he went on to complete his doctoral studies in both linguistics and psychology at Harvard in 1955. This was followed by three years of postdoctoral specialization at Harvard Medical School in both neurology and children's developmental disorders. This preparation and additional experience at the Children's Hospital Medical Center in Boston led directly to his now-classic monograph on the neuropsychology of language, *The Biological Foundations of Language,* which was published in 1967.

It is interesting to note that while each of the essays grows out of empirical evidence, all without exception attempt to attain a level of theoretical explanation and generalization which is frequently missing from experimental work per se. Here again Lenneberg's work was notable for the vigor with which he sought out explanations and theories from neuropsychological data. In particular, his thesis that "language is the manifestation of species-specific cognitive propensities" was a hypothesis which he drew from necessarily indirect evidence. Human neuropsychology studies the neurologically impaired population for whatever insight such study may offer into the normally functioning higher cortical processes. As Lenneberg often said, such generalizations are possible because pathology never adds complexity to brain function. Whatever the liabilities of this evidence, it did not deter Lenneberg from theorizing about the biological constraints that appear to guide normal language development. His concept of a critical period for language is at present the most widely discussed aspect of this theory.

Lenneberg also symbolizes a continuity in the European tradition of a more organic, holistic theory of the brain. Jackson and Goldstein are more clearly his predecessors than their American counterparts in neurology. Lenneberg's life in a sense reflects this bridging of European and American traditions. Born in Düsseldorf, Germany, in 1921, the son of a physician, he spent his formative years experiencing the intellectual and artistic life of that community. However, in the early thirties, when Lenneberg was 12 years of age, the family was forced to emigrate to Brazil, where he remained until 1945. It was only then, when he came to the United States, that he was able to begin his formal studies in higher education. Later, he was to participate in the intense theoretical climate of Harvard in the mid-fifties when the distinguished American linguist Noam Chomsky was developing many of his ideas. All of this, it could be argued, led to Lenneberg's interest in the biological and theoretical substrata of language and the brain.

There are many theoretical differences that separate the contributors to this volume—both from each other and from the particular conception of neuropsychology propounded by Lenneberg. However, all would undoubtedly agree that Lenneberg's theoretical contribution to the field has been substantial and probably of lasting value. And, as Chomsky notes in the closing section of his essay, what unites the group is the belief that "the study of the biological basis for human language capacities may prove to be one of the most exciting frontiers of science in coming years."

New York   *Eric Brown and R. W. Rieber*

CONTENTS

Noam Chomsky

ON THE BIOLOGICAL BASIS OF LANGUAGE CAPACITIES

My title, of course, is taken from Eric Lenneberg's major study of language and biology, now recognized as a classic in the field (Lenneberg, 1967, pp. 393–394). He set himself the task of studying lan guage as "an aspect of [man's] biological nature, to be studied in the same manner as, for instance, his anatomy." The purpose of this study was "to reinstate the concept of the biological basis of language capacities and to make the specific assumptions so explicit that they may be subjected to empirical tests." Adopting this point of view, we may regard the language capacity virtually as we would a physical organ of the body and can investigate the principles of its organization, functioning, and development in the individual and the species. Personally, I feel that this is just the right way to approach the study of human language. I would like to make a few remarks on the program that Lenneberg outlined and developed, concentrating on two theses that seem to me of particular significance.

In his concluding discussion, Lenneberg presented two important observations on the nature of the inquiry into language and biology. He noted in the first place that "the rules that underlie syntax (which are the same for understanding and speaking) are of a very specific kind, and unless man or mechanical devices do their processing of in-

Noam Chomsky · Massachusetts Institute of Technology, Cambridge, Massachusetts.

coming sentences in accordance with these rules, the logical, formal analysis of the input will be deficient, resulting in incorrect or random responses. When we say rules must have been built into the grammatical analyzer, we impute the existence of an apparatus with specific structural properties or, in other words, a specific internal organization."

He then observed that the fundamental question in the study of the biology of language is: "Just what is postulated to be innate in language behavior?" Evidently, "we must assume a biological matrix with specifiable characteristics that determines the outcome of any treatment to which the organism is subjected." The evidence, he argued, points "to great specificity of the underlying matrix." The "only thoroughly interesting problem" is to determine the range of possibilities that might be realized under given environmental conditions, this range evidently determined by the biological matrix. It is, he emphasized correctly, "entirely an empirical question"; there is no room for dogmatic preconceptions or *a priori* argument. Biology, he observed, "does no more than to discover how various forms are innately constituted, and this includes descriptions of a creature's reactions to environmental forces. Research into these reactions does not eventually free us from the postulation of innate features but merely elucidates the exact nature of innate constitutions. The discovery and description of innate mechanisms is a thoroughly empirical procedure and is an integral part of modern scientific inquiry."

When I met Eric Lenneberg as a graduate student, just 25 years ago, these basic concerns were beginning to take shape in his mind. He wanted to see the study of language assimilated to the natural sciences, and he devoted his subsequent efforts to placing language in its biological matrix. From the point of view he was to adopt, the study of systems of grammar is concerned with the "specific internal organization" and "specific structural properties" of an "apparatus" to which we "impute existence" as one component in the system of cognitive structures developed in the course of individual growth. What many linguists call "universal grammar" may be regarded as a theory of innate mechanisms, an underlying biological matrix that provides a framework within which the growth of language proceeds. There is no reason for the linguist to refrain from imputing existence to this initial apparatus of mind as well. Proposed principles of universal grammar may be regarded as an abstract partial specification of the genetic program that enables the child to interpret certain events as linguistic experience and to construct a system of rules and principles on the basis of this experience.

To put the matter in somewhat different but essentially equivalent terms, we may suppose that there is a fixed, genetically determined initial state of the mind, common to the species with at most minor variation apart from pathology. The mind passes through a sequence of states under the boundary conditions set by experience, achieving finally a "steady state" at a relatively fixed age, a state which then changes only in marginal ways. The initial state of the mind might be regarded as a function, characteristic of the species, which maps experience into the steady state. Universal grammar is a partial characterization of this function, thus a partial characterization of the initial state. The grammar of a language that has grown in the mind is a partial characterization of the steady state attained.

So viewed, linguistics is the abstract study of certain mechanisms, their growth and maturation. We may impute existence to the postulated structures at the initial, intermediate, and steady states in just the same sense as we impute existence to a program that we believe to be somehow represented in a computer or that we postulate to account for the mental representation of a three-dimensional object in the visual field. Evidence bearing on empirical hypotheses such as these might derive from many and varied sources. Ultimately, we hope to find evidence concerning the physical mechanisms that realize the program, and it is reasonable to expect that results obtained in the abstract study of the system and its operation should contribute significantly to this end (and in principle, conversely).

In the case of study of language the question is complicated in practice by the obvious fact that the system of language is only one of a number of cognitive systems that interact in the most intimate way in the actual use of language. When we speak or interpret what we hear, we bring to bear a vast set of background assumptions about the participants in the discourse, the subject matter under discussion, laws of nature, human institutions, and the like. Continuing to think of the system of grammatical rules as a kind of "mental organ," interacting with other mental organs with other functions and properties, we face a rather typical problem of natural science, namely, the problem of appropriate idealization and abstraction. In an effort to determine the nature of one of these interacting systems, we must abstract away from the contribution of others to the actual performance that can be observed. Steps taken in this direction are not without their hazards; they are also inescapable in rational inquiry. We therefore proceed to experiment with idealized systems, always bearing in mind the possibility that another approach might lead us closer to an understanding of the various systems that constitute the human mind.

There is much discussion in the literature of linguistics and psychology of the "psychological reality" of the linguist's constructions. I take it that the question at issue is whether it is legitimate to "impute existence" to the "apparatus," the properties of which are characterized by particular grammars or by universal grammar (which is of course not a grammar but rather a system of conditions on the range of possible grammars for possible human languages). The discussion of "psychological reality" sometimes seems to me to be rather misleading. Perhaps I can explain my misgivings by an analogy.

Consider the problem of determining the nature of the thermonuclear reactions that take place in the interior of the sun.* Suppose that available technique only permits astronomers to study the light emitted at the outermost layers of the sun. On the basis of the information thereby attained, they construct a theory of the hidden thermonuclear reactions, postulating that light elements are fused into heavier ones, converting mass into energy, thus producing the sun's heat. Suppose that an astronomer presents such a theory, citing the evidence that supports it. Suppose now that someone were to approach this astronomer with the following contention: True, you have presented a theory that explains the available evidence, but how do you know that the constructions of your theory have physical reality—in short, how do you know that your theory is true? The astronomer could only respond by repeating what he had already presented: Here is the evidence available and here is the theory that I offer to explain it. The evidence derives from investigation of light emitted at the periphery. We might want to place a laboratory inside the sun to obtain more direct evidence, but being unable to do so, we must test and confirm our theory indirectly. One might argue that the evidence is inconclusive or that the theory is objectionable on some physical (or, conceivably, methodological) grounds. But it is senseless to ask for some other kind of justification for attributing "physical reality" to the constructions of

* The analogy is modeled on an account given by Bahcall and Davis (1976).

the theory, apart from consideration of their adequacy in explaining the evidence and their conformity to the body of natural science, as currently understood. There can be no other grounds for attributing physical reality to the scientist's constructions.

Suppose now that an ingenious experimenter hits upon a more direct method for studying events taking place at the interior of the sun: namely, study of the neutrinos that are released by the assumed thermonuclear reactions in the solar interior and that escape into space. Using this new evidence, he may substantiate the old theory or construct a better one. Has this more "direct" investigation of events in the interior of the sun now answered the original objections? Are we now entitled to attribute "physical reality" to the constructions only postulated before? Not really. No empirical evidence can be conclusive. Again, we can only say that with our more direct and more conclusive evidence, we may now be more confident than before that the entities and events postulated are physically real—that the theoretical statements in which reference is made to these entities, processes, and so on are in fact true. But again, there is little sense to the contention that we still do not know that what is postulated is physically real, as if there were some further standard that might be achieved in some qualitatively different way. The enterprise in question is empirical science, not mathematics; we can at best settle on one of indefinitely many possible theories that account for crucial evidence, attributing physical reality to whatever is postulated in that theory.

Our investigation of the apparatus of the language faculty, whether in its initial or final steady state, bears some similarity to the investigation of thermonuclear reactions in the solar interior limited to evidence provided by light emitted at the periphery. We observe what people say and do, how they react and respond, often in situations contrived so that this behavior will provide some evidence (we hope) concerning the operative mechanisms. We then try, as best we can, to devise a theory of some depth and significance with regard to these mechanisms, testing our theory by its success in providing explanations for selected phenomena. Challenged to show that the constructions postulated in that theory have "psychological reality," we can do no more than repeat the evidence and the proposed explanations that involve these constructions. Or, like the astronomer dissatisfied with study of light emissions from the periphery of the sun, we can search for more conclusive evidence, always aware that in empirical inquiry we can at best support a theory against substantive alternatives and empirical challenge, not prove it to be true. It would be quite reasonable to argue against a claim for psychological reality—i.e., truth of a certain theory—on the grounds that the evidence is weak and susceptible to explanation in different terms; needless to say, the evidence that supports the linguist's constructions is incomparably less satisfying than that available to the physicist. But in essence the problems are the same, and the question of "psychological reality" no more and no less sensible in principle than the question of the "physical reality" of the physicist's theoretical constructions.

The literature takes a rather different view. Certain types of evidence are held to relate to psychological reality, specifically, evidence deriving from studies of reaction time, recognition, recall, etc. Other kinds of evidence are held to be of an entirely different nature, specifically, evidence deriving from informant judgments as to what sentences mean, whether they are well formed, and so on. Theoretical explanations advanced to explain evidence of the latter sort, it is commonly argued, have no claim to psychological reality, no matter how far-reaching, extensive, or persuasive the explanations may be, and no matter how firmly founded the observations offered as evidence. To merit the attribution of "psychological reality," the entities, rules, processes, components, etc. postulated in these explanatory theories must be confronted with evidence of the former category. If these theoretical constructions can be shown to play a role in the study of reaction time, etc., then perhaps we may attribute to them psychological reality. Note that what is apparently claimed is that there is some conceptual distinction between two kinds of theories based on the evidence advanced to support them, not a distinction based on the reliability of the evidence or the depth of the theories.

Let me illustrate with a concrete example, much simplified for the purposes of exposition. Suppose that we are concerned with the process of sentence-formation in colloquial English and we note that while some questions are judged to be well formed, others are not. Consider the sentence (1):

(1) Violins are easy to play sonatas on.

This sentence might, for example, be the answer to the question (2):

(2) What instruments are easy to play sonatas on?

But the sentence (1) is not a possible answer to the question (3):

(3) What kinds of music are violins easy to play on?

In fact, (3) is not a well-formed question at all. Corresponding to the sentence (1) we have such questions as (4) but not (5):

(4) What violins are easy to play sonatas on?
(5) What sonatas are violins easy to play on?

The distinction between (4) and (5) has been repeatedly noted in recent discussion; let us assume that careful inquiry shows it to be well-founded. Thus (5), like (3), is just not a well-formed question of colloquial English. The problem with (5) and (3) cannot be that the questioned term—*sonatas* in (1)—is too far toward the end of the sentence, or that it is within a verb phrase complement, or the like. Thus there is nothing wrong with the question (6) corresponding to (7) as (5) corresponds to (1):

(6) What sonatas did John want Bill to play on the violin?
(7) John wanted Bill to play sonatas on the violin.

Evidently, (6) conforms to the rules of English grammar, as these are represented somehow in our minds, in a way in which (5) does not. Many facts of this sort have been noticed in the literature of linguistics. Clearly, they call for explanation. If an interesting explanation is forthcoming, then these observations will have been demonstrated to be significant for the insight they provide into mental representations and the computations involving them.

Suppose now that someone were to advance the following explanation for the facts noted.* We know that *wh*-clauses are "islands" in the sense of Ross (1967); in particular, the rule of *wh*-movement that forms questions and relatives by moving such expressions as *who, what, what sonatas*, etc., to the left of a clause cannot be applied in general to a *wh*- expression within a *wh*-clause. For example, given the sentences (8) we cannot form the corresponding questions of (9), questioning *the book:*

(8) (a) We wondered [to whom John gave the book].
    (b) We found out [who wrote the book].
    (c) We did [what you asked us to do about the book].

---

* I think, incidentally, that the explanation outlined is essentially correct, but that does not matter with respect to the point at issue. For discussion, see Chomsky (1976b).

(9) (a) What book did we wonder to whom John gave?
    (b) What book did we find out who wrote?
    (c) What book did we do what you asked us to do about?

In sentences comparable to (8) but without the bracketed *wh*-clause, the phrase *the book* is accessible to the *wh*-movement rule forming questions; compare (9′):

(9′) (a) What book did we say that John gave to Bill?
    (b) What book did we find out that John wrote?
    (c) What book did we ask you to tell Bill to do something about?

From such examples, we might conclude that expressions that lie within *wh*-clauses, such as those bracketed in (8), are not accessible to the rule of question-formation. More generally, *wh*-clauses are "islands," immune to such rules as *wh*-movement. The explanation for this and other island phenomena lies in still deeper properties of rules of grammar, I believe, but we may put this matter aside for now.

    Returning to sentence (1), suppose that the expression *to play sonatas on* in (1) is the residue of a *wh*-clause in the mental computation by which (1) is formed, in particular, the same clause that appears as an infinitival relative in (10), analogous to the finite relative in (11):

(10) I found [$_{NP}$ a violin [$_S$ to play sonatas on]].*
(11) I found [$_{NP}$ a violin [$_S$ that you can play sonatas on]].

Suppose, in other words, that we postulate that there really is a *wh*-clause, perhaps the clause represented as in (12), at the stage of computation at which *wh*-movement applies to give ultimately the sentence (5):

(12) [$_S$ which for PRO to play sonatas on *t*].†

---

* Assume here a conventional representation of phrase-markers, with a string between paired brackets assigned to the category labeling the bracket. Thus in (10) the phrase *to play sonatas on* is categorized as an S (sentence); *a violin to play sonatas on* as an NP (noun phrase); etc. Other bracketing is omitted here and below for simplicity of exposition.

† Take *t* to be the "trace" left by movement of *which* from the position where *t* appears in (12), in accordance with the trace theory of movement rules; cf. Chomsky (1975a, 1976a), and references cited there. Take PRO to be an abstract "pronominal" form, which can in fact be regarded as an "uncontrolled trace"; cf. Chomsky (1976b) for discussion.

Then the rule of question-formation cannot apply to the phrase *sonatas*, just as it cannot apply to the phrase *the book* in (8), and for the same reason: Application is blocked by the *wh*-clause island constraint, and ultimately, by the deeper properties of grammar from which this constraint derives.

Tentatively accepting this explanation, we impute existence to certain mental representations and to the mental computations that apply in a specific way to these mental representations. In particular, we impute existence to a representation in which (12) appears as part of the structure underlying (5) at a particular stage of derivation, and to the mental computation that produces this derivation, and ultimately produces (5), identified now as ungrammatical because the computation violates the *wh*-island constraint when the rule of *wh*-movement applies to *sonatas* in (12). We attribute "psychological reality" to the postulated representations and mental computations. In short, we propose (tentatively, hesitantly, etc.) that our theory is true. Have we gone beyond the bounds of what is legitimate and proper, in so doing?

I think not. Granting the vast differences in the nature of the evidence, the depth and explanatory power of the postulated principles, etc., still the argument sketched seems to me analogous in the relevant respects to that of the physicist postulating certain processes in the interior of the sun. Of course, there are differences; the physicist is actually postulating physical entities and processes, while we are keeping to abstract conditions that unknown mechanisms must meet. We might go on to suggest actual mechanisms, but we know that it would be pointless to do so in the present stage of our ignorance concerning the functioning of the brain. This, however, is not a relevant difference of principle. If we were able to investigate humans as we study other, defenseless organisms, we might very well proceed to inquire into the operative mechanisms by intrusive experimentation, by constructing controlled conditions for language growth, and so on, thus perhaps narrowing the gap between the language example and the astronomical example. The barriers to this direct investigation are ethical. We must be satisfied with quite indirect evidence, but no particular philosophical problems arise from this contingency, just as no such problems arise in the case of the astronomer limited to investigation of light emissions from the sun's periphery as compared with the astronomer studying neutrinos escaping from the solar interior.

There are many questions that may legitimately be raised about the hypothetical explanation that I have briefly outlined. Thus one might ask how firm is the evidence, and how well supported independently are the principles on which the explanation is based. Let us examine these questions.

Consider first the question of the nature of the evidence. There is no reason why we cannot proceed to test and refine the initial judgments of well-formedness for colloquial English. For example, we might devise experimental tests of acceptability, and if these tests met appropriate empirical conditions, we might decide to rely on these tests to determine the adequacy of the judgments to which we have appealed here, recognizing, however, that "well-formedness" is a theoretical concept for which we cannot expect to find a precise set of necessary and sufficient operational criteria, a fact of no great moment in itself. Notice that it is a trivial point, though one often overlooked, that any test of acceptability must itself meet certain empirical conditions, just as an explanatory theory must meet such conditions (cf. Chomsky, 1964, for some comments). Some linguists have been bemused by the fact that the conditions that test the test are themselves subject to doubt and revision, believing that they have discovered some hidden paradox or circularity of reasoning (cf. Botha, 1973; Ney, 1975). In fact, they have simply rediscovered the fact that linguistics is not mathematics but rather a branch of empirical inquiry. Even if we were to grant that there is some set of observation sentences that constitute the bedrock of inquiry, immune to challenge, it nevertheless remains true that theory must be invoked to determine to what, if anything, these pure and perfect observations attest, and here there is no Cartesian ground of certainty. All of this is, or should be, obvious. Many argue that the problems of empirical uncertainty can be overcome by restricting attention to a corpus, and some (e.g., Ney) seem to believe that this has been the practice of traditional grammar. That is untrue. A corpus may contain examples of deviant or ungrammatical sentences, and any rational linguist will recognize the problem and try to assign to observed examples their proper status. Futhermore, any serious work on language uses "elicited" material, often "self-elicited," as, e.g., in Jespersen's classic works and other work that deserves serious attention. And insofar as a corpus is used as a source of illustrative examples, we rely on the same intuitive judgments to select examples as in devising relevant examples with the aid of an informant (or oneself). Restriction of grammatical analysis to a real corpus would be about as sensible as restriction of physics or biology to motion pictures of events happening about us in our normal lives.*

To consider what appears to be a more productive (as well as intellectually far more interesting) approach, we may turn to the second of the two questions raised above and try to put the principles used in the explanation to independent empirical test. One way to approach this question is by trying to explain the *wh*-clause island constraint itself in terms of deeper principles of grammar that have other consequences, thus opening the proposed explanation to a broader empirical challenge. Or, we may try to find other evidence bearing on the postulated analysis of (1), with the underlying mental representation including (12) and the mental computation postulated (cf. Chomsky, 1976b, for discussion).

Suppose that both of these approaches prove eminently successful. Thus we establish the reliability of the judgments and give substantial independent evidence for the theoretical constructions, showing that the postulated principles explain many other facts of a similar nature, withstand empirical test in English and other languages, etc. Would we then have provided evidence for the psychological reality of the mental representations and mental computations postulated? If I read the literature correctly, many would still reject this conclusion, arguing that something else is needed to carry us over that qualitative barrier of principle that distinguishes purely hypothetical constructions from others to which we may properly attribute "psychological reality."

Suppose now that someone were to devise an experiment to test for the presence of a *wh*-clause in underlying representations—let us say, a recognition or recall experiment. Or let us really let down the bars of imagination and suppose that someone were to discover a cer-

---

* To avoid a possible confusion, recall here that we are considering the problem of discovery of linguistic theory and of particular grammar, two enterprises that go hand in hand. Given a linguistic theory, it should be possible for the grammar to be determined merely from the kind of primary linguistic data available to the child. If linguistic theory (universal grammar) is regarded along the lines sketched above, as a function mapping experience into the final state attained, then linguistic theory must provide a "discovery procedure" for grammar from a corpus (along with whatever else is essential for the language learner). Each child provides an existence proof. For discussion and an outline of a possible theory of this general sort, see Chomsky (1955/1975c).

tain pattern of electrical activity in the brain that correlated in clear cases with the presence of *wh*-clauses: relative clauses (finite and infinitival) and *wh*-questions (direct and indirect). Suppose that this pattern of electrical activity is observed when a person speaks or understands (1). Would we now have evidence for the psychological reality of the postulated mental representations?

We would now have a new kind of evidence, but I see no merit to the contention that this new evidence bears on psychological reality whereas the old evidence only related to hypothetical constructions. The new evidence might or might not be more persuasive than the old; that depends on its character and reliability, the degree to which the principles dealing with this evidence are tenable, intelligible, compelling, and so on. In the real world of actual research on language, it would be fair to say, I think, that principles based on evidence derived from informant judgment have proven to be deeper and more revealing than those based on evidence derived from experiments on processing and the like, but the future may be different in this regard. If we accept—as I do—Lenneberg's contention that the rules of grammar enter into the processing mechanisms, then evidence concerning production, recognition, recall, and language use in general can be expected (in principle) to have bearing on the investigation of rules of grammar, on what is sometimes called "linguistic competence" or "knowledge of language." But such evidence, where it is forthcoming, has no privileged character and does not bear on psychological reality in some unique way. Evidence is not subdivided into two categories: evidence that bears on reality and evidence that just confirms or refutes theories (about mental computation and mental representations, in this case). Some evidence may bear on process models that incorporate a characterization of linguistic competence, while other evidence seems to bear on competence more directly, in abstraction from conditions of language use. And, of course, one can try to use data in other ways. But just as a body of data does not come bearing its explanation on its sleeve, so it does not come marked "for confirming theories" or "for establishing reality."

It is not uncommon to draw a line separating the two disciplines, linguistics and psychology, in terms of the kinds of evidence they prefer to use and the specific focus of their attention. Thus, linguistics is the field that relies on informant judgments, eliciting, whatever limited use can be made of an actual corpus, and so on, to try to determine the nature of grammar and universal grammar. Its concern is competence, the system of rules and principles that we assume have in some manner been internally represented by the person who knows a language and that enable the speaker in principle to understand an arbitrary sentence and to produce a sentence expressing his thought; and universal grammar, the principles that specify the range of possible human grammars. Psychology, in contrast, is concerned with performance, not competence; its concern is the processes of production, interpretation, and the like, which make use of the knowledge attained, and the processes by which transition takes place from the initial to the final state.

To me, this distinction has always seemed quite senseless. Delineation of disciplines may be useful for administering universities or organizing professional societies, but apart from that, it is an undertaking of limited merit. A person who happens to be interested in underlying competence will naturally be delighted to exploit whatever understanding may be forthcoming about process models that incorporate one or another set of assumptions about linguistic knowledge. Futhermore, it seems evident that investigation of performance will rely, to whatever extent it can, on what is learned about the systems of knowledge that are put to use. The theory of particular and universal grammar, so far as I can see, can only be sensibly regarded as that aspect of theoretical psychology that is primarily concerned with the genetically determined program that specifies the range of possible grammars for human languages and the particular realizations of this schematism that arise under given conditions. One may perfectly well choose to study language and grammar with other purposes in mind and without concern for these questions, but any significant results obtained will nevertheless be a contribution to this branch of psychology. I take it that this is one major point that Lenneberg was putting forth in his work. It seems to me entirely correct.

Not everyone agrees, or so a literal reading might suggest. It is illuminating to see how opposing views are put in the literature. In one recent text on cognitive psychology, Kintsch, Crothers, Glass, Keenan, McCoon, and Monk (1974) argue that the "strict separation" between competence and performance "permits the linguist to deal with convenient abstractions, uninhibited by psychological reality, and it provides the psychologist with the facetious argument that linguistic theories have nothing to do with processes anyway. As long as linguistic theory is strictly a competence theory, it is of no interest to the psychologist. Indeed I doubt that it should be of much interest to linguists either, but that is for them to decide" (Chap. 1).

These remarks, which are not untypical, reflect deep-seated confusions. The approach that Kintsch criticizes, as his references make clear, is the one outlined above: the approach based on the assumption that a person's knowledge of language can properly be represented as a system of rules of grammar, and that process models concerned with language use will incorporate such representations of linguistic competence. On this assumption, which is of course not God-given but must be evaluated in terms of its empirical consequences, the goal of the investigator will be to determine the nature of the competence system that expresses what it is that the mature speaker knows, and to develop process models that show how this knowledge is put to use.

Kintsch asserts that study of the abstracted competence system is "uninhibited by psychological reality"; only processes have "reality." Someone who lacks his special insight into what is real will have to retreat to normal scientific practice, imputing existence, subject to verification and test, to whatever structures and processes are postulated in the effort to explain significant facts. The enterprise is not "uninhibited by psychological reality," but is rather concerned with specific aspects of psychological reality. Kintsch's psychologist has "no interest" in explanatory theories, no matter how far-reaching and well confirmed, dealing with these aspects of knowledge of language and the basis for its acquisition (particular and universal grammar). In short, fundamental questions of cognitive psychology are to be excluded from the concern of the psychologist (or for Kintsch, the concern of anyone). Note that these positions are taken on purely *a priori* grounds, not on the basis of alleged empirical or conceptual inadequacies of the approach he rejects as compared with some alternative. It is difficult to imagine comparable dogmatism in the natural sciences.

Kintsch's psychologist not only declares his lack of interest in this central domain of human psychology; he decides, *a priori*, that a characterization of the system of knowledge attained can be of no relevance for investigation of the process models to which he limits his attention. Note that this is what a literal reading of Kintsch's remarks implies, for if indeed the study of competence models along the lines he rejects (namely, those outlined above) were to bring to light a system embedded in processing models in the way that Lenneberg (and others) propose, then clearly results attained in this study would be of great relevance for the investigation of process models. Again, such astonishing dogmatism about matters so poorly understood can hardly be imagined in the natural sciences. One might put forth a rational hypothesis that perhaps expresses what Kintsch has in mind: namely, one might propose that once process models are developed we will find that all relevant facts are explained without any abstraction to a rule system that articulates the speaker-hearer's knowledge of his language. This thesis might prove correct. To reject it out of hand would be as irrational as Kintsch's dogmatic stand. But the dogmatic insistence that it must be correct and that alternatives must be discarded on *a priori* grounds, as a literal reading of Kintsch's remarks implies, is simply a reflection of the irrationality that has hampered investigation in the human sciences for many, many years.

Note that the "strict separation" between competence and performance that Kintsch deplores is a conceptual distinction; knowledge of language is distinguished from behavior (use of this knowledge). This conceptual distinction is surely quite "strict," though one might argue that a different conceptual framework would be preferable. In fact, Kintsch adopts throughout the conceptual distinction that he believes he rejects, where his discussion is coherent.* The main concern of his book is "the study of the properties" of a certain "level of representation in memory, both theoretically and empirically," namely, representation of a sentence "conceptually in terms of its meaning," which he takes to be a "propositional" representation. This is the study of a certain aspect of linguistic competence. Kintsch simply presupposes some system of rules that generates the representations he postulates, in particular cases. And like everyone else, Kintsch tries to gain some understanding of this "level of representation" through the study of performance and tries to show how it figures in process models. In short, while Kintsch believes that his approach "has no use at all for the competence-performance distinction," in fact, he invokes it in

---

* It often is not. As one of many examples, consider the discussion of definite and indefinite description on p. 48, or the account of quantificational structure a few pages later. But where the discussion is coherent, it makes use of representations of the sort assumed in one or another competence model, and develops the kinds of arguments that might be used in connection with representations of linguistic competence and the process systems in which they find their place.

pretty much the conventional way. This is not surprising, given that no coherent alternative framework of concepts has been proposed in this domain, to my knowledge.

My remarks so far have been directed to the first of the two conclusions cited from Lenneberg's study of the biology of language. Let me now turn to the second, namely, his conclusion that "the discovery and description of innate mechanisms is a thoroughly empirical procedure and is an integral part of modern scientific inquiry." The study of innate mechanisms leads us to universal grammar, but also, of course, to investigation of the biologically determined principles that underlie language use, what has sometimes been called "pragmatic competence," and cognitive structures of other sorts that enter into the actual use of language.

In drawing his conclusions concerning the investigation of innate mechanisms, Lenneberg felt that it was necessary to emphasize the empirical nature of this research because "there was a time when 'innateness' was on the index of forbidden concepts," and "there are still many scientists who regard the postulation of anything innate as a clever parlor trick that alleviates the proponent from performing 'truly scientific' investigations," a position, he noted, that "is odd to say the least," but one that has had and in fact still retains quite a grip on the modern imagination.

It is easy to illustrate the persistence, to this day, of serious qualms concerning explanations that rely on postulated innate mechanisms, though I entirely agree with Lenneberg that these reservations are "odd to say the least." Of course, specific proposals may be open to all sorts of legitimate objections. But I am referring now rather to the commonly expressed belief that there is some objection in principle to such an approach. Such objections have been expressed in an extreme form by a number of philosophers. I have argued elsewhere that their objections are groundless, and will have nothing to say about this here.* Similar doctrines sometimes appear in the linguistic literature as well (e.g., Peizer and Olmsted, 1969, note 1), also, to my knowledge, without valid supporting argument.

Appeal to innate mechanisms is also regarded with great suspicion by many psychologists, and not—contrary to widespread belief— only those who regard themselves as "behaviorists," whatever that

* For detailed discussion of the views of several contemporary philosophers, see Chomsky (1968, 1975a), and references cited there.

designation may mean today, if anything. Consider, for example, the objections raised by Piaget and his colleagues. Piaget argues that the postulated innate mechanisms are "biologically inexplicable" and that what can be explained on the assumption of fixed innate structures can be explained as well as "the 'necessary' results of constructions of sensorimotor intelligence . . ." (Plaget, 1975). However, he offers no argument at all that the postulated mechanisms are any more "inexplicable" than mechanisms postulated to account for physical development; indeed, even the most radical "innatists" have suggested mechanisms that would add only a small increment to what any rational biologist would assume must be genetically determined. Piaget's complaint would be correct if he had said "biologically unexplained" instead of "biologically inexplicable," but then the same might be said about the current theory of development of physical organs of the body. As for Piaget's further claim that the facts for which an explanation has been offered in terms of a postulated genetically determined universal grammar can also be explained as the "necessary" results of constructions of sensorimotor intelligence, I will only say the obvious: The literature contains no evidence or argument to support this remarkable factual claim, nor even any explanation of what sense it might have. Again, we see here an instance of the unfortunate but rather common dogmatic insistence on unsupported factual doctrines in the human sciences.

The same doctrine is advanced by Piaget's colleagues. Consider, for example, the discussion of this point by Inhelder, Sinclair, and Bovet (1974, p. 8). Citing Piaget, they put forth "the basic hypothesis of developmental constructivism," which "postulates that no human knowledge, with the obvious exception of the very elementary hereditary forms, is preformed in the structures of either the subject or the object." In particular, they reject the hypothesis that certain principles of language structure (and other cognitive structures) are "not only present at an extremely early age, but hereditary." * The postulated principles, they insist, are not "preformed" (i.e., governed by geneti-

---

* Inhelder et al. attribute to "rationalist psycho-linguists" the view that "linguistic competence" and "cognitive structure" are hereditary. Presumably by 'linguistic competence" they mean what these psycholinguists call "universal grammar." Surely no one holds 'linguistic competence"—e.g., knowledge of English—to be hereditary. Similar remarks may be made about cognitive structure. What has been proposed is that specific properties or conditions on cognitive structures attained are hereditary.

cally determined factors) but rather arise through the child's activity, and are explained by "regulatory or autoregulatory mechanisms." These are, however, described in terms so vague that it is hard to know what is intended. Taking the hypothesis of "developmental constructivism" literally, they are claiming that such principles as the *wh*-island constraint, or the deeper principles from which it derives, must arise on the basis of the same kinds of principles that account for the child's early sensorimotor constructions and the like. While one cannot dismiss this contention out of hand, it seems a most astonishing claim and surely is backed by no argument or evidence.

The persistence of such empirical claims in the absence of any argument or even an intelligible formulation can perhaps be explained in terms of another doctrine of the Geneva school. Thus, Inhelder *et al.* "agree with Piaget" that the approach they attribute to neonativists "does not help to solve any problem; all it does is to transfer the question from the psychological to the biological level by formulating it in terms of biological development." If this argument had any merit, it would apply as well to standard accounts of physical development. Suppose that someone postulates that binocular vision or the fact that we grow arms instead of wings is genetically determined. By the argument of the Geneva school, this assumption "does not help to solve any problem," but only transfers the question from the psychological to the biological level.

Plainly, no one would take this argument seriously, nor would the Geneva psychologists advance it in the case of physical development. If the general structure of binocular vision (etc.) is genetically determined, then naturally we must seek to explain its origin in terms of biological (evolutionary) development rather than in terms of learning. In short, we must "transfer the question [of development] from the psychological to the biological level." Exactly the same is true when we turn to cognitive structures or the (unknown) physical mechanisms that underlie them. If, say, we find extensive evidence that the *wh*-island constraint or the principles that underlie it belong to universal grammar and are available to the language learner without relevant experience, then it would only be rational to suppose that these mechanisms are genetically determined and to search for a further account in terms of biological development. The Geneva school doctrine seems to be that no matter how substantial the evidence in favor of such a thesis may be, and no matter how weak the argument for ontogenetic development, nevertheless we must maintain the thesis that the principles in question are derived by "regulatory or autoregulatory mechanisms" in accordance with the hypothesis of "developmental constructivism." At least, I see no other way to read their proposals, since the arguments they put forth are in no way empirical but rather purely *a priori*. All of this again simply seems to constitute a chapter in the history of dogmatism.

Notice that I do not suggest that the Piagetians cannot be correct in their contentions. Rather, I ask why they insist that they must be right, whatever the evidence seems to show, and why they propose arguments in the case of mental development of a sort that they would never accept in the case of physical growth of organs. Why, in short, must the normal procedures and assumptions of scientific inquiry—in particular, its open-mindedness—be abandoned, when we turn to cognitive structures and their development?

To mention one last case, consider the recent critique of "nativist" linguistics and psycholinguistics by the distinguished Russian neuropsychologist A. R. Luria (1975). He insists that the natural place to seek the origin of principles of universal grammar * say, the *wh*-island constraint, to make the discussion concrete—is "in the history of our society and in the active forms of man's relations with reality." Just how the principles of universal grammar might arise in this way, Luria does not tell us, even in the most vague and hypothetical way. Rather, like Piaget and others he offers a purely methodological argument. The assumption that certain principles of universal grammar are genetically determined, he asserts, "makes a postulate out of a problem and this in itself means that all further study in the area can lead us nowhere."

Once again, if this *a priori* argument were valid, then it would hold as well for the development of physical organs; that is, it would show that the hypothesis that the growth of arms rather than wings is genetically determined makes a postulate out of a problem and guarantees that further inquiry will lead us nowhere. Since Luria would obviously not accept this conclusion, we are left with only one way of interpreting his argument: Cognitive development must, on *a priori* grounds, be fundamentally different from physical development in

---

* Throughout the discussion, Luria mistakenly identifies "universal grammar" and "deep structure." There are other misinterpretations of this sort, but they are easily corrected. The point he is making is clear.

that it has no genetic component. It is an *a priori* truth that cognitive development is "decoupled" from biology in this basic respect. Luria goes on to make a series of empirical claims about what "we must" assume and where "we must look" for an account of the origin of linguistic universals: namely, "in the relations between the active subject and reality and not in the mind itself." Note that no argument is advanced to show that this *is* true, or even any hint of an argument. Rather, it *must* be true; argument is therefore superfluous. If, indeed, investigation shows that the *wh*-island constraint derives from principles of universal grammar and is available to the language learner without relevant experience, we must nevertheless insist that this constraint (or the underlying principles) is acquired by the child through "the active relationship between the subject and the world" or "active reflection on the objective world." Note that the reference to "the history of our society" is entirely beside the point, since however language has evolved, a given child must acquire it on the basis of the evidence available. What is most curious of all, perhaps, is that all of this is offered as the "genuinely scientific" approach, the "scientifically philosophical manner" of studying the question at hand. One can imagine how comparable dogmatism would be regarded in the natural sciences.

Perhaps these citations suffice to show that Lenneberg was quite right to take the trouble to emphasize that "the discovery and description of innate mechanisms is a thoroughly empirical procedure and is an integral part of modern scientific inquiry," and to insist that there is no room here for dogmatism or *a priori* doctrine. It is significant fact that this simple observation seems so difficult for many researchers to accept. Rather, the normal canons of scientific methods and procedure have met with great resistance in the study of mind and cognition, and there has been a compulsion to adhere to *a priori* theses, whether they are those of associationism, S-R psychology, developmental constructivism, etc. The belief expressed by Luria, that "all patterns present in the human mind are simply a reflection of the interaction between the subject and the outside world," can be traced directly back to scholastic doctrine, and is often attributed, probably erroneously, to Aristotle. It is interesting to ask why this doctrine is regarded as so sacrosanct. I think that a history of the study of these questions in the modern period will show that such doctrines have been proposed not as bold empirical hypotheses, to be developed and tested, but rather as necessary truths that it would somehow be dangerous to abandon, whatever inquiry may reveal. It seems evident that no science can advance unless it frees itself from intellectual shackles of this nature.

It is interesting to note, in this connection, that the approach that Lenneberg and others recommend—the approach often designated by its opponents as "nativism," though "open-mindedness" would seem a more accurate term—has not met with comparable objections from natural scientists, to my knowledge. Conclusions that have been tentatively advanced by "neonativists" seem to be regarded as unexceptionable in principle, though perhaps incorrect as formulated, by many biologists speculating on questions of language and mind (e.g., Monod, 1970; for references and comment, cf. Chomsky, 1971, pp. 11 ff.; Jacob, 1973, p. 322; Luria, 1973, pp. 137 ff.; Stent, 1975). Furthermore, assumptions similar to those of the "neonativist" psychologists and linguists are proposed without special comment by neurophysiologists quite regularly. To cite one case, in a recent review of research on vision two neurophysiologists formulate what they call the "principle of restricted potential" in the following terms: "By this we mean to emphasize that the developing nervous system is not a tabula rasa, free to reflect whatever individual experience dictates. Rather, the development of the nervous system is a process sharply constrained by a genetic program. At certain points, the genetic program permits a range of possible realizations, and individual experience acts only to specify the outcome within this range" (Grobstein and Chow, 1975).

In particular, they suggest, "there appears to be a small range within which individual experience operates to assure proper binocular fusion," though the general character of binocular vision in cat and monkey is genetically determined; and "there is some genetically determined range of possible orientation specificities for an individual neuron within which the actual orientation specificity is realized by experience." I have no independent judgment as to whether these suggestions are correct. My point, rather, is that no one would argue that by thus attributing some general restrictive principles to the genetic program they are violating some methodological canon, turning a problem into a postulate, aborting further inquiry, etc. Why then should we take a different stance when it is proposed that universal grammar, genetically determined, permits "a range of possible realiza-

tions" and individual experience acts only to specify the outcome—
namely, as a particular grammar and performance system—within this
range?

The answer is: We should not. Specific arguments with regard to
native endowment should be assessed on their merits, without in-
trusion of *a priori* doctrine as to the nature of legitimate idealization,
the structure of mind, the character of mental representations and
mental computation, the role of history and experience, etc. There is,
in short, no reason to adopt the common view that the human mind is
unique among the systems known to us in the biological world in
that, in its higher cognitive functions, it is unstructured apart from
some minimal "hereditary forms" or "quality space."

One might be disinclined to suppose that a principle such as the
wh-island constraint, assuming it to be a principle of universal grammar, is genetically programmed as such. Perhaps such a principle, if
indeed genetically determined, arises from the interaction of other
more basic properties of the language faculty. I think that this is in fact
the case, as noted earlier. I have suggested elsewhere that the *wh*-
island constraint follows from quite general properties of rule systems
that have many other consequences as well. Suppose that we can show
that these or other principles of comparable generality are well confirmed in human language and suffice to explain such principles as the
wh-island constraint, and thus to explain why the sentences described
earlier are interpreted as they are. We might then ask whether these
deeper principles are specific to the language faculty or apply to the
operation of other "mental organs" as well. Thus, these deeper principles might result from some sort of organism–environment interaction, difficult as it is to imagine at present how this might come about,
or more plausibly they might be characteristic of a broad class of cognitive processes, reflected in various ways in particular cognitive domains. Lenneberg has some interesting speculations along these lines.
In discussing the general principles of organization of grammar, he
suggests that phrase structure and transformational systems may be
"simply special applications of general modes of organization, modes
that are common to the organization of the behavior of all higher
animals," though these systems must be "highly adapted biologically"
in humans (Lenneberg, 1967, p. 302). It remains an open question,
and an interesting one, to determine whether there really are significant analogies between the principles of mental representation and

computation that seem well motivated in the study of language, and other mental operations, in other domains. Personally, I am rather skeptical; I see no interesting analogies in other cognitive domains, but so little is known that we can really say very little.

In this connection too, it seems to me that one must deplore the common tendency to insist that the mechanisms of language must be special cases of "generalized learning strategies" or general cognitive mechanisms of some sort. Perhaps this will prove true, but there is for the moment little reason to suppose that it is. I see nothing surprising in the conclusion, if it proves correct, that the principles of rule organization that underlie the *wh*-island constraint are special properties of the language faculty, just as distribution of orientation specificities is a special property of the visual cortex. Similarly, it would not come as a great surprise to find that in some respects the human auditory system is specifically adapted to speech or that general principles of semantic structure and organization derive from the language faculty. At the level of cellular biology, we hope that there will be some account of the properties of all organs, physical and mental. There seems little reason to suppose, for the moment, that there are general principles of cognitive structure, or even of human cognition, expressible at some higher level, from which the particular properties of particular "mental organs" such as the language faculty can be deduced, or even that there are illuminating analogies among these various systems. Of course, we do expect to find that some systems—say, the systems of memory—enter into a variety of cognitive processes, but that is another matter altogether.

There are many barriers to progress in the study of the biological basis for human language capacities, among them, the impossibility of direct experimentation on humans to answer many questions that arise. In the case of some systems, such as the visual system, investigation of other higher animals helps to overcome this limitation, but the lack of significant analogs to the language faculty in other species—which, I suspect, will become clearer and better understood as research with language-like symbolic systems in apes advances—forecloses this option in the case of language, so it appears. The abstract study of competence systems and the study of process models offers a great deal of promise, I believe, and can place significant conditions on the biological mechanisms that enter into the language capacities. Eric Lenneberg, in his very productive work, developed a range of other approaches that seem very promising, as have other researchers in several related disciplines. The study of the biological basis for human language capacities may prove to be one of the most exciting frontiers of science in coming years.

References and Bibliography

Bahcall, J. N., and Davis, R., Jr. Solar neutrinos: A scientific puzzle. *Science,* 1976, *191,* 254–257.

Botha, R. P. *The justification of linguistic hypotheses: A study of nondemonstrative inference in transformational grammar.* The Hague: Mouton, 1973.

Chomsky, N. *Current issues in linguistic theory.* The Hague: Mouton, 1964.

Chomsky, N. *Language and mind.* New York: Harcourt Brace Jovanovich, 1968 (extended edition, 1972).

Chomsky, N. *Problems of knowledge and freedom.* New York: Pantheon Books, 1971.

Chomsky, N. *Reflections on language.* New York: Pantheon Books, 1975. (a)

Chomsky, N. On cognitive structures and their development. Proceedings of the Royaumont Conference on Phylogenetic and Ontogenetic Models of Development, 1975. (b)

Chomsky, N. *The logical structure of linguistic theory* (1955). New York: Plenum Publishing Corp., 1975. (c)

Chomsky, N. Conditions on rules. In Chomsky, N. (Ed.), *Essays on form and interpretation.* American Elsevier, 1976. (a)

Chomsky, N. On *wh*-movement. Proceedings of the Conference on Formal Syntax of Natural Languages, June 1976. (b). To appear in Akmajian, A., Culicover, P., and Wasow, T. (Eds.), *Formal syntax.* New York: Academic Press.

Grobstein, P., and Chow, K. L. Receptive field development and individual experience, *Science,* 1975, *190,* 352–358.

Inhelder, B., Sinclair, H., and Bovet, M. *Learning and the development of cognition.* Cambridge: Harvard University Press, 1974.

Jacob, F. *The logic of life.* New York: Panthon Books, 1973.

Kintsch, W., Crothers, E. J., Glass, G., Keenan, J. M., McKoon, G., and Monk, D. *The Representation of meaning in memory.* New York: Wiley & Sons, 1974.

Lenneberg, E. H. *Biological foundations of language.* New York: Wiley & Sons, 1967.

Luria, A. R. Scientific perspectives and philosophical dead ends in modern linguistics. *Cognition,* 1975, *3*(4).

Luria, S. E. *Life: The unfinished experiment.* New York: Scribners, 1973.

Monod, J. *Le hasard et la necessité,* Paris: Editions du Seuil, 1970.

Ney, J. W. The decade of private knowledge: Linguistics from the early 60's to the early 70's. *Historiographia Linguistica,* 1975, *II*(2).

Peizer, D. B., and Olmsted, D. L. Modules of grammar acquisition. *Language,* 1969, *45*(1), March.

Piaget, J. La psychogenèse des connaissances et sa signification epistémologique. Proceedings of the Royaumont Conference on Phylogenetic and Ontogenetic Models of Development, 1975.

Ross, J. R. *Constraints on variables in syntax.* Doctoral dissertation, M.I.T., 1967.

Stent, G. Limits to the scientific understanding of man. *Science,* 1975, *187,* 1052–1057.

2

Eric R. Brown

NEUROPSYCHOLOGICAL INTERFERENCE MECHANISMS IN APHASIA AND DYSLEXIA

This chapter is one of a series of papers devoted to the development of an explanatory model of reading. An explanatory model might be expected to delineate the process as a whole, order most of the known data, explain certain puzzling anomalies, and predict the dimensions of successful methods for teaching children to read (Brown, 1970). Furthermore, following Sperling (1970), we can propose that components of an information-processing model ought to have three types of potential verification: structural, functional (or behavioral), and neurological. Structural verification requires that the component must be essential to the logic of the explanation; functional or behavioral verification requires that the component be open to experimental investigation (e.g., perceptual or psycholinguistic studies); and neurological verification requires that the component have potential neuronal equivalents in the form of spatiotemporal physiological events (Lenneberg, 1974). It is this last level of explanation which will be the primary domain of this discussion.

In 1970 the present author first proposed a theory of reading that attempted to delineate the normal process in terms of the integration

Eric R. Brown · New York University, New York, New York.

of perceptual, linguistic, and psychological components. This was a deterministic, procedural model of the information-processing variety. In particular, following Chomsky and Halle's (1968) suggestion, it was proposed that the realization of adult reading competence in English involves a rather low-order transition from orthography to equivalent phonological segments at the level of syntactic surface structure and phonological base forms. Reading, in this model, is seen as a clearly derivative process, dependent upon a prior functioning oral language competence. This competence appears to develop with little reference to traditional psychological learning theory (Lenneberg, 1967), and by inference would sharply limit the ways in which a child "learns" to read. Furthermore, by proposing such a low-order transition, it is possible to take advantage of more fully developed language-processing models in delineating an explicit theory of reading. Coding in short-term memory takes the form of abstract distinctive articulatory features which have the potential for higher-order referencing of peripheral mechanisms (Liberman, Cooper, Shankweiler, and Studdert-Kennedy, 1967; Cooper, 1972). Subsequent processing of short-term memory contents consists of analysis-by-synthesis algorithms for determining acceptable deep structures hypotheses. A generated match of the contents of short-term memory is finally accepted as the appropriate analysis on the basis of decision theory, which invokes various psychological criteria for accuracy.

While this theory has been recently revised to incorporate changes since 1970 in linguistic theory and to better account for certain perceptual problems (Brown, 1976), the model is capable in its earlier form of delimiting a number of problems associated with reading acquisition (Brown, 1971). It follows from the theory that there are four types of reading problems that we would want to associate with the inability of some intelligent children to profit from reading instruction; they are peripheral, cultural, developmental, and neurological in character. Peripheral problems refer to correctable disorders in vision and hearing; cultural problems are in the domain of sociolinguistic issues, an area which is by now well established in the discussion of reading disabilities; developmental problems refer to the entire issue of selective maturational lags which may affect the reading process; neurological problems, or specific reading disability, remain as the black box of a psycholinguistic theory of reading. If indeed there are children with such selective neurological dysfunctions that they only affect a narrow band of learning behaviors including reading, then we have little hope of explaining the reading disorders of these children within the framework of a language-dependent, central processing theory of reading. Instead, it is far more likely that something is amiss in the first few steps of the reading process which has to do with the visual-to-auditory or visual-to-motoric transformation, or the access, coding, and contents of short-term memory structures prior to language interpretation.

An important theoretical distinction must be drawn between developmental and neurological problems. At present, the dyslexia syndrome is so variously defined that it is very difficult not to overdiagnose this disorder. It is hypothesized for the purposes of this study that a distinction can be drawn between developmental and residual dyslexias. The developmental type is defined as the possibility of differential rates of maturation within the perceptual and cognitive systems (Birch, 1962; Bender, 1958; Kinsbourne, 1973, 1975); the residual disability is for the present operationally defined as those specific reading disabilities that do not show marked improvement by the time the child has reached age 9–11, hence, an inferred neurological dysfunction. Together, these two types of problems would specify the dyslexia syndrome in its broadest possible sense; therefore, such problems as hyperactivity (Denckla, 1973), overt brain damage (Mattis, French, and Rapin, 1975), developmental apraxias (Gubbay, 1975), and developmental aphasias (Lenneberg, 1964), while possibly related to this syndrome, would need to be separately considered. It should also be noted that much of our concern with developmental dyslexia may be artefactual to our culture-specific demand that all children be reading by the end of their sixth chronological year. As Dr. Birgit Dyssegaard has recently reminded me, a number of West European countries do not begin formal schooling until age 7, nor is any special attention given to reading problems until the end of the second year (age 9).

If it follows that the neurological or residual disorder is the more serious condition, then type and degree of neurological dysfunction becomes an important variable in the diagnosis, prognosis, and management of this disorder. That is, if dyslexias or specific learning disabilities are something more than a manifestation of cultural anxiety over later-maturing children, then we must be able to find a significant if specific level of neurological dysfunction. One possible way of evaluating this deduction would be to study instances of unequivocal, documented adult brain damage, especially those cases affecting higher cortical functions, and argue by analogy to childhood, developmental disorders. Most notably, soft sign, secondary sensory, and more global neuropsychological nuisance variables associated with such disorders as aphasia, apraxia, and visual neglect could be correlated or clustered with dyslexia syndromes (Denckla, 1973). The dangers inherent in making such comparisons are real—obviously, focal or diffuse acquired lesions in adult populations, with their concomitant behavioral losses, are not the same as failure of functions to appear in childhood, stemming from a relatively unknown etiology. However, neither is it unreasonable to expect that such comparisons ought to exist if there is a significant degree of neurological dysfunction in such children.

As a first approximation, we might propose that the adult aphasic syndrome offers the closest analogy to childhood dyslexia. Both disorders involve a selective language impairment with no other necessarily associated cognitive or perceptual disabilities. Furthermore, they both appear to be affected by many of the same neuropsychological "nuisance" variables that selectively interfere with performance. Therefore, in the context of this study, dyslexia will be examined and interpreted as an "instance of aphasia." This theoretical gambit may allow us to draw certain parallels between aphasia and dyslexia, not only in the manifestations of the respective disorders, but also, more importantly, in the management of the consequences of these problems. This latter problem has been an especially trying issue in light of the increased recognition of the dyslexia syndrome, for in spite of the elaborated differential diagnosis of dyslexia, very little is known of specific remedial therapeutic techniques that will map onto these diagnoses. For example, the often-noted visual perceptual anomalies of these children have not responded well to perceptual training activities, when the results of such training have been evaluated in terms of potential gain in reading skills (Masland and Cratty, 1970). Therefore, we will examine the behavioral consequences of aphasia in some detail, hoping that experience in this domain may help us better understand the therapeutic process in dyslexia.

The Aphasia Study

At the time of Eric Lenneberg's death, he was working on several projects, including a research program on comprehension deficits in aphasia. The present author had the privilege of collaborating on the implementation of this work, and although the program as a whole remains incomplete, the theoretical structure, with some supportive data, has been published (Lenneberg, Pogash, Cohlan, and Doolittle, 1976). What follows is a description of this research approach to aphasia, a paradigm that we jointly elaborated upon, and made more specific, in the context of our work.

Lenneberg assumed that many aphasic patients have a relatively intact language competence or knowledge system which is masked or blocked by the selective interference of more global cognitive or neuropsychological factors. These factors could be summarized as problems associated with simultaneity and sequencing of verbal stimuli. We were working with comprehension tasks, rather than the more traditional speech tasks, because we believed that comprehension more directly accesses the true language knowledge of the patient. In the course of the study we hoped to find those conditions where we could considerably attenuate the effect of those neuropsychological factors which appear to block verbal performance. Furthermore, where possible, we hoped to directly manipulate these factors in order to determine their effect on language understanding.

Subjects

All subjects are stroke patients who have been admitted to the neurological unit of Burke Rehabilitation Center, a Cornell University-affiliated teaching hospital. Minimum time post onset of the traumatic event is 4 weeks. All are clear cases of left cerebral vascular accidents, often accompanied by significant right-sided motor involvement, but no other serious complications. Cases of severe global aphasia, apractagnosia, or suspected organic brain syndrome have been eliminated from the study. Finally, all patients are involved in daily programs of physical, occupational, and speech therapy.

Tasks

The tasks consist of commands that the patient responds to behaviorally by manipulating such items as a glass, plates, cups, spoons, a comb, a key, etc.; or, at another level of abstraction, arranging tokens which vary in shape, size, and color. An example of a more complicated command with concrete items would be, "Give me the cup before you give me the box." Substituting more abstract items in the same grammatical frame we obtain, "Give me the circle before you give me the square." Every attempt was made to keep the commands short and syntactically uncomplicated in order to reduce the memory load for the patient. The tasks instead concentrate on the order of difficulty of certain relational concepts. Some of the concepts tested include:

> Gestures—"Open your eyes." "Raise this hand."
> Body Identification—"Point to your mouth." "Point to your nose."
> Object Identification
>> Concrete—"Give me the glass (comb, spoon, etc.)."
>> Abstract—"Give me the green square."
> Relational Concepts
>> Spatial (over, into, beside, etc.)
>>> Concrete—"Put the pencil beside the box."
>>> Abstract—"Put the circle beside the square."
>> Temporal (before/after, first/then, etc.)
>> Quantitative (more/less, any, some/all, etc.)
>> Comparative (either/or, both, small/large, etc.)
> Temporal and Quantitative Questions
>> Concrete—"Does OT come after lunch?" "Is 50¢ more than a dollar?"
>> Abstract—"Does June come after April?" "Is 50 more than 100?"

Correct responses to all of these items are either the appropriate behavioral manipulation or, in the last category of questions, a yes–no response or nod of the head.

Variables

These are the factors we wished to manipulate in a behavioral sense. They included:

Degree of Abstraction of the Material. This is reflected in the use of either environmental objects or colored tokens within the same syntactic frame. Kurt Goldstein (1948) described a principle behavioral deficit associated with brain damage as loss of the abstract attitude.

Degree of Environmental Support. This variable is related to the above concept. In short, are we asking the patient to do something which he can relate to his own immediate or past experience?

Size of Stimulus Field. This variable refers to problems the patient may have with simultaneity of visual stimuli. This has sometimes been called simultanagnosia. For example, the patient may be able to carry out a simple command involving object discrimination and identification when there are only several objects in the visual field; however, if we simply add other irrelevant objects to the field, the patient may fail with the same task.

Timing of Tasks. These are the sequential problems that complicate the performance of some aphasic patients. The rapidity with which a sequence of tasks is presented and the spacing between tasks is a variable that can be manipulated.

Order of Presentation. This variable refers to the order of difficulty of a sequence of tasks. If more difficult items are presented first, then a catastrophic reaction may ensue which reduces all subsequent performance for that testing session.

All of these variables have been systematically manipulated in the context of the presentation of these verbal comprehension tasks. Their cumulative effect can perhaps best be summarized in an example drawn from the self-report of a middle-aged, well-educated man who suffered a stroke with subsequent expressive language loss, but who also eventually recovered and was able to make the following observations concerning his initial speech evaluation following the stroke. He said in part that he had been greatly shaken by this experience, and that during the testing he felt constantly "pushed to the limit." He further observed that his performance would have been better if the situation as perceived could have been less stressful and the testing more incidental. Finally, he spoke of the great mental fatigue he experienced in maintaining vigilance, finding appropriate words, speaking clearly, and, in general, attempting to conceal his problem. It is probable then that each of the above-mentioned variables can facilitate or interfere with the verbal performance of an aphasic patient. They do so by selectively interacting with whatever compensatory strategies the patient may invoke in the recovery process.

Analysis of Performance Errors

Most importantly, when patients do make errors in understanding, we wish to attribute the source of these errors to factors in addition to the possibility that the patient simply did not know the item. The patient may "know" the item only under certain conditions

that are open to behavioral manipulation. Therefore, we have attempted to code patients' errors as the effect of global neuropsychological factors which may have interfered with performance. These factors
are those same variables first delineated by Goldstein (1948). Some of
the error patterns of interest include:

Simultanagnosia. This has been defined as "a form of visual agnosia in which the patient is able to perceive parts of a pattern or picture, but fails to recognize the meaning of the whole." In a similar
vein, a patient may be unable to focus his attention on a limited
domain within a larger and potentially confusing visual field. We can
attempt to code this behavior by asking if the patient seems overwhelmed or confused in the presence of many visual stimuli.

Perseveration. Perseveration is the involuntary, pathological repiti-
tion of some behavioral activity. For example, a patient may respond
correctly to a task, but continue to perform the exact same response in-
appropriately on all subsequent tasks.

Catastrophic Reaction. The catastrophic reaction may take a
number of different forms, but essentially the patient appears defeated
and/or agitated by his failure to perform certain initial tasks, and all of
his subsequent behavior is negatively affected.

Depression. This factor refers to noticeable differences in the
overall quality of performance between different testing sessions with
the same patient. The patient's attitude, demeanor, and consequent
performance may all be significantly depressed throughout a particular
testing session.

Fatigue. This condition refers to those occasions when the patient's performance begins to deteriorate toward the end of a testing
session. An item which may have been completed successfully earlier
in the session, can now no longer be performed. As Goldstein notes,
this condition may result from feelings of distress that arise when
tasks become too difficult; however, in this context, the observed or
reported fatigue that emerges during the testing session is the behavioral cue. This is undoubtedly the same "mental fatigue" reported by
the aphasic patient in the prior example. It grows out of extended effort as a function of physiological condition, motivation, and arousal.

Arousal. This is basically a part of physiological condition; in this
instance the patient seems more alert, responsive, and involved than
is his custom—his level of arousal is judged significantly higher than
normal. At the other end of the scale, on a particular day, the patient

may be completely lethargic and uninvolved with his surroundings. It might be possible to get some indication of substantial changes in the degree of arousal by checking such autonomic functions as pulse and blood pressure.

It is obviously the case that these proposed neuropsychological interference mechanisms, while intended as a fairly exhaustive set of descriptive categories, are not mutually exclusive. In fact, it could be argued that they are simply differing manefestations of the same disturbing conditions—problems with simultaneity and sequencing. However, the behaviors associated with these problems suggest distinctive category names, and we shall see that these distinctions are especially useful in the discussion of how best to manage the consequences of these problems.

Expected Results

The preliminary results from this experimental approach to comprehension deficits in aphasia have been reported elsewhere (Lenneberg et al., 1976). Eventually, one would hope to be able to confirm an overall order of difficulty for the tasks themselves, not only in terms of a stability in the performance of a particular patient from session to session, but also in the sense that some items are more difficult for all patients studied. Furthermore, one would expect a substantial correlation between these results and those obtained from the administration of standardized aphasia tests of expressive ability, and at least a partial correlation with child language acquisition data. And yet the most important result of this approach to aphasia and brain damage is the most difficult to quantify, determining the source of patients' fluctuations in performance on verbal comprehension tasks. It is the failures of these patients that present the most interesting phenomena. As was earlier stated, we want to know under what conditions the patient knows or does not know a particular item, and if some of these conditions can be systematically varied. By inference then, the ultimate research goal is to determine what neuropsychological factors interfere with verbal comprehension in brain-damaged patients. Finally, there may be possible inferences from this type of study to our understanding of dyslexic or learning disabled children, insofar as there is the possibility of true neurological dysfunction in such children.

Parallels with Dyslexia

The dyslexic or learning disabled child undoubtedly possesses the same relatively intact language competence system that has been observed in many adult aphasics. This is reflected in the fact that such children will often be able to communicate and understand quite freely, if in something other than a very stressful situation. Peripheral perceptual and memory functions are often at issue in such children, or there is a general slowing or hesitation in the entire process that is not unlike apraxia. Yet none of this necessarily affects the basic language comprehension process, as was made abundantly clear in Lenneberg's classic (1962) presentation of a congenitally anarthric boy who could nevertheless understand language.

Learning to read, on the other hand, involves a conscious, sequential referencing of rather abstract language units (Kavanagh and Mattingly, 1972; Brown, 1976), a highly tenuous process which is not open to everyone to the same degree, and a process which is especially suceptible to disruption by the neuropsychological nuisance factors under discussion. Even minimal dysfunctions in "abstract attitude," sequencing, or the sense of simultaneity can lead to serious consequences in reading acquisition. But as in the parallel case of aphasia, we will see that the conditions that so often appear to block a child's performance in reading are also partially open to our behavioral manipulation.

Behavioral Manipulations in Diagnosis and Remediation

The theme of this approach is to concentrate on how to get the best performance from a dyslexic child—how we can help him cope with his reading problem. The behavioral parallels with aphasia and brain damage are as follows:

Degree of Abstraction. The degree of abstraction of the content of reading materials, holding language structure constant, affects the reading performance of dyslexic children. While this is true to a lesser extent for all readers, and has generally been acknowledged as a major deficiency in most readability formulas, the problem is particularly acute with the dyslexic child. With minimal dysfunction, the crux of the issue is not an inability to deal with abstractions per se, but the additional burden this places on the child who is simultaneously attending to relatively inaccessible abstract language units necessary for the decoding of orthographic materials. Therefore, in general, we will want to avoid presenting more abstract materials to these children in the context of reading instruction.

Size of Stimulus Field. As in the brain-damaged adult, the dyslexic child can often be overwhelmed by a complex visual field with multiple, simultaneously competing stimuli, a set of symptoms we have called simultanagnosia. In this case it would appear that many students are unable to cope with an entire page of closely spaced print. They are either unaware of or cannot activate the appropriate scanning patterns for English orthography. Symptoms may take the form of either a complete blockage and confusion or a partial visual neglect of one half or the other of the visual field. For these children, we might pay special attention to the visual format of reading materials, including legibility, spacing, and size of type. It may even be necessary to intially present orthographic material in a line-by-line or word-by-word format, but at all costs avoiding a visually cluttered stimulus field.

Timing of Tasks. In diagnosing and testing dyslexic children, the examiner must be aware that pressing or hurrying the student may lead to a perservative response pattern. This will of course affect our evaluation of what the child knows or does not know. The tendency toward perserverative responses was aptly described by an acquaintance of mine who had herself experienced many symptoms of dyslexia as a child. She noted that these interfering factors in the reading process stem from "the inability to disconnect the attention from the stimulus and activate a transfer from visual to speech equivalents." In all events, if we are hoping to obtain an optimal performance from a child, we must allow him time to resolve and consolidate visual and verbal stimuli. Certainly it would be a serious error to prematurely stress fluency or speed.

Degree of Environmental Support. The degree of environmental support can clearly affect the reading performance of the dyslexic child. While this concept is clearly related to problems with abstraction, it is not one and the same. For some time now, writers about reading instruction have stressed that all reading must be in a "meaningful" situation; it must be purposeful and relevant to the reader. Indeed, relevancy may be the essential psychological construct necessary for reading acquisition. While this may be true of the normal child, it is of even greater importance for the dyslexic. Both the reading act and the contents of reading materials must be brought within his personal sphere. Just as the aphasic patient can sometimes complete an item at bedside that he has missed in the laboratory, the dyslexic child may learn or know a difficult concept if placed in a more relevant context.

Order of Presentation. Material to be learned or used as the basis of testing ought to be in some idealized order from easy to more difficult items. By starting with easier materials, we build the confidence of the reader, and make testing more incidental in character. All of this may help both the aphasic patient and the dyslexic child avoid catastrophic reactions which either block performance completely or cause it to deteriorate to such an extent that further testing is useless. It is the inability of the child to cope with a situation that leads him to either risk nothing further or fail to consciously integrate his intellectual functioning. The childhood apraxia syndrome (Gubbay, 1975) suggests that it is voluntary, conscious, fine-motor activities which are susceptible to neuropsychological interference mechanisms or stress. The child is no longer willing to flexibly adapt, compensate, or cope with the situation.

Cross-Modal Extinction. This new variable is introduced as a variation on the problems of both simultaneity and sequencing. In 1952, in the context of his study on double simultaneous stimulation, Morris Bender noted the phenomenon of cross-modal extinction. Quite simply, this was the observation that while many brain-damaged patients could perceive a simple signal stimulus in the auditory, visual, or tactual realms, when presented with simultaneous pairs of stimuli in different modalities, patients would "extinguish" one of the modalities. More recently, Linda Chapanis (1974), working in Lenneberg's laboratory, rediscovered this phenomenon and has undertaken a systematic investigation of the extinction effect in right-hemisphere-damaged stroke patients. Her work thus far indicates that about 50% of such patients show signs of cross-modal extinction. Furthermore, there are no distinctive neuroanatomical correlates of this problem, and the only related functional disability appears to be a disorientation in time, or problems with the ordering of events.

These latter functional disabilities have frequently been noted in the symptomotology of dyslexia, and it was immediately suggested that manifestations of cross-modal extinction might also be found in this population. Failure to apprehend simultaneity implies a loss of abstracting ability, a more general sign of significant brain damage. True to this prediction, only a small subset of a sample of older dyslexic children thus far tested by Chapanis and the present author show positive signs of cross-modal extinction. This group may, however, correspond to those children suffering from significant neurological dysfunction, or the hypothesized residual dyslexic condition. Therefore, signs of cross-modal extinction could be an important early indicator of serious (nondevelopmental) cases of dyslexia.

If these initial findings of a cross-modal extinction effect should hold up under further experimental elaboration (and Connors, 1976, has reported compatible evoked potential data with dyslexic children), then several important inferences follow for the educational management of such children. First, we should help these children avoid situations involving competing, simultaneous stimuli. This is a commonly held teaching strategy, advocated by many educators, for dealing with learning disabled students. The second and more important inference concerns the multimodality approaches to reading instruction which are widely used with this same population. Typically, these techniques may involve tracing a word and saying it simultaneously, on the assumption that the information presented in two modalities has an additive perceptual salience. Nothing could be further from the truth for children who exhibit problems with simultaneous cross-modal stimulation. For them, additional mental energy and vigilance would be required to suppress one of the two competing stimulus modalities.

Depression, Fatigue, and Arousal. Emotional lability is one of the hallmarks of diffuse brain damage, and it is certainly true that dyslexic children will also have really bad days when they appear markedly depressed. It is perhaps best to understand these occasions for what they are, transient alterations in mood that affect performance, rather than actively combating them or attributing the problem to materials or teaching technique. Signs of fatigue should tell us to either stop working with the child or turn to easier tasks where chances for success are greater. Above all, we would do well to shorten most teaching and testing sessions if we desire to have the optimal involvement and performance of the child. Finally, at the physiological level, we need to realize that the child's arousal can vary not only as a function of factors outside the teaching–testing situation, but also as a consequence of his interest and involvement in the learning paradigm. The student will read more productively in an area where he has a real or special interest.

Theoretical Interpretation

Theoretically, we can relate these global neuropsychological interference mechanisms to the normal adult reading process by demonstrating at just what points blockages are likely to occur. As was earlier stated, many of these dysfunctions appear to especially affect the early stages of the reading process. In particular, they are often associated with attentional and preattentive processes in the visual perception act, scanning patterns in readout from the visual icon, articulatory motor and auditory scanning patterns in subvocal rehearsal, and in the apperception of phonological segments and syntactically based logical form (Chomsky, 1975). (This latter awareness comes rather late in the reading act.) Furthermore, there is a greater-than-normal and perhaps selective short-term memory decay function for phonological segments and extrasentential referents necessary for the semantic interpretation of surface structure. With respect to this last point, the most frequently noted instructional complaint with dyslexic children is that they cannot follow directions, a task that is uniquely defined by a linear dependency in discourse which is in turn based upon the correct assignment of pronoun referents, and the determination of presupposition and anaphora as they affect the interpretation of logical form. Finally, there is a dysfluency in the reading process as a whole which may be manifested in dysnomia and developmental apraxia. Rapid sequencing of mental tasks can produce overlapping and confounding interference patterns from one task to the next, leading to perseverative responses. The child may know the appropriate coding or lexical access skills; it simply takes him longer to execute these functions—so long in fact, that often the decoded information has faded from short-term memory prior to final interpretation.

An elaborated model of the reading process with special reference to the syndromes of dyslexia is presented elsewhere (see Brown, 1976). This model combines many of the aforementioned components together with additional short-term and long-term memories, coding devices, analysis units, and comparators, to form an analysis-by-synthesis information-processing paradigm representing the normal act of reading. The interfering factors first affect attentional states needed for the activation of scanning patterns. These scanning units typically convert orthography to corresponding articulatory feature segments, or speech musculature motor plans, which are stored in a recognition buffer memory (Sperling, 1970). However, as Sperling points out, the actual conversion or scanning must be preceded by prescan activities, including locating the area of the visual icon where scanning is to be done, then calling the processing capacity to these locations. This second activity may be called attention, and failure of attention is another level of explanation for perseveration, catastrophic reaction, and other neuropsychological problems.

Another problem is the failure of abstract attitude or level of awareness of abstract language units. At one level, this may mean that children are not able to isolate phonemic contrasts or later synthesize or blend them for realization in oral or subvocal reading. At another level, this may mean that children are not able to abstract away the phonetic detail and redundancy necessary for an appreciation of English orthography at the systematic phoneme or phonological base form level. At a later point in the reading process, there may be a failure to grasp more involved abstract structures of logical form prior to a final semantic reading. Many educators speak of the persistent difficulties teen-agers and young adults experience with enriched and complex surface structures associated with logical form.

Another aspect of abstract attitude is the perception of simultaneity. Kurt Goldstein (1948) proposes that impairment of abstract attitude (the highest and most easily disturbed mental function) is reducible to a failure in "simultaneous function." Simultaneous function is the capacity to have "two things in mind at the same time; separated and combined in one view, to distinguish them and to synthesize them to a new whole" (p. 118). In cases of minimal and diffuse brain damage, one might expect some loss of this function. An analysis-by-synthesis approach to reading requires that initial information be held in short-term memory while heuristic analyzers attempt to generate a facsimile of that information. Comparator units then decide if the approximation or fit of the generated match meets the accuracy criteria of the reader's expectations. To make such judgments, the comparator unit must bring together many different processes from subcomponents functioning at different rates and at different points on a relative time continuum. These events must be perceived as simultaneous and coequal within a mathematical moment or zero span of time if the reading process is to function. One can predict that dyslexic children will show many other deficits in the perception of "simultaneity," in addition to simultanagnosia and cross-modal extinction.

Therapeutic Implications

As was earlier noted, it is proposed that there are at least two types of dyslexic disorders: developmental and residual. Developmental dyslexia again is a consequence of a general slowing or immaturity of cognitive and perceptual development. Recent theoretical research has suggested that such problems as immaturity in levels of awareness of phonological segments are resolved with further maturation, thus allowing these children to read quite naturally at age 9 or 10. Residual dyslexia suggests a true neurological, organic dysfunction attributable to such factors as genetic disorders, complications of pregnancy or birth, childhood disease, or actual head injury. While often confused with the developmental disorder, in the residual condition symptoms do not subside at age 9 or 10, but continue to be a source of difficulty for the reader well into adult life. At present we are unable to differentiate these disorders in early childhood. Certainly an important research goal is to be able to reliably make such discriminations earlier in the life of the child, because there are important remedial consequences.

For the developmental condition we might draw the following parallels from the course of recovery in aphasia: In speech recovery with aphasics, therapy seems to have little to do with rate of recovery in the first 3 months following the accident (Ludlow, 1974). Rather, a central, spontaneous, organic recovery process ensues. The particular therapy or skills developed during this period appear to be relatively unimportant. Instead, it is the generally supportive, interpersonal relationship between therapist and patient which promotes recovery. In other words, that therapy succeeds with which the therapist feels most comfortable.

In an exactly parallel fashion, we can make the following observations concerning the course of reading acquisition in developmental reading disorders: With delayed readers, we must also be patient and allow maturation to take its course, especially in the first 2 to 3 years of schooling. The specific therapy or skills taught is not causative or even particularly important. What is important is the supportive interpersonal relationship between teacher and child. And finally, the teacher will succeed with that technique with which he or she feels most comfortable and certain.

With the residual or more serious reading disorder, we need to think increasingly in terms of compensatory strategies. As Eric Lenneberg (1974) showed in one of his last publications on developmental aspects of language and the brain, in cases of real organic damage, the organism at a certain level of developmental complexity can no longer reconstitute the mechanisms underlying the original function in question. The organism must instead use alternative means to achieve the functional goal—in this instance, reading competence. The residual dyslexic must learn to compensate for whatever organic losses or dysfunctions he may experience. Unfortunately, just what the character of these compensatory strategies might be is not yet clear. Ozer (1976) has recently presented a model of the neuropsychological examination of dyslexic children that emphasizes an interactive assessment of the child's learning strategies, including a determination of those environmental conditions in which a child may learn. While not yet definitive, this would appear to be the most appropriate diagnostic research strategy.

In conclusion, we can observe that most residual dyslexics successfully make such compensations as are necessary for a functional literacy sometime in the preteen years. However, we can help them make these adjustments by being aware of those factors that so often serve to block their best performance: simultanagnosia, perseveration, depression, extinction, etc.—in short, by helping them circumvent all those neuropsychological problems which have been discussed within the context of this chapter.

Acknowledgments

This chapter is based upon the present author's contribution to a joint presentation on dyslexia undertaken with Dr. Lenneberg and delivered to The International Reading Association, New York, May 1975.

The research work leading to the original paper was supported by a grant from The Spencer Foundation, National Academy of Education. The author also wishes to thank Burke Rehabilitation Center, Cornell Medical Center, and in particular Drs. Joel Feigenson and Fletcher McDowell for their extended research cooperation.

The author has received an additional appointment as Visiting Fellow in Psychology, Cornell University, 1974–1976.

References

Bender, L. Problems in conceptualization and communication in children with developmental alexia. In F. H. Hock and J. Zubin (Eds.), *Psychopathology of communication.* New York: Grune & Stratton, 1958.

Birch, H. Dyslexia and the maturation of visual function. In J. Money (Ed.), *Reading disability.* Baltimore: Johns Hopkins Press, 1962.

Brown, E. The bases of reading acquisition. *Reading Research Quarterly,* 1970, *6,* 49–74.

Brown, E. Implications of a theory of reading. In F. Greene (Ed.), *Reading: The right to participate.* Milwaukee: National Reading Conference, 1971, *20,* 355–367.

Brown, E. A model of the reading process. In preparation, 1976.

Chapanis, L. *Intramodal and cross-modal pattern recognition in stroke patients.* Doctoral dissertation, Cornell University, 1974.

Chomsky, N. *Reflections on language.* New York: Pantheon, 1975.

Chomsky, N., and Halle, M. *The sound pattern of English.* New York: Harper & Row, 1968.

Connors, K. Pre-convention institute presentation on learning disabilities. International Neuropsychology Society Meetings, Toronto, February 1976.

Cooper, F. How is language conveyed by speech. In J. Kavanagh and I. Mattingly (Eds.). *Language by ear and by eye.* Cambridge: M.I.T. Press, 1972.

Denckla, M. Research needs in learning disabilities. *Journal of Learning Disabilities,* 1973, *6,* 43–52.

Goldstein, K. *Language and language disturbances.* New York: Grune & Stratton, 1948.

Gubbay, S. *The clumsy child: A study of developmental apraxia and agnosic ataxia.* Philadelphia: W. B. Saunders, 1975.

Kavanagh, J., and Mattingly, I. *Language by ear and by eye.* Cambridge: M.I.T. Press, 1972.

Kinsbourne, M. Minimal brain dysfunction as a neurodevelopmental lag. *Annals of the New York Academy of Sciences,* 1973, *205,* 268–273.

Kinsbourne, M. Models of learning disability: Their relevance to remediation. *CMA Journal,* 1975, *113,* 1066–1068.

Lenneberg, E. Understanding language without ability to speak. *Journal of Abnormal and Social Psychology,* 1962, *65,* 419–425.

Lenneberg, E. Language disorders in childhood. *Harvard Educational Review,* Spring 1964, *34*(2), 152–177.

Lenneberg, E. *Biological foundations of language.* New York: Wiley, 1967.

Lenneberg, E. Language, speech, and speakers. In E. Lenneberg (Ed.), *Language and brain: Developmental aspects. Neurosciences Research Program Bulletin,* 1974, *12*(4) *(December)*.

Lenneberg, E., Pogash, K., Cohlan, A., and Doolittle, J. Comprehension deficts in acquired aphasia. *Proceedings of the Academy of Aphasia,* 1976. In press.

Liberman, A., Cooper, F., Shankweiler, D., and Studdert-Kennedy, M. Perception of the speech code. *Psychological Review*, 1967, *74*, 431–61.

Ludlow, C. L. *The recovery of syntax in aphasia*. Doctoral dissertation, New York University, 1974.

Masland, R., and Cratty, B. The nature of the reading process, the rationale of non-educational remedial methods. In E. Calkins (Ed.), *Reading forum*. Washington: NINDS Monograph No. 11, 1970.

Mattis, S., French, J., and Rapin, I. Dyslexia in children and adults: Three independent neuropsychological syndromes. *Developmental Medicine and Child Neurology*, 1975, *17*, 150–163.

Ozer, M. Levels of interaction in the assessment of brain function. *The INS Bulletin*, March 1976, 9–11.

Sperling, G. Short-term memory, long-term memory, and scanning in the processing of visual information. In F. Young and D. Lindsley (Eds.), *Early experience and visual information processing in perceptual and reading disorders*. National Academy of Sciences, 1970, 198–215.

3

R. W. Rieber, Neil Smith, and Barbara Harris

NEUROPSYCHOLOGICAL ASPECTS OF STUTTERING AND CLUTTERING

The phenomena of stuttering and cluttering have been observed clinically since the time of Hippocrates. Although these disorders have some factors in common, they differ in many respects.

Stuttering

Stuttering is a communication disorder which usually begins during childhood, between the ages of 4 and 5. Throughout early medical history stuttering was observed and treated by professionals who had their own theories about the disorder and set about to cure their patients in the light of these theories. Amman, a Swiss physician in the late 17th century, who believed that "hesitantia" was a horrible tongue habit, recommended tongue exercises and gymnastics.

Not until the 19th and 20th centuries have serious investigation and observation led to the acquisition of substantial and helpful information on the etiology and symptomatology of this affliction.

One researcher in the early 19th century viewed stuttering as a linguistic transitional phenomenon, i.e., the inability to shift from one

R. W. Rieber · John Jay College, CUNY, New York, New York; and Columbia University, College of Physicians and Surgeons, New York, New York. *Neil Smith* · John Jay College, CUNY, New York, New York. *Barbara Harris* · Allen Memorial Institute, Montreal, Canada. A part of this article is based on an unpublished M.A. thesis by B. Harris completed in the Department of Psychology, John Jay College, CUNY.

sound to another. Otto in 1832 defined stuttering as "the utterance of a sound unit, syllable or word, made faulty by severance, extension or repetition of the initial sound" (Sheehan 1970, p. 40). Otto felt that in normal nonfluency, the difficulty is with the whole word or phrase, while in stuttering the syllable is the problem area.

Wyllie (1894) described the development of symptom formation in stuttering. His explanation of the role of tension was a major contribution. Wyllie felt that most of the involuntary movements and spasms are produced by this tension. Following this lead, Treitel in the late 19th century was the first to divide the stuttering spasm into tonic and clonic blocks.

The research carried out on stuttering during the 19th century was not experimental in nature. Rather the phenomenon was observed clinically and subsequent theoretical conclusions were drawn from these observations. It was not until the turn of the present century that the most influential contributions through empirical research were made. Emil Froeschels, who from 1911 had written prolifically on the subject, provides present researchers with a wealth of experimental information. With respect to the etiology of the disorder, Froeschels drew his conclusions from experience with more than 1600 cases. He felt that stuttering begins in the child's search for words and thoughts, a search which creates syllable and word repetitions. These early repetitions are of normal tempo and without tension (primary clonus). Frustration and the need to make his wants known evoke tension, which alters the tempo of the repetitions and gradually causes them to turn into tensed articulatory prolongations (tonus). As he becomes aware of these repetitions and prolongations, he begins to struggle and then to avoid them, with distortion of the personality and anxiety following later.

According to Wingate (1962), Johnson's theory of stuttering involves the following three assumptions: (1) Most normal young children speak with a considerable amount of repetition and other breaks in fluency. (2) Adults differ in their standards of fluency, and some react to the hesitant speech of children with unusual intolerance. (3) Children who are penalized for normal nonfluencies are likely to develop stuttering.

Johnson's semantogenic approach to the problem of stuttering follows through on Froeschels's earlier postulations. Although this approach has been widely accepted, there are other equally credible approaches to the problem. For example, stuttering has also been regarded as a neurological problem, and as a reflection of an emotional or personality conflict.

Cluttering

Although cluttering has been mentioned in the literature of speech pathology for more than 2000 years, the actual amount of factual information on the disorder is meager. The predominant reason for this is that clutterers do not regard themselves as having a speech defect and therefore tend not to seek professional help. It has not been until the present century that the phenomenon of cluttering has received its due attention as an important debilitating speech defect. Even the most recent research, however, has been primarily clinical in nature. Weiss (1964) defines cluttering as "a speech disorder characterized by the clutterer's unawareness of his disorder, by short attention span, by disturbances in perception, articulation and formulation of speech and often by excessive speed of delivery. It is a disorder of the thought processes preparatory to speech and based on a hereditary disposition. Cluttering is the verbal manifestation of Central Language Imbalance, which affects all channels of communication (e.g., reading, writing, rhythm and musicality) and behavior in general."

Cluttering has long been recognized as both a part of the syndrome of stuttering and a separate entity. Bazin (1717) felt that the disturbance depended more upon the mind than upon the tongue. He felt that a clutterer's thoughts tend to race ahead of his speech, thus causing the thought and concept to be expressed all at once. The person then tends to become caught up on the initial syllables. The clutterer does not leave enough time to articulate his thoughts. The specific symptomatology of cluttering was not clearly differentiated from that of stuttering until the beginning of the nineteenth century. In the 1800s March Colobat used the French term *bredouillement* to demarcate "excessive rapidity leading to poor articulation" and *balbatiement* to indicate "hesitation resulting from inability to find the appropriate word or phrase."

Kussmaul (1881) describes cluttering as follows: "The clutterer exaggerates his speech, does not subdivide it into proper time intervals, swallows sounds, syllables and words with unrecognizable mumblings."

Kussmaul emphasized the principal diagnostic difference between stutterers and clutterers, which is based upon the patient's perception of his affliction. The more a clutterer dwells upon his speech, the better it becomes, whereas in order for a stutterer to improve, he should not think about his speech defect at all.

As mentioned previously, the research that has so far been carried out on cluttering has been primarily clinical in nature. Most researchers are in agreement that rapid tempo of speech is the most prominent symptom in cluttering (Froeschels, 1946; Freund, 1952; Weiss, 1964; Seeman, 1959; Luchsinger, 1957; and Arnold, 1960). Seeman (1959) points out that clutterers do not pause between words, i.e., that interverbal acceleration is one of the most important signs of cluttering. Luchsinger (1957) refers to the increase in temporal rate within the polysyllabic word as "intraverbal acceleration," while Weiss (1964) calls it "telescoping." Arnold (1960) states that cluttering is more noticeable in long words and longer sentences.

Many researchers (Weiss, 1964; Arnold, 1960; Rieber, 1975) cite the study done by Seeman and Novak (1963) in which they investigated the articulatory ability of 52 clutterers and 52 "normals." The subjects were divided into four age groups, being matched for age, sex, and intelligence. Each subject was asked to repeat rapidly the syllables "pah" and "tah." Results showed that as the groups increased in age, the differences between clutterers and nonclutterers also increased, clutterers speaking on the average between 100 and 180 more syllables per minute than the nonclutterers.

Beebe (1960) asked a group of 60 normal speakers to read and speak with excessive speed. For the most part the subjects were observed to produce behavior resembling cluttering. Weiss (1964) believes, however, that the diagnosis of cluttering cannot be made on the basis of speed of speech alone, the main criterion being the faulty integration of language, whether or not acceleration of speech is present. He characterizes cluttering as a "disorderly speech delivery, often over-hurried and without self-awareness. . . ." p. 238. In his article he discusses 12 symptoms, some or all of which may be found within the same individual. These include frequent repetitions of single syllables or short words, prolongations, interjections, vowel-stopping in the beginning of a word, excessive speed in speaking, poor articulation, (including omission of sounds, syllables, and whole words), inversion of the order of sounds, repetition of initial sounds and "telescoping longer words into one or two syllables, poor respiration, monotonous tone in speaking, lack of musicality, poorly integrated thought processes, poor concentration and attention span, delayed speech development, and difficulties with reading and writing, especially during the learning stages.

The above symptoms have been researched and modified by such experts in the field as Liebmann (1925), Froeschels (1961), Beebe (1960), Seeman (1955, 1959), Arnold (1960), and Luchsinger (1955, 1957), among others.

As summarized by Rieber (1975), research studies indicate that: (a) clutterers articulate syllables more rapidly than normal speakers; (b) clutters manifest a decrement or complete absence of the usual temporal rate within polysyllabic words; (c) most clutterers manifest the same symptoms in reading as in speaking.

Comparison of Stuttering and Cluttering

With respect to the comparison of the two speech disorders of stuttering and cluttering, the research that has been carried out up to date has, as in the case with cluttering, also been primarily clinical in nature.

Freund (1952) noted that stuttering and cluttering can frequently appear in the same individual. Weiss (1964) hypothesized that stuttering essentially begins as a reaction to the efforts of an individual in overcoming cluttering. West (1958), apparently in agreement with Weiss, says that "many a clutterer is a 'cured' stutterer who has made a compromise." Froeschels (1955b) in his clinical observations of stutterers and clutterers found that out of 231 stutterers, 23 or approximately 10% exhibited cluttering signs as well.

From initial observation, cluttering speech appears much like stuttering. There are repetitions, inhibitions, nonfluencies, and stumbling blocks. But their significance is entirely different. Whereas the true stutterer is acutely aware of his nonfluent self-expression, the clutterer is just as acutely unaware of his defect and cares little about his resulting carelessness.

Electroencephalographic studies of the two disorders have revealed data which may prove to be helpful, although they are as yet inconclusive. Luchsinger and Landolt (1955), the first to compare stutters and clutterers on a neurophysiological level, found that genuine stutterers tend to demonstrate a normal EEG. Clutterers, however, are characterized by a "slightly pathological" EEG 90% of the time. The same appears true for the stutterer-clutterer. Streifler and Gumpertz (1955), while confirming the high incidence of abnormal EEG findings among both stutterers and clutterers, did not find significant differences between the two groups. Langova and Moravek (1966) studied 253 subjects, 74 females and 179 males. There were 57 clutterers and 134 stutterers, and 62 stutterer-clutterers. The results showed that 13.5% of the stutterers exhibited abnormality, while 48% of the clutterers and 37% of the stutterer-clutterers had abnormal EEG tracings.

Langova and Moravek (1966) also studied groups of stutterers and clutterers comparing their responses to delayed auditory feedback and the effect of certain drugs. In the former investigation they studied the effects of delayed auditory feedback (DAF) on 59 stutterers, 28 clutterers, and 47 stutterer-clutterers. The results showed that 82% exhibited improvement in their speech, tonis and clonis disappearing and speech becoming continuous. Of the 28 clutterers, however, 85% manifested more severe cluttering behavior, and of the 47 stutterer-clutterers, 23% improved, 22% showed no change, and 56% became worse.

In the latter study, Langova and Moravek investigated the effects of chlorpromazine and dexfenmetrazine on 17 stutterers, 18 clutterers, and 17 stutterer-clutterers. The subjects read a 200-word passage before the administration of the drugs and again 25 minutes after taking the drugs. The following effects were reported with the administration of chlorpromazine: 66% of the 17 stutterers stuttered more severely, 44% exhibiting no change in speech or behavior. On the other hand 86% of the 18 clutterers improved with the drug, with 2 manifesting no changes. Of the 17 stutterer-clutterers 73% improved, 1 subject deteriorated, and 3 manifested no change. Conversely, dexfenmetrazine caused 78% of the stuttering group to improve, while 100% of the clutterers exhibited deterioration in their speech, and 35% of the stutterer-clutterers showed a reduction in the severity of their symptoms.

Another area in which investigators have explored the relationship between stuttering and cluttering is personality. Freund (1952) postulated a list of personality characteristics of stutterers, clutterers, and stutterer-clutterers. Pure clutterers are described as "aggressive, expansive, explosive, extroverted, impulsive, uncontrolled, hasty, and overproductive" (p. 162). The stutterer-clutterers tend to have characteristics of both stutterers and clutterers.

Rieber (1962) investigated the dependency–independency charac-teristics of stutterers and clutterers. His results showed that stutterers tend to be significantly more dependent than clutterers, and con-versely, clutterers tend to be more independent than stutterers.

The above review of the literature on stuttering and cluttering il-lustrates the fact that, although these two communication disorders have been investigated and compared in the past, very little in terms of empirical facts is really known.

The only research to date which has investigated the similarities and differences between stuttering and cluttering from a psycho-linguistic framework is that by Rieber, Breskin, and Jaffe (1972), and Rieber (1975). The latter study found that: (1) clutterers have a signifi-cantly higher rate of fluency failure than stutterers; (2) clutterers have a significantly higher temporal rate of speech than stutterers; however, both stutterers and clutterers show a progressive decrement in the frequency failure during massed oral readings, i.e., adaptation effect; (3) stutterers have a significantly greater mean pause time than clut-terers; on the other hand, the measure of mean phonation time did not significantly distinguish stutterers from clutterers; stutterers do, how-ever, have a trend toward lower mean phonation time; (4) both stut-terers and clutterers showed spontaneous recovery of fluency failure.

Purpose and Procedure

The present investigation was designed to explore the similarities and differences between stutterers and clutterers with respect to the loci of fluency failures in the sequential ordering of speech.

There is still much to be accomplished with regard to actual mea-surement of differences between stuttering and cluttering on such psy-cholinguistic variables as: (1) word position, either in the noun phrase or sentence, (2) word length, (3) initial phoneme class, and (4) gram-matical class. It is interesting to note that these variables have been researched with respect to stuttering only (Johnson and Brown, 1935; Brown, 1938a, 1938b, 1945; Brown and Moren, 1942; Hahn, 1952; Reid, 1946; Meissner, 1946; Quarrington, Conway, and Seigel, 1962; Con-way and Quarrington, 1963; Blankenship, 1964; Quarrington, 1965; Taylor, 1966; Silverman and Williams, 1967; Lanyon, 1969; Silverman, 1972). The general findings on these variables have shown the follow-ing: (1) Words which appear in earlier positions in the sentence, i.e., initial, tend to be stuttered more often than those in later positions (Brown, 1938a,b, 1945; Meissner, 1946; Quarrington et al., 1962; Conway and Quarrington, 1963; Blankenship, 1964; Quarrington, 1965; Taylor, 1966; Silverman and Williams, 1967). (2) Polysyllabic words tend to be stuttered more frequently than monosyllabic words (Brown and Moren, 1942; Brown, 1945; Meissner, 1946; Taylor, 1966; Silverman and Williams, 1967; Silverman, 1972). (3) Consonants tend to be stuttered more than vowels, and this fluency failure tends to occur at the beginning of a word rather than at the end (Brown, 1938a,b; Johnson and Brown, 1935; Hahn, 1952; Meissner, 1946; Quarrington et al., 1962; Taylor, 1966; Silverman and Williams, 1967). (4) Content words are more akin to stuttering than function words (Brown, 1945; Meissner, 1946; Quarrington et al., 1962; Quarrington, 1965; Taylor, 1966; Silverman and Williams, 1967).

The present investigation deals with three psycholinguistic variables. These are word length, word position in a sentence, and position of fluency failure within a word. "Word length" is defined as the number of syllables in the word. "Word position in the sentence" is defined as failures in the first, second, and final word of each sentence: initial, medial, and terminal. "Position in the word" is defined as four positions: initial sound (P1), first syllable (P2), remaining sounds (PS), and end position (S). The research is designed to investigate the following hypotheses: (1) The trend and patterns of fluency failures differ on word length among stutterers and clutterers. (2) There are differences in fluency failure with respect to word position in a sentence among stutterers and clutterers. (3) There are differences in fluency failure with respect to its position in the word among stutterers and clutterers.

Subject

Thirty persons,* ranging in age from 17 to 25, who have been previously classified as stutterers and clutterers, respectively, served as subjects.

---

* This experiment was based on the raw data generated from a study done by R. W. Rieber (1975). All subjects used in this study were the same subjects that participated in the above-mentioned study, and therefore the same definitions were used for the terms stuttering and cluttering as in that study (see Tables 1, 2, and 3).

Table 1. (See Figure 1.) Mean Frequency of Fluency of Failures by Length of Word for Stutterers and Clutterers across Five Trials

	Words		
	Monosyllabic	Bisyllabic	Polysyllabic
Stutterers			
Trial 1	6.45	8.72	20.
2	4.71	6.42	15.41
3	3.29	5.33	9.72
4	3.61	5.09	10.
5	3.38	5.70	9.17
Clutterers			
Trial 1	9.29	10.42	25.
2	7.41	8.97	16.25
3	6.76	7.15	14.58
4	6.82	7.75	14.58
5	5.99	7.15	13.33

Apparatus

Data were gathered from five successive readings of a standard controlled 304-word passage, recorded on a reel-to-reel Wollensak magnetic tape T-1500 tape recorder at the rate of 7½" per second. A plug-type Wollensak Model B microphone, as well as a foot switch,

Table 2. Mean Frequency of Fluency Failures for Stutterers and Clutterers According to Their Position in the Sentence

	Position		
	Initial	Medial	Terminal
Stutterers			
Trial 1	7.47	11.20	7.20
2	7.33	8.00	5.40
3	4.67	6.13	4.20
4	5.06	5.87	4.06
5	4.87	5.60	4.00
$\overline{X}$	5.88	7.36	4.97
Clutterers			
Trial 1	11.07	14.20	10.60
2	9.93	10.60	7.67
3	7.73	11.00	6.33
4	8.06	9.93	7.33
5	7.33	9.47	6.16
$\overline{X}$	8.83	11.04	7.13

Table 3. Mean Number of Fluency Failures for
Stutterers and Clutterers by Trial and Position within
a Word

	Position			
	p^1	p^2	P–S	S
Stutterers				
Trial 1	44.84	9.31	3.14	2.01
5	40.41	5.33	2.48	9.86
$\overline{X}$	42.63	7.32	2.81	5.93
Clutterers				
Trial 1	24.05	14.27	3.00	8.86
5	27.39	11.65	1.88	4.07
$\overline{X}$	25.72	12.96	2.45	6.46

Wollensak Model T. F. 404, were also utilized. Analysis of the data
was carried out by means of IBM 370:168 computer.

Procedure

The experiment was conducted in a soundproof room. The experimenter (E) was the only observer present and each subject was tested
individually. There was only one condition in this study, that condition consisting of five oral readings of a 304-word passage.

The reading passage used in this experiment had been controlled
for length, type-token ratio, Flesch readability, and Fries's seven parts
of speech.

The same reading passage was used for all subjects in the study.
Each subject read this passage five successive times, with a 20-second
interval after each of the first five readings.

After entering the experimental room the subject was seated at a
table with E seated at his right. The following instructions were given
to each subject: "Turn over the page which will be placed face down
before you. Read it aloud in your normal conversational manner.
When you have finished the entire passage place it face down in front
of you. Remember to speak in your normal conversational manner. Except for the oral reading you are not to speak at any time while the experiment is in progress. Are there any questions?"

Twenty inches to the right of the subject was a plug-type microphone which was connected to a tape recorder situated under the
table. In front of the E was a stopwatch and a folder containing the in-

structions and reading passages. After the subject was seated, he was instructed to begin oral reading. The E at this point activated the tape recorder by means of a foot switch.

The oral readings and tape recordings took place during trials one through six. During the oral reading the E followed along with a copy of the passage. At the completion of each oral reading the E took the reading passage from the subject. Just before the start of the next trial the E placed another copy of the passage face down before the subject.

Results

Hypothesis 1 states that the trend and patterns of fluency failures differ on word length among stutterers and clutterers.

A 2 (groups) by 5 (trials) by 3 (word lengths) analysis of variance (hereinafter, ANOVA) was performed to test the hypothesis. The two "groups" are stutterers and clutterers; the 5 "trials" are readings one through five; the three word lengths tested are monosyllabic, bisyllabic, and polysyllabic; word "failures" are represented as percentages of total fluency failures per trial.

Hypothesis 1 was confirmed, and an interaction effect appeared between word length and trials (or readings).

Table 4 is the summary source table for the mixed-model (groups

Table 4. Analysis of the Fluency Failure Variance by Stutterers and Clutterers, Trials and Word Length

Source of variance	Sum of squares	Degrees of freedom	Mean square	F ratio
Trials (T)	2230.38	4	557.59	9.70 [a]
Word length (L)	6735.90	2	3367.95	58.59 [a]
T × L	955.70	8	119.46	2.08 [b]
Error 1: Subjects within T and L	12070.30	210	57.48	
Groups (G) (S and C)	1069.79	1	1069.79	18.10 [a]
G × T	49.83	4	12.46	<1
G × L	92.64	2	46.32	<1
G × T × L	99.25	8	12.41	<1
Error 2: G × Subjects within T and L	12410.81	210	59.09	
Total	38274.81	449		

[a] $p < .001$.
[b] $p < .05$.

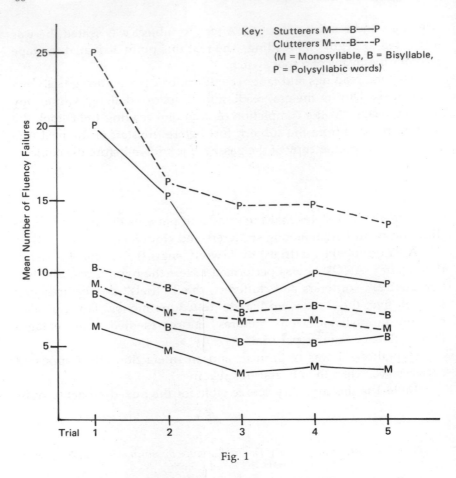

Fig. 1

by two repeated factors) ANOVA. Figure 1 is a plot of the profiles of the two groups on word length across the 5 trials. (Tables 1–3 present the mean fluency failures, the statistics for Figure 1.) The plot of the means summarizes the results of the ANOVA more clearly.

From Figure 1 it is clear, on the whole, that both groups experience the same pattern of failures for mono- and bisyllabic words, but quite a different pattern for polysyllabic words (word length (L): $F = 58.59$, $p < .001$). Second, there is a definite adaptation effect across trials, which is most marked for failures in polysyllabic words (trials (T): $F = 9.70$, $p < .001$). Thus the interaction between word length and trials is significant (TXL: $F = 2.08$, $p < .001$).

Table 5. The Observed and Expected Frequencies and Percentages of Fluency Failures for Stutterers and Clutterers by Number of Syllables (Trial One Only)

	Syllables					
	1	2	3	4	5	Total
Stutterers						
Observed	230	85	**34**	**9**	3	361
Expected	276.68	65.31	15.44	2.38	1.19	361
(Percent)	(63.7)	(23.6)	(9.4)	(2.3)	(1)	(100)
				$x^2 = 57.29$ at 4 df.		
Clutterers						
Observed	338	86	**49**	6	**6**	485
Expected	371.73	87.75	20.71	3.19	1.59	485
(Percent)	(69.7)	(17.8)	(10.1)	(1.2)	(1.2)	(100)
				$x^2 = 56.31$ at 4 $df.$		

Table 1 and Figure 1 also reveal that all interactions involving the two groups are not significant. That is, the pattern of failures across trials and different word lengths is not moderated by stutterer and clutterer differences. The plots of the means separate for each group show approximately parallel profiles.

To clarify further the pattern of differences for the stutterers and clutterers as the length of the words increased, chi square analysis of the raw frequencies of fluency failures were performed.* Table 5 presents the results for both groups. Since there were no groups by trials, nor groups by word length by trials interaction, there is little to be gained by examining all five trials for syllabic effect. Hence, only reading trial one was analyzed, using one-sample chi square.

For convenience, major observed-to-expected differences in frequencies are shown in Table 5 in boldface type. Thus, the table shows that the largest deviations from chance occur among three- and four-syllable words for stutterers (three-syllable $x^2 = 22.31$, 39% of total x^2; four-syllable $x^2 = 18.41$, 32% of total x^2; and among three- and five-syllable words for clutterers (three-syllable $x^2 = 38.5$, 68% of total x^2; five-syllable $x^2 = 12.23$, 22% of total x^2). Hence, stutterers and clutterers do differ in their failures from what one would expect to observe

* We would like to thank Dr. Sam Anderson of the New York Psychiatric Institute for his suggestion that we examine closely the direction of fluency failure by syllable length from expectation.

by chance alone. An examination of the percentages, however, suggests that the two groups are similar to each other in terms of their pattern of failures for reading one only.

Hypothesis 2 states: There are differences in fluency failure between stutterers and clutterers with respect to word position in the sentence.

A 2 (groups) by 5 (trials) by 3 (positions) ANOVA was performed to test the hypothesis. The three "positions" are initial, medial, or terminal, defined as the number of fluency failures observed in the first, second, and final third of each sentence. Hypothesis 2 was confirmed in all its main effects. There were no significant interaction effects. Table 6 is the summary source table for the mixed-model ANOVA.

As in hypothesis 1, there is again an adaptation effect ($F = 7.94$, $p. < .01$), with a leveling off in the mean of failures after reading 3 (10.3, 8.2, 6.7, 6.7, 6.2). (Tables 1–3 contain the mean fluency failures for hypothesis 2.) There is a significant position effect ($F = 10.38$, $p < .05$), with the greatest mean failure in both groups occurring at the medial position in the sentence (7.4, 9.2, 6.3). Again the clutterers (C) far outdo the stutterers (S) in mean failures, regardless of word position in the sentence (S = 6.07, C = 9.16; $F = 44.6$, $p < .001$).

Table 6. *Analysis of the Fluency Failure Variance By Stutterers and Clutterers, Trials and Position of Fluency Failure in a Sentence*

Source of variance	Sum of squares	df	Mean ratio	F ratio
Trials (T)	992.37	4	248.09	7.94 [a]
Position in a sentence (P)	649.12	2	324.56	10.38 [a]
T×P	78.96	8	9.87	<1
Error 1: Subjects within T and P	6564.32	210	31.26	
Groups (G) (S and C)	1073.39	1	1073.39	44.59 [b]
G×T	15.49	4	3.87	<1
G×P	21.42	2	10.71	<1
G×T×P	26.81	8	3.35	<1
Error 2: G × Subjects within T and P	5055.10	210	24.07	
Total	26098.51	449		

[a] $p < .05$.
[b] $p < .001$.

Table 7. Analysis of the Fluency Failure Variance by Stutterers and Clutterers Trials and Position of Fluency Failure within the Word

Source of variance	Sum of squares	df	Mean square	F ratio
Trials (T)	38.42	1	38.42	<1
Position in a word (P)	36602.43	3	12200.81	73.81 [a]
T×P	176.29	3	58.76	<1
Error 1: Subjects within T and P	18514.68	112	165.31	
Groups (G) (S and C)	461.81	1	461.81	<1
G×T	14.80	1	14.80	<1
G×P	4308.55	3	1436.19	2.26 (n.s.)
G×T×P	818.62	3	272.87	<1
Error 2: G×subjects within T and P	71120.50	112	635.00	
Total	42360.38	239		

[a] $p < .001$.

Hypothesis 3 states that there are differences in fluency failures between stutterers and clutterers with respect to position in the word.

A $2 \times 5 \times 4$ (positions) ANOVA was performed to test the hypothesis. The four "positions" investigated are: initial sound (P1), first syllable (P2), remaining sounds (PS), and final sound (S). Hypothesis three was partially confirmed. Table 7 is the summary source table for the ANOVA. Differences did appear between positions (P1 = 34.17, P2 = 10.14, PS = 2.63, S = 6.19; $F = 73.81$, $p < .001$), but not between groups or between trials. Thus, both stutterers and clutterers during all attempts show greatest failure at the initial sound of words, and least failure at the near-end or end of words.

Had the initial sound (P1) been contrasted against all other positions in the word, a significant groups-by-position effect would have been obtained (Figure 2). (Tables 1 3 contain the statistics used to construct Figure 2).

Discussion

This study has examined the relationship between stuttering and cluttering on three psycholinguistic variables. We investigated whether there were significant differences between the two groups in the measurement of fluency failures on word length, word position in a sentence, and position of fluency failure within a word.

Clutterers exhibited a significantly higher frequency rate of fluency failure than stutterers. This result is in agreement with that found by Rieber (1975). Moreover, both groups show a progressive decrement in the fluency failures over time, i.e., adaptation effect. The greatest difference in both groups occurs between trial one and trial five. With respect to whether there is a difference between the two groups regarding the frequency rate of fluency failure on word length,

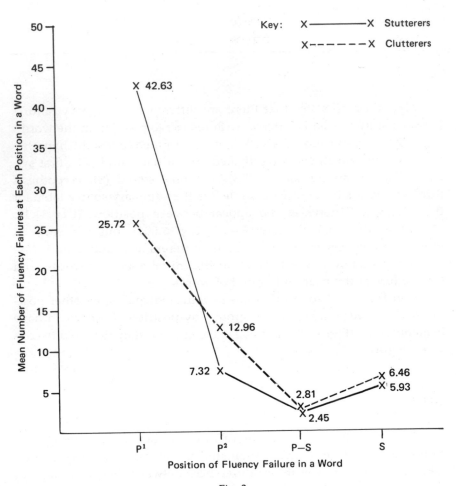

Fig. 2

previous research dealing with stuttering indicates that long words are stuttered more often than short words. Quarrington (1965) confirms Brown's (1945) assertions that stuttering on a word is a function of its information value. On the other hand, Lanyon (1969) and Taylor (1966) report that this longer-word fluency failure relationship tends not to be a function of how much information the word carries, but rather the length of the word itself. It is not clear what method Lanyon used in defining long words as opposed to short words, but Taylor designated as short words those containing five or less letters, and as long words those containing six or more letters. We have clearly demonstrated in this study that the variable of word length can be utilized to illustrate both the similarities and the differences between stutterers and clutterers. The results of the present investigation show that both stutterers and clutterers exhibit the same trend in frequency rate of fluency failure with respect to word length. The results clearly suggest that as syllabic length increases from monosyllabic to bisyllabic to polysyllabic, there is a significant increase in fluency failures. The means for the clutterers, however, were significantly greater than those for stutterers.

The basic distinguishing factor between stutterers and clutterers, as pointed out previously, is manifested in the difference regarding fluency failures in respect to word position in the sentence. All the main effects of the data show that the means of the clutterers were greater than the stutterers in all three positions within the sentence. A very interesting factor, however, arises when we examine this further. A number of studies (Conway and Quarrington, 1963) have indicated that fluency failures in stuttering tend to occur more frequently within the initial positions of words in a sentence as opposed to medial and terminal positions. Conway and Quarrington's results corroborate Brown's (1938b) original study of the positional variable. Quarrington (1965) further explains this word position effect in terms of Sheehan's (1958) approach-avoidance hypothesis. He postulates that the initial word of a sentence is approached with a high avoidance gradient, thus there is an association of stuttering with the initial word. If stuttering does occur, then the fear is reduced, and the rest of the sentence can be produced more fluently. The present study shows that there are significant differences in fluency failure when you look at the position within a sentence. However, the frequency rate of fluency failure for both stutterers and clutterers is higher for words occurring in the medial position in the sentence as opposed to the initial and terminal positions. Thus our results are contrary to the previously mentioned research. While our findings are interesting, the reason for it is not apparent at this time.

The mean frequency rate of fluency failure is significantly higher for initial sounds as opposed to medial and final for both groups. However, a significant difference arises here between stutterers and clutterers; that is, stutterers tend to have a higher rate of fluency failure on the initial sound in the word whereas clutterers tend to have a higher rate of fluency failure at all other points.

From a neuropsychological point of view, we may pose the following questions: (1) What aspects of neurophysiological brain function can account for the findings of our investigation? (2) Furthermore, we may ask how might these processes be related to the individual's psychological reactions and/or to the attention he may exhibit to his own communicative behavior.

In answer to the above questions we would like to suggest the following theoretical position.* The human brain can be understood as having certain biological interdependent neurophysiological mechanisms. The first of these mechanisms might be referred to as a temporal ordering process, and the second a spatial ordering process. The temporal function provides an overall time frame for a given utterance such as a syllable, word, or sentence, etc. The spatial or serial sound production provides the appropriate sequence of motor events, i.e., articulation within a given time frame during the communicative act. The above-mentioned interdependent processes interact with one another in order to achieve the complex event of producing the smooth flow of speech during this communicative act. This event is often referred to as fluency or fluent speech. If we assume that the above-mentioned functions may be malfunctioning or out of phase with one another, the most likely result would be a specific kind or class of fluency failure. The manner in which fluency failure manifests itself would also be dependent upon the organism's reaction to or anticipation of this failure in fluency. The quality of attention and/or expectation of the organism's response to this fluency would be a crucial de-

---

* This theoretical model will be elaborated in a forthcoming chapter which will appear in a book edited by R. W. Rieber and D. Aaronson *Psycholinguistic Research*, to be published late 1976 (New York: L.E.A.).

terminant of the type of behavior exhibited. When attention and/or expectation is shifted from its appropriate operation of cognitive planning to the operation of phonetic production, this tends to de-automize the communicative behavior. The result is usually a symptom such as stuttering or cluttering and perhaps certain types of aphasia. As our study has shown, this fluency failure is more than likely to occur on the first sound of a word rather than at any other point. And furthermore, it is more likely to occur in a polysyllabic word rather than a monosyllabic word. The reason for this phenomenon may be due to the relatively higher order of operational complexity involved in both the temporal and serial ordering of polysyllabic utterances. It should also be noted that not only are monosyllabic words much simpler to program in time and space, but they are also the most frequently used words in spoken and written English (Thorndike and Lorge, 1944).

Monosyllabic words are not only the most frequently used words in the language but are among the first words learned in ontogenetic development. Psychological factors such as attention, expectation (hope and/or fear), familiarity (frequency of written or spoken use), self-confidence in speaking ability, and self-awareness of one's speech are important variables related to acquisition and maintenance of linguistic fluency. Thus fluency as a function of word length is probably determined by psychological factors in the environment as well as neurological factors within the organism.

Conclusion and Implications for Future Research

The implications of our present study for future research are striking. First, from our experience, word length should be dichotomized into one- and two-syllable versus three- or-more-syllable words. Second, position in the word should be analyzed as initial-sound failures versus all other position failures. And third, the combination of independent variables which best predicts fluency failures is: class of fluency failures (stuttering vs. cluttering) and the interaction of length of word by position within the word. Specifically, the highest fluency failures will occur among clutterers who fail on the initial sounds of long words. In multiple regression terms (the actual general linear equation, $FF = a + b_1x_1 + b_2x_2$, is expressed as two equations for illustrative purposes) the hypothesis to be tested is:

$$\text{High } FF = a + b_1C + b_2IxL$$
$$\text{Low } FF = a + b_1S + b_2NxS$$

where FF = fluency failure, C = a Clutterer, I – an initial sound, L = a long word, S = a Stutterer, N = not an initial sound, and S = a short word.

We are presently engaged in carrying out a study which will test this multiple regression hypothesis.

Another possible research approach, also in progress, is to determine which of the independent variables (position in the word, length of the word, position by length interaction, and reading trial) best discriminates between stutterers, clutterers, and normals. A discriminant analysis will be used to test our hunches. It is our hope that our suggested research will provide insight for better understanding of the phenomena of linguistic fluency and its neuropsychological foundations.

References and Bibliography

Arnold, G. E. Present concepts of etiologic factors. In *Studies in tachyphemia*. New York: New York Speech Rehabilitation Institute, 1960. Pp. 3–25.

Arnold, G. E. Signs and symptoms. In *Studies in tachyphemia*. New York: New York Speech Rehabilitation Institute, 1960. Pp. 23–47.

Bazin, D. *De lingua et vitiis ejus morbosis*. Basel, 1717.

Beebe, H. H. Voluntary tachylalia. *Folia Phoniatrica, 1960, 12*, 223–228.

Blankenship, J. Stuttering in normal speech. *Journal of Speech and Hearing Research, 1964, 7*, 95–97.

Bloodstein, O. *Handbook of stuttering*. Chicago: National Easter Seals Society for Children and Adults, 1969.

Bloodstein, O., Jaeger, W., and Tureen, J. A study of the diagnosis of stuttering by parents of stutterers and non-stutterers. *Journal of Speech and Hearing Disorders, 1952, 17*, 308–316.

Brown, S. F. A further study of stuttering in relation to various speech sounds. *Quarterly Journal of Speech, 1938, 24*, 390–397. (a)

Brown, S. F. Stuttering with relation to word accent and word position. *Journal of Abnormal and Social Psychology, 1938, 33*, 112–120. (b)

Brown, S. F. The loci of stutterings in the speech sequence. *Journal of Speech Disorders, 1945, 10* (September) 180–192.

Brown, S. F., and Moren, A. The frequency of stuttering in relation to word length during oral reading. *Journal of Speech Disorders, 1942, 7*, 153–159.

Conway, J. and Quarrington, B. Positional effects in the stuttering of contextually organized verbal material. *Journal of Abnormal and Social Psychology, 1963, 67*, 299–303.

Freund, H. Studies in the interrelationship between stuttering and cluttering. *Folia Phoniatrica*, 1952, *4*, 146–168.

Froeschels, E. Pathology and therapy between stuttering and cluttering. *The Nervous Child*, 1943, *12* (January) 148–161.

Froeschels, E. Cluttering. *Journal of Speech Disorders*, 1946, *11*, 31.

Froeschels, E. The significance of symptomatology for the understanding of the essence of stuttering. *Folia Phoniatrica*, 1952, *4*, 217–230.

Froeschels, E. The core of stuttering. *Acta Oto-Laryngologica*, 1955, *45*, 115–119. (a)

Froeschels, E. Contribution to the relationship between stuttering and cluttering. *Logopaedie en Phoniatrie*, 1955, *4*, 1–6. (b)

Froeschels, E. New viewpoints on stuttering. *Folia Phoniatrica*, 1961, *13*, 187–201.

Hahn, E. F. A study of the relationship between stuttering occurrence and phonetic factors in oral reading. *Journal of Speech Disorders*, 1952, *7*, 143–151.

de Hirsch, K. Diagnosis of developmental language disorders. In *Studies in tachyphemia*. New York: New York Speech Rehabilitation Institute, 1960. Pp. 47–54.

Jaffe, J., Anderson, S. W., and Rieber, R. W. Research and clinical approaches to disorders of speech rate. *Journal of Communication Disorders*, 1973, *6*, 225–246.

Johnson, W., and Brown, S. F. Stuttering in relation to various speech sounds. *Quarterly Journal of Speech*, 1935, *21*, 481–496.

Johnson, W. A study of the onset and development of stuttering. *Journal of Speech Disorders*, 1942, *7*, 251–257.

Kussmaul, A. *Speech disorders*. New York: William Wood & Co. 1881.

Langova, J., and Moravek, M. An experimental study of stuttering and cluttering. *Academia*, Praha, 1966, *70*.

Lanyon, R. Relation of non-fluency to information value. *Science*, 1969, *164*, 451–452.

Liebmann, A. *Vorlesungen über Sprachstörungen* (2nd ed.). Berlin: Coblentz, 1925.

Luchsinger, R. Phonetics and pathology. In L. Kalser (ed.), *Manual of phonetics*. Amsterdam: North Holland Publishing Company, 1957. Ch. 22, pp. 339–363.

Luchsinger, R., and Landolt, H. Cluttering and cluttering-stammering *Folia Phoniatrica*, 1955, *7*.

Meissner, J. H. The relationship between voluntary non-fluency and stuttering. *Journal of Speech Disorders*, 1946, *11*, 13–23.

Pearson, L. Dysrhythmia in cluttering associated with congenital language disability (I). In *Studies in tachyphemia*. New York: New York Speech Rehabilitation Institute, 1960. Pp. 54–63. (a)

Pearson, L. Auditory discrimination in cluttering associated with general language disability. In *Studies in tachyphemia*. New York: New York Speech Rehabilitation Institute, 1960. Pp. 92–100. (b)

Pearson, L., and Douglas, D. B. Dysrhythmia in cluttering associated with congenital language disability. (II). In *Studies in tachyphemia*. New York: New York Speech Rehabilitation Institute, 1960. Pp. 101–108.

Quarrington, B. Stuttering as a function of the information value and sentence position of words. *Journal of Abnormal Psychology*, 1965, *70*, 221–224.

Quarrington, B., Conway, J., and Siegel, N. An experimental study of some properties of stuttered words. *Journal of Speech and Hearing Research*, 1962, *5*, 387–394.

Reid, L. Some facts about stuttering. *Journal of Speech Disorders*, 1946, *11*, 3–12.

Rieber, R. W. An investigation of dependent and independent characteristics of stutterers and clutterers. (A Pilot Study) *International Association of Logopedics and Phoniatrics*. Proceedings of the XII International Speech and Voice Therapy Conference, Padua, 1962. L. Croatto, Ph.D. and C. Croatto-Marino, LLI, PhD. (Eds.).

Rieber, R. W. A study in psycholinguistics and communication disorders. *Linguistics, An International Review,* 1975, *160* (September).

Rieber, R. W., Breskin, S., and Jaffe, J. Pause time and phonation time in stuttering and cluttering. *Journal of Psycholinguistic Research,* 1972, *2,* 149.

Rochester, S. R. The significance of pauses in spontaneous speech. *Journal of Psycholinguistic Research,* 1973, *2,* 51–81.

Seeman, M. *Speech disorders in childhood.* Halle. A. D. Saale: C. Marhold, 1959.

Seeman, M., and Novak, A. Motor ability in clutterers. *Folia Phoniatrica,* 1963, *15.*

Sheehan, J. G. Conflict theory of stuttering. In J. Eisenson (Ed.), *Stuttering, a symposium.* New York: Harper, 1958.

Sheehan, J. G. *Stuttering: Research and therapy.* New York: Harper & Row, 1970.

Sheehan, J. G. Stuttering behavior: A phonetic analysis. *Journal of Communication Disorders,* 1974.

Sheperd, G. Phonetic description of cluttered speech. In *Studies in tachyphemia.* New York: New York Speech Rehabilitation Institute, 1960. Pp. 24–33.

Silverman, F. H. Disfluencies and word length. *Journal of Speech and Hearing Research,* 1972, *15,* 788–791.

Silverman, F. H., and Williams, D.E. Loci of disfluencies in the speech of stutterers. *Perceptual and Motor Skills,* 1967, *24,* 1085–1086.

Streifler, F., and Gumpertz, M. Cerebral potentials in stuttering and cluttering. *Confinia Neurologica,* 1955, *15.*

Taylor, I. K. The properties of stuttered words. *Journal of Verbal Learning and Verbal Behavior,* 1966, *5,* 112–118.

Thorndike, E., and Lorge, I. The teacher's word book of 30,000 words. New York: Bur. Pub., Teacher's College, Columbia University, 1944.

Weiss, D. A. *Cluttering.* Englewood Cliffs: Prentice-Hall, 1964.

Weiss, D. A. Similarities and differences between cluttering and stuttering. *Folia Phoniatrica,* 1966, *19,* 105–109.

Weiss, D. A. Cluttering. *Folia Phoniatrica,* 1967, *19,* 233–263.

West, R. W. An agnostic's speculation about stuttering. In J. Eisenson (Ed.), *Stuttering, A Symposium.* New York: Harper, 1958.

Wingate, M. E. Evaluation and stuttering, Part I: Speech characteristics of young children. *Journal of Speech and Hearing Disorders,* 1962, *27* (May), 106–119.

Wyllie S., *Disorders of speech,* London: Oliver & Boyd, 1894.

4

Jason W. Brown

CONSCIOUSNESS AND PATHOLOGY OF LANGUAGE

There are two basic orientations in neuropsychological research. The one holds that psychopathology is simply a malfunction of a normal mechanism, and that the pathological has meaning only to the extent to which it relates to a hypothetical normal capacity. The other approach maintains that the laws of pathological change bear an inner relationship to those of normal function, that the pathological is not a fragmentation but a lawful unraveling of normal cognitive structure. Here the pathological does not simply point to something but represents a level in normal cognition. In this view, pathological change is of aid in the understanding of the nature of cognition, and needs to be contemplated each step of the way in the construction of psychological theory.

The cognitive approach to psychopathology found one of its most thoughtful and articulate spokesmen in Eric Lenneberg. In fact, his work presents a historical challenge to materialism in psychology at the same time that it lays the groundwork for a formal theory—a system—of neuropsychology. This chapter is offered in the spirit of this work and in dedication to the memory of a dear friend and colleague.

I will begin with a brief description of a structural model of cognition and then attempt to relate this model to some observations on

Jason W. Brown · New York University Medical Center, New York.

pathological alterations of consciousness. The model was developed through studies of aphasic phenomena (1972, 1975a) and the anatomical organization of language (1975b) and will be more fully elaborated in a forthcoming monograph (Brown, 1977).

A Structural Model of Cognition

The series of levels through which cognition is elaborated recapitulates a sequence of evolutionary plateaus. Moreover, there is a correspondence between each level in the cognitive series and each plateau or stage in the evolutionary sequence, such that it is possible to describe a dynamic, formative structure built up in the course of evolution and continued on into maturation which supports and elaborates the mental life.

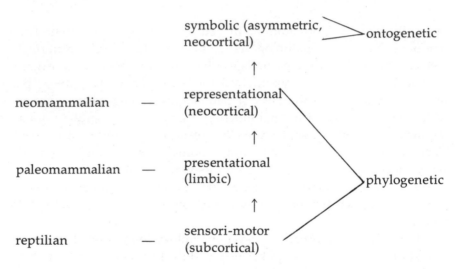

In this structure, four more or less arbitrary levels can be defined, each having an anatomical and a psychological aspect. The former has to do with the distribution and physiology of the system, the latter with action, perception, and inner experience. These levels are conceived as "closed systems" in that each represents, or represented at some point in evolutionary time, an endstage of cognitive development. But each level is also a transitional phase. The incessant flow of cognition, the continual appearance and disappearance of new form at each moment of our waking and sleeping life—these are manifestations of the activity of the structure as a whole, as it achieves one or another level of realization.

Of the four levels of structural organization which can be distinguished in man, three are phylogenetic and correspond roughly to stages described by MacLean (1972). The earliest of these is designated the *sensorimotor*, the next the *limbic-presentational*, the third the *cortical-representational*. The fourth level, the *asymmetric-symbolic*, is achieved for the most part in the course of ontogenetic development.

These levels are in no sense "separate brains," but rather are widely distributed systems which develop *seriatim* out of one another, serving to transform cognition to successively more differentiated states. Moreover, the levels are to some extent arbitrary, each probably comprising several—perhaps innumerable—subsystems. Nor are there clear transitions from one level to another, since it is not certain whether the levels develop as quantal achievements or on a continuum of evolutionary change.

The structure most likely develops out of a foundation of visceral activity, corresponding in part with the innermost visceral stratum in the hierarchy of Yakovlev (1948). The visceral is at the frontier of the transition from the physical to the psychological. It is also at the point of differentiation of somatic and extrasomatic space out of the wholly intrasomatic space of autonomic function.

Anatomical Organization

1. The sensorimotor stage of the reptilian forebrain incorporates, in mammals, much of the reticular formation, midbrain, tectum and basal ganglia, and brainstem systems concerned with sleep and wakefulness. The level also embraces other constituents of the extrapyramidal action system, nonspecific thalamic groups, and, possibly in primates, centremedian, pulvinar inferior, or in other mammals lateralis posterior.

2. The paleomammalian stage comprises structures usually included as part of the limbic lobe, *viz*, hypothalamus, anterior thalamic nuclei, cingulate gyrus, hippocampus and their interconnections (i.e., the Papez circuit), as well as orbitofrontal, pyriform and perhaps insular cortex, and various subcortical groups, e.g., amygdala, septal nuclei, and (medial) dorsomedial nucleus of thalamus.

3. The neocortical or neomammalian stage comes as a relatively late development with continued expansion over the mammalian series to man. Sanides (1970) has commented that the phylogeny of neocortex occurs through a process of "growth rings," new cortex developing as a core and displacing the previous core to a ringlike structure. Moreover, in this series of stages of neocortical development, sensorimotor koniocortex, which differentiates out of the preceding paralimbic growth ring, may be a more recent development than parietal or frontal "integration" cortex. The latter regions serve as a more generalized ground within which the sensorimotor areas appeared. Thus, classical sensorimotor cortex may represent an *endstage* evolutionary differentiation out of a parainsular/paralimbic and integration cortex field. This evolutionary process has an emergent character with new strata appearing as core differentiations within older more diffusely organized zones.

4. The asymmetric–symbolic level: The phylogenetic trend toward core differentiation discussed in relation to neocortex is continued, in the course of maturation, in the development of cerebral dominance or lateralization. Asymmetry represents a further continuation of this trend. In fact, the recent findings of anatomical asymmetry of the cerebral hemispheres in stillborns (Wada, Clarke, and Hamm, 1975; Teszner, Tszavaras, Gruner, and Hecaen, 1972) may be interpreted as a first anatomical sign of this evolutionary process thrust into ontogeny. Asymmetry is a prolongation of encephalization into ontogenetic development; it is a solution to the problem of size limitations imposed upon an expanding brain. Hemispheric dominance or lateralization is one expression of this "asymmetrizing" process.

Fundamentally, there is no difference between lateralization and localization; these are different ways of looking at a unitary process. Lateralization comes about through a process of core differentiation within the generalized "association" neocortex of one (the left) hemispheric speech zone. This process of intrahemispheric differentiation transforms language (cognition) to a level beyond that attainable through the generalized neocortex of both hemispheres. Lateralization is the result of this transformational property of left hemisphere. Through this dynamic process the "speech zone" is eventually constructed. Moreover, the realization of a new structural level entails an adaption (asymmetrization) of earlier bilaterally organized levels. In this way the acquisition of language acts to transform structure.

Cognitive Organization

1. The *sensorimotor* level represents an initial stage in the emergence of cognition, characteristics of which can be recovered from the study of human psychopathology. The cognitive form unfolds into somatic activity centered in the body itself. Sensation is incorporated into a perceptual space-model and develops into a generalized, undifferentiated preobject. The space of the perception moves outward from the space of the body but there is still a unitary space field. Motility is effected in axial body-on-body motor patterns as the action accompanies the preobject out into primitive perisomatic space. In fact, we may say that perception, action, and space together reach out into the body surround. The body may be conceived as the global somatic referent of the thought which seeks to realize itself in action.

2. The *limbic–presentational* level is characterized by a semantic operation applied to emerging contents. There is a transition toward a specific content, whether perceptual, motoric, or linguistic. This transition can be thought of as a selectional operation, if by this is meant a striving toward a final form and not just a choice between elements. At this level the object in perception will have the nature of an image, since the process leading to the image—or the hallucination—is the same process as that which leads to the perception. The differentiation of the object also corresponds to a differentiation of the forming action pattern which like the object proceeds from body-on-body organization, axial and proximal musculature out into the space of the distal limbs. The space-field achieves an extrapersonal but still subjectively intrapsychic character. The drive-character of the previous level also begins to settle into partial expressions.

3. At the *cortical–representational* level, perceptual and action systems show a progressive resolution of both object and action. The perception achieves a delimitation in abstract space as a veridical object; the action undergoes an increasing specification toward a discrete performance with the distal extremity on objects in a space apprehended as real and extrapersonal. The object has exteriorized and seems to dissociate from the self. Yet as the object proceeds outward, space also becomes more articulated. The object, and the space of the object, "separate" together.

This perceptual development is accompanied by a progression of the action to an asymmetrical motility on exteriorized objects. The action develops with the perception. The graded externalization of the object corresponds to a graded externalization of an action upon that object. The "deception" of the perceived object taken as real has a counterpart in the "deception" of the action on that imagined object.

More highly individuated emotional states emerge with the new perceptual and action forms. Actually, the affect is occasioned by (realized through) these new forms. As the object exteriorizes with its space, the object draws out or extends from within the range of feeling. The object and its affective component are like arborizations of the affect-laden image which precedes them.

4. The designation of the final level as *symbolic* conveys more than the usual sense of an idea standing for something; it implies a mode of thought in which "standing for" is understood. The idea is a symbol not when it is simply an idea but when the idea can be conceptualized *qua* symbol. The symbol is an attainment beyond the representational; the representation—the act or the perception—takes on a new value.

Action has exteriorized to a position in extrapersonal space. Speech is a higher form of action and seems to inhabit a different space. This is also true of speech perception. The new space of language develops in the intrapersonal component and not in the extrapersonal field achieved by the previous level. One can say that language permits an articulation of mind in the same way that the world was articulated by objects. The fate of these components, of action, perception, language, and affect in symbolic-level cognition, and the relation of these components to consciousness is the subject of the following section.

Comment

These four briefly described levels form the basis for the attempt which follows toward an account of the microgenesis of consciousness. Though we must focus on these levels in order to provide a stable framework for a necessarily complicated discussion, the reader should be aware that the levels are probably only arbitrary phases in a continuously unfolding pattern. They have meaning only insofar as they guide our thinking on the underlying process which is involved.

This process appears to have the nature of a continuous wave-front reiterated at sequential points (levels) in a transformational pattern. The concept of an ascending reduplication of a unitary process avoids the alternative of a piecemeal construction out of separate partial mechanisms. Each structural level may thus be thought of as solution to the problem of carrying an emerging abstract representation one further transformation. The forward direction of the process is maintained by its tendency to unfold, i.e., by its transformational nature. The process tends toward a finalmost stage. In a sense, then, the microgenesis of cognition and consciousness is a capsule of the whole evolutionary process.

Neuropsychological Studies of Consciousness

In general we may say that awareness is not a state or an attitude attached to performance but has a developmental character. Piaget has commented that awareness in the young child begins not as an awareness of objects or an awareness of activity, but rather as an undifferentiated state out of which more highly developed levels emerge. For the reason of this developmental character it is difficult to give a definition or description of awareness as such, since the various manifestations of awareness—e.g., vigilance, wakefulness, arousal, attention, set or orientation, self-awareness, or consciousness-of—refer rather to different *levels* in a unitary formative process than to independent systems.

Not only does awareness develop over several levels, but at each level awareness occurs as an inner part of that cognitive stage. Awareness is another aspect of the microgenesis of action, perception, and language and differs according to the development of these components. This is why it is misleading to say that a content *enters into* consciousness, or that one is or is not conscious *of* a particular content. This gives the erroneous impression that consciousness seizes the content from outside, or that the content gains access to consciousness. The content is as much *in* consciousness as consciousness is *in* the content. And like the content, consciousness is also a momentary achievement, a kind of product that needs to be continuously renewed.

Introspection refers to a consciousness of a content: *consciousness-of*. The idea of consciousness-of, however, does not necessitate the logical possibility of a series of compounded introspective states. Consciousness-of refers to a real psychological event. The idea of a con-

sciousness of that consciousness-of comes from a false understanding
of consciousness as something external to the content. The opposition
between consciousness and content which seems to be implied in
consciousness-of is, in fact, the mode of presentation of the conscious
state and not an aspect of its underlying nature. In this respect, Bren-
tano has written that "the consciousness which accompanies the presentation (of a sound) is a consciousness not so much of this presentation as of the whole mental act in which the sound is presented, and
in which the consciousness itself exists concomitantly."

It may fairly be asked whether there exist planes of awareness between a consciousness of objects or of activity and true introspection.
Ontogenetic studies suggest a gradual transition from one level to the
next. The evidence from pathological cases also seems to point in this
direction, that is, to a series of levels in a continuum and not to a
sharp break between radically different forms. However, one cannot
apprehend states of consciousness in oneself other than the immediate
state; i.e., the state can only know itself. For this reason prior levels
may be misrepresented as nonconscious rather than primitively conscious. The concept of an ascending series of levels of consciousness
avoids to some extent this problem, i.e., whether consciousness is a
product of primitive consciousness or of a nonconscious state, since
the problem results from the idea of consciousness as extrinsic to content and the consequent importance of consciousness-of as *sine qua
non* of any conscious state.

The existence of preliminary forms of consciousness can be inferred from the behavior of patients. Since only the final stages of consciousness are readily accessible through private introspection or in-
terrogation of others, earlier levels have to be reconstructed from the
pathological material. Our most objective means of achieving this reconstruction is through the use of behavioral and verbal performances,
but even here research into the nature of the preliminary stages is
largely intuitive. Even the private recollections of dreams may not adequately represent the experience of the dream state since the latter, to
achieve introspection, have passed on to a further genetic level; i.e.,
the introspected content is realized to a level beyond that which is
taken to be the object of the introspection. We can no more be sure
that what is recalled of a dream is a faithful copy of the actual dream
than that our consciousness-of, the state of introspection, is the endstage of cognition. In dream there is no awareness of the subsequent

(waking) level. The dream state is a closed system of reality, a universe. Waking, there is only a dim apprehension of the preceding stage, possible only because the latter gives rise to (indeed, is necessary as a part of) the introspective level. Yet, like dream, introspection is also a closed system. We cannot even guess at what conscious forms might lie beyond.

The Idea of Levels in Consciousness Formation

Awareness refers to the configuration of components within a particular cognitive level. It is this configuration which determines the constitution of the awareness state. If one could specify everything about these components—i.e., about action, perception, and language at a specific level in cognition—the total phenomenal realization of those specifications would constitute the awareness experience.

Affect is like form to the content of a particular component at a particular cognitive stage. There is a close relationship between affect and awareness. Awareness is like form to all components at a given moment at one level in cognition. In a sense, therefore, awareness can be identified with the total affective content, that is, awareness is the affective aspect of all components simultaneously.

Affect and awareness *seem* to have a reciprocal relationship. From the genetic point of view, however, this apparent reciprocity is a sign of an inner identity. Intense affective states do not preclude consciousness (in the sense of consciousness-of), the affective state *is* the consciousness experience at that particular level, the affect pointing to a stage where consciousness-of does not yet exist.

If affect is the *experience* of consciousness, then the *content* of that experience is determined by the primary components (i.e., action, perception, and language). For example, the degree of perceptual realization will determine whether consciousness is organized about the dream state or the object world.

Four levels—arbitrary phases—in consciousness formation can be distinguished which correspond to the described cognitive stages. *Sensorimotor* cognition would be characterized by an action series ranging from simple wakefulness or arousal to states of drive or motivation, and a perceptual expression in dreamless sleep. The immediacy of the performance and its enactment within a single, probably atemporal, somatic space field would not permit a "private" experience. Indeed, in a sense the behavior *is* the private experience. A comparison with pathological conditions at the same structural level such as coma or coma vigil is suggestive. In the *limbic* stage, the developing extrapersonal space both extends and begins to "fill in" the consciousness experience. The semantic transition of this level does not yet permit an object-consciousness, but the emergence of forming (isolating) contents achieves the initial step of an "opposition" between these various contents, as well as between the level and the prefigurating ground. Dream and psychotic hallucinosis and partial expressions such as derealization or depersonalization are manifestations of this level. The *neocortical* level achieves a stable object world. The organism perceives and acts in that world. This object or action consciousness is directed outward. This is because the exteriorization of the object has "left behind" an intrapersonal component that is not yet a parallel formation. For this reason the intrapersonal, the self, cannot yet serve as an object for cognition. At the *symbolic* level consciousness of self (consciousness of intrapersonal content, not self-recognition) is achieved by means of language. This occurs through the cognitive advance accompanying language production, and concerns a progressive articulation by language of a new intrapersonal space developing against (out of) the exteriorized space of the "outside world" and apprehended as intrapsychic. The articulation of this new space occurs through a kind of objectivization of intrapersonal content beyond that already achieved in the formation of the extrapersonal object.

Though language recapitulates earlier stages in action and perception it does not seem to uniquely contribute to the formation of consciousness at these early levels. Yet the utterance is an important means of access to preliminary stages in the private world of consciousness. In pathological states, the utterance is a representative of preliminary cognition and thus of the consciousness elaborated at that stage. In organic cases this can best be studied in disorders where the alteration of consciousness, in relation to language, is in the foreground of the clinical tableau: hemispheric disconnections (the so-called "split-brain" model), denial syndromes, aphasia, and the confusional state.

The Split-Brain Model of Consciousness. Following surgical section of the human forebrain commissures, special testing of patients has suggested a separate awareness-experience restricted to events occurring within each hemisphere. The evidence for this interpretation, which is of great importance to contemporary study of the nature of consciousness, is so well known that the reader is simply referred to two recent monographs (Gazzaniga, 1970; Dimond, 1972) and the paper on consciousness by Sperry (1969).

Characteristically, a "callosal" patient (with eyes closed) is unable to name objects placed in his left hand. Generally the patient does not say, "I don't know," but either does not respond at all or more commonly gives paraphasic or confabulatory answers. For example, a patient of Sperry's called a pencil held in the left hand a "can opener" and a "cigarette lighter," a patient of Geschwind and Kaplin (1962) identified a ring in the left hand as an "eraser," a watch as a "balloon," and a screwdriver as a "spoon" or a "piece of paper." If the patient is then asked to select with the left hand the (still unseen) object from a group of objects, he will tend to select—if it is present—the object named in the confabulation. Thus, if a key has been placed in the left hand and identified verbally as a comb, the left hand will select the comb from the object group. If the procedure is repeated nonverbally, the correct object is selected. I have also observed this in personal cases. We see that the "left hemisphere" confabulation determines the left hand ("right hemisphere") response. Moreover, the patient appears not only unaware of right hemisphere events but also of the erroneous nature of the misnaming, a product allegedly of the left hemisphere.

This failure of the patient to *admit* a lack of awareness for experiences presumably restricted to the right hemisphere is only one indication that the stimulus object has undergone *bihemispheric* processing. The confabulation is also a sign that the object has developed in both hemispheres. The lack of awareness for the erroneous nature of the confabulation reflects the fact that the object name is realized in right and left hemisphere only to a semantic level. The response, the confabulation or paraphasia, is comparable to the semantic paraphasias of standard aphasics, where there is also a lack of awareness for the incorrect performance. This verbal response in the left-hand test situation, e.g., "eraser" for ring, is proof that the content has developed to an intermediate stage in *left* hemisphere. Moreover, the nature of the paraphasia, whether categorical or asemantic, will reflect the degree of microstructural development within left hemisphere, a level which is determined by, and is continuous with (i.e., part of the same ground as) right hemisphere language capacity. This capacity is in turn related to the degree of lateralization which varies from one individual to another (Brown and Hecaen, 1976).

The correct nonverbal identification or selection of the object with the left and not the right hand points again to the state-specific nature of the performance and not to a separate hemispheric localization or "lack of transfer." The *endstage* cognitive level of the successful right hemisphere/left-hand performance is continuous with an *intermediate* stage in left hemisphere. Therefore the performance (cognitive) level of the patient in the right-hand/left hemisphere situation represents a stage beyond that to which the content has been processed in right hemisphere, even though this processing achieved a correct "nonverbal" response. In other words the correct right hemispheric selection corresponds to a content in left hemisphere preterminal to the actual performance level. It should be emphasized in this regard that the lack of a verbal element in the test situation—i.e. so-called nonverbal matching—does not indicate that the performance occurs exclusively through nonverbal systems. The absence of the verbal element is an absence on the test *and not in cognition.*

According to this analysis, the hemisphere act *as one* up to a certain cognitive stage which will vary according to the degree of lateralization. Beyond this level asymmetric structures carry cognition to a further level in one (the left) hemisphere only. There are several clinicopathological disorders which confirm this interpretation of the surgical material. One such disorder is the left-sided (so-called sympathetic) apraxia which occurs with left frontal lesion, usually in the presence of a right hemiparesis and some degree of aphasia. The condition has been attributed to an interruption of fibers passing from left to right frontal region which are concerned with movement of the left side to verbal command. The explanation is therefore much the same as that advanced for left-sided apraxia after surgical section of the corpus callosum. However, the nature of the impaired performance is quite different in the two conditions. In the former there are clumsy or dyspraxic approximations to the target action while in the surgical case, action is dextrous but more or less unrelated to the command. In "sympathetic" apraxia the action pattern is further along in its development and therefore closer to the goal. The awareness which accompanies this action is also further developed and so there is some recognition of error. In the surgical case the action pattern points to a more preliminary stage. The dislocations or parapraxes reflect a semantic level in the developing action comparable to the semantic-level origin of the confabulatory misnamings discussed above, and as in confabulatory misnaming the incorrect performance—the action—is not accompanied by a awareness of error.

An identical set of observations can be made in regard to the condition of agnosic or "pure" alexia. This disorder occurs with lesion of the left occipital lobe and splenium of corpus callosum. There is a right visual field defect. The central feature of the disorder is an impairment of reading in the intact left visual field, i.e., in the right hemisphere. The classical interpretation is identical to that of the left visual field alexia in the surgical patient, namely an interruption in the flow of written material from minor (right) hemisphere to language areas on the left side. However, closer attention to the reading difficulty in these two forms indicates that this common explanation is incorrect.

The reading difficulty in the clinical case contrasts with that of the surgical patient. Most patients with agnosic alexia can read single letters and construct simple words through a process of letter-by-letter spelling. Errors in reading tend to reflect morphological relationships to the correct words. There is awareness of error and some degree of frustration. In contrast, words flashed briefly in the left visual field of the surgical case evoke confabulatory and paralexic readings. While the former patient might read the word *chair* as "chase," showing a closer approximation to the target item, the surgical patient might say "throne" or "sofa," or give a confabulatory answer. Moreover, readings in the surgical patient are more facile and effortless than the slow, labored readings of the agnosic alexic, and are not accompanied by so acute an awareness of error.

These differences between the surgical and clinical patients in regard to disorders of action (apraxia) and perception (e.g., alexia) represent aspects of performance in the two groups in which all grades of transition occur, both moment to moment in testing and from one patient to another. These transitions are indication of the momentary "depth" of the performance, i.e., whether it is closer to the semantic level, as in paralexia or parapraxia, or to the final (target) action or perception. Moreover, in these transitions one observes also a change in awareness of content, as well as of affect; e.g., euphoria becoming frustration. These findings indicate that the performance of such patients reflects the genetic level achieved by a particular content in cognition and not its hemispheric isolation. Indeed, within the extremes of performance illustrated by the clinical and surgical "callosal" patients is to be found a wide range of aphasia symptomatology. Such cases argue for the view that awareness is specific to cognitive stage and that instances of what appear to be separate awarenesses point rather to multiple levels in a unitary process.

The Syndrome of Denial. Denial or lack of awareness of disease (anosognosia) is a common manifestation in both organic and functional disorders. The first description was by von Monakow (1885) in respect of two cases of cortical blindness, while the term *anosognosia*, often applied to this phenomenon, was coined by Babinski (1914) for lack of awareness of hemiparesis. Lack of awareness is also characteristic of several aphasic forms, e.g., jargon, stereotypy, and echo-responses. In general, three types of denial are recognized: partial or complete unawareness of a deficit; explicit denial of the deficit or, in the case of hemiplegic denial, of the very existence of the hemiparetic limbs; and denial associated with distortions, hallucinations, or other illusory phenomena referrable to the impaired body zone (e.g., phantom or reduplicated limbs, visual hallucination).

The view that denial is a reaction of the personality as a whole to the disorder is contradicted by the selective nature of the symptom. Thus, patients with left hemiplegia may deny weakness in the arm but admit to weakness in the leg. This occurs when there is a return of threshold sensory or motor function in the lower extremity while the arm remains fully paralyzed. Similarly, there may be catastrophic depression over subtotal cortical blindness with persistent denial of a hemiplegia. One patient with a left hemiplegia and previous amputation of the first two fingers of the left hand was able to correctly explain why he could not move his amputated fingers, but when asked to move the other (paralyzed) fingers of the same hand refused to admit the paralysis. Stengel (1946) described a case of cortical blindness with denial for the totally blind right visual field and awareness of visual loss on the left side where only minimal vision remained (motion and light perception). Thus, denial may spare a less recent disorder, may involve one of two (usually the more severely involved) hemiparetic limbs, and may spare deficient performances referrable to the same body zone depending on the reason for the deficiency.

In patients with denial there is commonly some degree of disorientation, recent memory loss, and a confabulatory trend. There appears to be a relationship between the severity of the perceptual deficit and the confabulation. Cases of denial with fair visual or somaesthetic perception will have a marked Korsakoff syndrome, whereas the more severe the perceptual impairment, the less prominent need be the Korsakoff and confusional state. In those cases where confabulatory denial is accompanied by hallucination in the impaired modality—e.g., visual hallucination in patients with cortical blindness—the hallucination, like the confabulation, should be viewed not as a cause of the denial but as a manifestation of the same level of disruption.

An interpretation of denial begins with the view that *awareness for a content is always related to the genetic level achieved by that content*. A somaesthetic or a visual percept is thus not outside of awareness but realized—with the awareness form bound to that content—only to an incomplete stage. Thus, when a cortically blind patient claims that he can see (the so-called Anton's syndrome) he is, in fact, correct, though his perception, and the awareness for that perception, are at a preobject level. Moreover, the confabulation that characterizes many such patients points also to a preliminary level, and in this respect is comparable to the confabulatory naming of "split-brain" patient to objects in the left hand or visual half-field.

Language and Awareness. There are three major forms of aphasic language which are characterized by deficient insight. These are the stereotypy, the echo-response, and certain forms of jargon-speech, including semantic paraphasia.

The stereotypy or recurrent utterance is a feature of Broca's and global aphasia. The utterance may consist of single words, such as *yes, no,* or *fine,* oaths or profanities, brief phrases such as *Oh my God,* or a few words in unintelligible jargon. There is an important difference between stereotypic and volitional speech. Stereotypies are well articulated, brief latency, or explosive, and often show preservation of speech melody, stress, and intonation. During the utterance, the patient may be excited or euphoric and gives no evidence of awareness of the stereotypic content. In contrast, the volitional speech of a patient with stereotypic utterance is slow, labored, and dysarthric with acute self-awareness and frustration. Moreover, patients who recover from a Broca's aphasia do not recall the stereotypic content, but may painfully recollect their initial attempts to produce their own name.

A transition occurs between the stereotypic and the volitional utterance. The stereotypy evolves from complete automaticity without awareness, through modification and then blocking, which is at first partial and incomplete. At a later stage, the stereotypy may alternate with some volitional speech; finally, the complete inhibition of the stereotypy signals the return of volitional speech.

There is some tendency to attribute the stereotypy to the action of right hemisphere, given a lesion on the left side. However, the stereotypy is not a phenomenon in isolation but undergoes a gradual change with the return of volitional speech. Nor is the stereotypy sharply demarcated from awareness. It is neither the residuum of damaged left hemisphere nor the highest vocal achievement possible in the intact right hemisphere, but a product of both acting in unison at a preliminary language level.

There is a close relationship between the stereotypy and the echo-reaction. Echolalia is also a brief-latency, well-articulated, often explosive iteration without awareness seen in focal aphasic disorders as well as in diffuse organic states. The short, one- to two-word echolalic repetitions of the posterior (jargon) aphasic are, in fact, exactly analogous to the stereotypies of the anterior patient. When both posterior *and* anterior regression occur, the result is echolalia and stereotypy as a more or less isolated feature of language performance, the so-called isolation syndrome (see Brown, 1975c, for further discussion).

Echolalia is clearly not a simple audioverbal reflex but like the stereotypy is in relation to other language performances. Thus echolalia occurs only when the patient is addressed, there is personalization of the iteration (e.g., asked, "How are you?" the patient responds, "How am I"), and given incorrect presentations the patient produces a correct grammatical form. Moreover, there is often a relation between the fidelity of the repetition (the echo) and the degree to which it is understood. Patients may show echolalia for nonsense words or a foreign language and paraphasic repetition for the mother tongue. In some patients, a transition can be seen between the echo and normal repetition. This transition takes place over four stages: (1) initial brief latency, explosive echo-responses accompanied by euphoria or labile emotionality and a lack of awareness for the echoed content; (2) echo-like responses with surprise or uncertainty (partial awareness) of the performance; (3) repetition with paraphasia, especially phonemic paraphasia, with moderate awareness and efforts at self-correction;

and (4) complete failure of an anomic type with acute self-awareness, frustration, and at times catastrophic reactions. These several forms of repetition may coexist and alternate in a single patient, just as the Broca's aphasic may have concurrent stereotypy and volitional speech.

The inner relationship between language and awareness is also apparent in the transition of semantic jargon to anomia. A clear progression occurs from the lack of awareness for speech in semantic (asemantic) jargon, through the minimal insight of semantic paraphasia to the partial awareness of verbal (categorical) paraphasia and finally to anomia or amnesic aphasia with improved awareness of the speech difficulty. The evolution from a stage of impaired word-meaning, lack of awareness, and euphoria to one of preserved word-meaning, acute awareness and frustration, occurs gradually through a series of intermediate stages. These stages can be observed from one moment to the next even in the same patient.

From cases such as these, of echolalia, stereotypy, or paraphasia, we learn that awareness is linked to the momentary realization level of the utterance, and that the *pathological alterations of awareness do not just represent disorders of the normal process but levels that have been achieved.* This assertion, which appears evident on a study of language-bound alterations of consciousness, can also be explored through an investigation of changes in consciousness which accompany more generalized regressive states, including the acute confusional state and the derealization complex.

The Confusional State. This condition is easy to recognize but quite difficult to define. There is a disorder of attention with rapid shifts of interest and inability to establish and maintain an attentional set. The patient seems confused. There is a loosened contact with the surround. He is unable on direct or multiple-choice questions to give an account of his location in geographic space (e.g., the hospital, city, or state) or the current date (the day of the week, year, or season). This is referred to as a "disorientation in space and time."

Confabulation may occur and establishes a relationship with the Korsakoff syndrome. While the attentional disorder and the appearance of perplexity in the patient are the most striking features, the syndrome ordinarily—perhaps invariably—occurs in the company of impairments in memory and affect. The disorder may occur acutely or may appear as a stage in the deterioration of a dementia. In either case, however, the disruption is generally uniform across the cognitive level, though the relative emphasis on one or another component may determine special features in an individual case—e.g., hallucinations accompanied by a more dreamlike or oneiric attitude pointing to a shift toward perceptual systems at the limbic level; excitation, as in manic confusion, pointing to the action component; confabulation to language involvement; and so on.

The awareness of such a patient is intermediate between that of dream and consciousness of self. The patient gives the impression of a closer contact than the dreamer to the shared world around him. Ey has written that "the essential symptom consists in an incapacity to achieve a sufficient synthesis and differentiation of the psychic contents, which are mixed and agglutinated. This accounts for the lack of lucidity and clarity in the field of consciousness." The confusional state can be explained as a reflection of this preobject cognitive level. Since both object and object consciousness develop together, the incomplete resolution and exteriorization of the object will entail an attenuation (failure of development) of consciousness of that object. This is the basis of the impairment of attention. One might say that object consciousness is distributed over the diffuse preobject field.

The confusional state, therefore, represents a more or less global dissolution of cognition at the cortical–representational level. However, the confusion itself is in large part a reflection of the gap between the cognitive level of patient and examiner and does not completely reflect an inner confusion, i.e., the consciousness experience of the patient is appropriate to his (not the examiner's) genetic level of object formation.

Derealization and Depersonalization. The loss of a sense of reality of the object world (derealization) accompanies the regression of that world back to a preobject level. Derealization therefore can be a partial element of a confusional state though it may occur independently. It is also a sign of incipient hallucination. The incomplete formation and exteriorization of objects leading to a feeling of estrangement from the world is really a partial withdrawal back into the intrapersonal space of imagery.

In derealization it is not the object but the object-experience that seems unreal. Federn (1952) has argued that in psychotics the loss of reality by objects is accompanied by a gaining of reality by thoughts. As the object recedes back into the intrapersonal sphere it becomes more like a thought, while the thought seems to have objectified. This coming-to-the-fore of the cognitive aspect of perception is just another feature of the incomplete object exteriorization. This feature, moreover, helps to bring derealization into relation with *déjà-vu*. This phenomenon is a kind of brief derealization and points to a predominance in the object of its mnemic (i.e., cognitive) aspect. In other words, *déjà-vu* is the momentary experience of an incomplete object formation. The feeling of familarity develops out of the greater immediacy to the cognitive matrix within which the object (any object) develops.

In depersonalization there is a feeling of will-lessness, of an inability to go out and meet the (generally derealized) object-world. There is a failure of the action to fully exteriorize and so its imaginal character is regained. This regression is associated with a reduction in the volitional attitude which accompanies the action development. The loss of volition, moreover, entails a greater prominence of more automatic performances.

The anxiety and fear which are a part of derealization and depersonalization experiences are not simply reactions to the loss of the object or the active self but are manifestations at the same cognitive level. Psychoanalytic accounts of estrangement stress the withdrawal of libido from objects. In ego psychology there is a withdrawal of the libidinal component from the cathexis of the ego boundary. However, the affective change is not a causal effect or a determining factor but just another phenomenon in parallel with the failure of complete object and action development.

Derealization and depersonalization occur in a variety of organic, toxic, and functional states tending to implicate pathology of the temporal lobes. This is also true of *déjà-vu* experiences. A continuum exists from *déjà-vu* to derealization and from these to loss of the object world, hallucination, and psychotic regression. Similarly, depersonalization may be a first step toward schizophrenic inertia and loss of Will.

These various phenomena are partial manifestations of the limbic–presentational level in cognition. The more complete expression of the level occurs in dream or profound psychotic regression. In a sense, therefore, the consciousness of dream, and its discussed partial manifestations, represent a stage preliminary to that corresponding to the confusional state, while the latter is transitional to consciousness of self.

Further Considerations on the Model of Consciousness

The various alterations of consciousness which have been discussed can be brought into relation with a general model of cognitive
formation, according to which consciousness is a manifestation of
both the achieved cognitive level and the full series of cognitive levels
at a given moment in psychological time. Thus, consciousness corresponds to stages in the development of the object world. However, the
realization of an object world has the implication of a *purposeful* behavior in that world. The realization of an object accompanies the actual or implicit realization of an action on that object. This provides
the basis of a motility that is *directed toward an object.* In perception
the object appears as an endstage, in action as a goal. In perception
the object is a kind of product which seems passive to the act, while in
action motility is the product and seems active in relation to the object. When one perceives in another this orientation of both action and
object toward a common goal the behavior is judged *purposeful.*

Through language purposeful behavior can become *volitional.* The
distinction here is between an action which is ostensibly directed or
motivated toward a goal and an action which is obediant to a will.
Purposeful behavior is not necessarily willed behavior, as in trance or
fugue states or automatisms, but volitional behavior always incorporates purposefulness. It is in the idea of the will that one sees the
microgenetic advance over representational level cognition afforded by
language. Volition is an act of reflection that has an action for its object. Will is a way of describing the self in this reflective state. The
problem of volition can be considered not only as an advance over
purposefulness but in relation to the formation of self.

Volition and the Idea of Self. We have discussed how language
becomes to mental space as objects are to public space, stressing that
this is not the old space of imagery before the external world had
formed but a space beyond that achieved in the formation of the
world. In a very real sense, the initial distinction of world from self
leads, through language, to a distinction of self from world. The separation of the world leads only to a consciousness of the world and of
self *qua* object in that world. Self-awareness requires a further differentiation within self. Language fulfills this need. Words do not exist
in the world psychologically in the same way as do acts or objects. The
object *seems* to exist in itself, to impinge on mind from outside; the ac-

tion seems to have an effect in that object space. Words "interact" in a different space; and we are conscious of the fact that the word has to be thrown out into that space from its position in the mind. Thus language begins to populate a new intrapsychic domain. The exteriorization of both object and action provides a common space which can be set against this emerging intrapsychic component. This common space, together with action and object (goal) as purposeful behavior—all of this as a unit, a level in cognition—is incorporated within the experience of volition as a kind of already materialized content beyond (out of) which the language-act will emerge.

Another aspect of this transition from purposeful to volitional action concerns the attitude of "activity" created by the very process through which the action unfolds. While the space of perception constantly draws away from the subject, finally "detaching" as the object exteriorizes, the subject is drawn into the space of action. This is part of our experience of the temporal or successive nature of action. Seriality brings to action a striving for completion. In contrast to the immediacy of perception, action seems to build up a meaning or a signification over time. The feeling of activity in action development is somehow created through a complex of these factors; the seeming pursuit of meaning, the orientation and progression toward an object, and the temporal unfolding of the action plan. The feeling of activity is then transformed into the idea of an active self; the seriality of action and the increasing separation from the action help to create the deception of a will as causal instigator; and the apparent inexhaustibility of the meaning-content of action development gives the impression of actions planned for a future.

The self in a volitional act has to be built up in the same way as any other cognitive component. We have spoken of the cognitive *form* as the experience of consciousness and the level-specific *components* as determining the conscious content. Self is this content realization together with the awareness form; it is the composite of these two aspects of consciousness. Will is a prominence of self in the context of an action (or an inaction). The corresponding state in perception is reflection or a higher type of object-consciousness. Thus, the self in will and the self in consciousness-of-self (reflection) are expressions of this coming together of the experience and content of consciousness when the latter, the content, is oriented toward action or perception, respectively. However, this orientation concerns the linguistic representatives of action and perception rather than action and perception as such. The consciousness of self in will and reflection is a transformation of the consciousness of activity and objects of a previous level. Consciousness of objects is a consciousness of a world that has already exteriorized. Self looks on this world of its creation. But this is an earlier self than self-in-consciousness. In the latter, in reflection, there is a new self and a new object. Self in consciousness-of-self (reflection) is to an idea or image as self in consciousness of objects is to an exteriorized object. Yet all levels in cognition have a share in the self. The traces of innumerable past cognitive traversals, the "selves" of earlier ontogenetic times no longer realized as final contents, the whole body of experience built into structural form, this complex historical and microgenetic organization lies behind, generates, and contributes to the ephemeral self-in-consciousness.

The Psychoanalytic Theory of Consciousness. A state-specific theory of consciousness is not just a theory of different conscious states, but rather states specific to content and ordered in a series which corresponds to—indeed recapitulates—the formative process through which consciousness develops. Moreover, specificity to content does not refer to the particular content of an act of cognition but to the prominence of certain components (action, perception, language) within that cognitive act. From a variety of conditions it appears that more than one such conscious state can exist in one individual. This is true not only for the more dramatic instance of the "split-brain" patient, but also for dream consciousness, hysteria, dissociative states, etc., where contents persist not as "subconscious ideas" but as incompletely realized levels. From the point of view of psychopathology, these levels consist of: (1) sensorimotor consciousness, as in sleep, wakefulness, and drive-related states; (2) presentational consciousness, where consciousness is in behavior at a preobject level, as in psychosis or dream; (3) representational consciousness, where there is consciousness of object and activity, disrupted as in the confusional state; and (4) symbolic consciousness, where the self which is realized in consciousness-of-self (reflection) and will (volition) is threatened with loss, as in depression and apathy, or will-lessness (the *Willenlosigkeit* of German authors).

This concept of pathological levels in a process of realization is to some extent incorporated in psychoanalytic formulations of subconscious, preconscious, and conscious strata. However, the emphasis is usually on a two-level system with complex mechanisms of interaction postulated between levels. In contrast, Rapaport (1951) has written, "We have no reason to assume theoretically that these (Cs, subCs) are the only two kinds of consciousness possible. Observation and experience, on the other hand, suggest that there is a group of such states of consciousness ranging between the hallucinatory consciousness characteristic of the dream and waking consciousness (et seq.)." Psychopathological case study indicates at least one interpolated level. However, it is likely that any schema of levels will be somewhat arbitrary, the different consciousness states representing phases in the unfolding of cognition rather than distinct systems of consciousness.

According to Freud (SE * 18:7), consciousness and memory do not appear in the same system, consciousness arising in place of the memory trace. This notion comes from the view of memory as a deep-level store acted upon by other processes. Thus, it is inconsistent with the idea of a "trace" at each level of mnemic realization, i.e., that memory is also something to be achieved.

The term ego (Ich) generally connotes a province of mind, though it was employed also for the self or self-concept. In the former sense the ego (consciousness) is the differentiated surface of the psyche between the instincts and perception. Freud (SE 19:25) says, "For the ego, perception plays the part which in the id falls to instinct. The ego represents what may be called reason and common sense, in contrast to the id, which contains the passions." Thus, ego (self) and consciousness have both a receptive and an inhibitory effect positioned between psyche (subconscious) and external world. More recently, Hartmann and others have developed the idea that the ego has an adaptive role built up around the objects and acts of the real world. Hartmann has rightly called attention to the importance of nonconflictual activity in the ego, but at the same time has added to the weight of assumed ego functions.

However, the ego (or consciousness) is not a function or a functional division, it is only a possibility, an achievement that must be continually renewed. There are no "ego functions." These are the diverse manifestations of a cognitive level simultaneously realized. The view of ego as a frontier of the psyche thrust against the external world is an application to ego of the conflictual organization of the

* Standard Edition

"lower centers." Conflict points to incomplete resolution, and thus to preliminary cognition, rather than to interaction and competing interests. The ego does not act in the world. World and ego are represented cotemporally in the same cognitive plane. Ego is not a site where action is initiated but the terminal point, the outcome, of an action development.

Ego as self-in-awareness becomes manifest only when cognition is completely unfolded. Yet at any given moment, the endstage cognitive level determines the ego experience, each such level modeling the world up to a certain point. Reality is determined by the degree of modeling achieved. There is no "reality principle," only stages in private space which correspond to levels in the formation of a world always "real" to the viewer at each level of its formation. However, reality also refers to a shared world constructed by all of the members of a group. A concensus about this shared world is achieved through access to others inhabiting the same cognitive endpoint.

Some General Considerations

On Free Will. Volition is a stage in the course of an action development, rather than a motive force which stands behind the act. The traditional idea of free will requires an actor or agent who acts. However, since the actor (the self) has, like the action, a developmental history, there is no agent who initiates the action. Both actor and action are realizations of this developmental history.

The idea of free will would also seem to demand that a choice is available to a conscious self. However, the conscious self, or self-in-awareness, does not cause another cognitive state; it does not choose something but rather *gives way* to another state rising from below. In a very real sense, each conscious moment dies at the instant of its birth, dissolving away in the continual emergence of new form.

On the "Mental" and the "Physical." Mind is not attached to structure but is itself a kind of organism that undergoes growth and change. Structure is dynamic, structure is only one brief moment in the life of process. Mind as organic form approaches structure viewed as process. Both mind (or cognition) and structure (or process) unfold according to the same evolutionary law.

Cognition develops over a series of phylogenetic levels. Ontogeny extends the development of both structural and cognitive form. These genetic stages are again recapitulated each moment in cognitive microgenesis. The process which supports this cognitive form, this series of transformations from one level to the next, is inwardly inseparable from the cognitive form which it supports. This is not an argument for "identity," it is an argument for parallelism.

The old distinctions between inner and outer, extension and lack of extension, do not take us very far toward a solution, or even a true definition, of this problem. Certainly, neuropsychological study seems to confirm a Kantian point of view. Even at the level of retina the object has undergone some construction. But the final object in perception is no closer to the "real" object than this retinal construct. At each level in the construction of the world the "real" object is accurately rendered by cognition. There is no solid physical object waiting to be perceived. Stages in object realization correspond to a hierarchy of physical existences of the "real" object. This "real" world is the stage in cognition which happens to crystallize. In mind there is no physical *and* psychic, only psychic. The physical is an inference about the origins of cognition; it is therefore a kind of evolutionary myth.

The model of cognition seems to lead to the following conclusions about the mind–brain problem. The brain process(es) which mediates cognitive development is an *emergent* process which may or may not conform to causal laws. Each brain-state is also a mind-state, *provided that* the brain-state occurs within the framework of the described cognitive structure. There is no additive or one-to-one relationship between brain activity and mind "stuff"; mind is not constructed out of component elements. An isolated, electrically active slab of cortex does not generate a partial mind-state. The mind-state occurs as an *epiphenomenon* of the brain-state when the brain-state is both global and embedded in cognitive formation. There is a succession of mind-states elaborated as another aspect of (i.e., having the same referent as) a corresponding succession of brain-states, but as epiphenomena, mind-states have no influence on these brain-states or on other mind-states.

On Other Forms of Consciousness. Each conscious state in the cognitive series is to the preceding state as a kind of endstage, and to the subsequent state a ground in which it will develop. A conscious state may thus contain some apprehension of a preceding level, since this preceding level has gone into its (the next level's) formation. However, there can be no knowledge of a state which lies beyond, since to any given conscious state the subsequent state does not yet exist. Thus waking consciousness has an intuition of the dream experience, but dream consciousness, a more preliminary level, cannot foresee the waking state. From this it follows that waking consciousness (self-in-consciousness) could be a point *en passage* to a still higher stage of which it, waking consciousness, is unaware. It is not inconceivable that certain psychic phenomena, extrasensory experiences and the like, may represent fleeting realizations of this higher level. Nor is it inconceivable that such a level of consciousness could participate in some sort of collective fabric. In this respect, the concept of a noösphere should not be lightly dismissed. Finally, if it is true that every mind-state requires a brain-state, as well as the preliminary brain-states out of which the final brain-state developed, consciousness could not persist independent of brain-states. For this reason it seems unlikely that brain death permits a transcendence to this possible higher level.

References

Babinski, J. Contribution a l'etude des troubles mentaux dans l'hemiplegie organique cerebrale (anosognosie). *Revue Neurologique*, 1914, *27*, 845.

Brown, J. *Aphasia, apraxia and agnosia: Clinical and theoretical aspects.* Springfield, Illinois: Charles C. Thomas, 1972.

Brown, J. On the neural organization of language. *Brain and Language*, 1975, *2*, 18–30. (a)

Brown, J. Aphasia and Neuropsychiatry. In S. Arieti and M. Reiser (Eds.), *American handbook of psychiatry* (Vol. 4). New York: Basic Books, 1975. (b)

Brown, J. The problem of repetition: A study of "conduction" aphasia and the "isolation" syndrome. *Cortex*, 1975, *11*, 37–52. (c)

Brown, J. *Mind, brain, and consciousness: A study in the neuropsychology of cognition.* New York: Academic Press. In press. 1977.

Brown, J., and Hecaen, H. Lateralization and language representation. *Neurology*, 1976, *26*, 183–189.

Dimond, S. *The double brain.* London: Churchill-Livingstone, 1972.

Federn, P. *Ego psychology and the psychoses.* New York: Basic Books, 1952.

Gazzaniga, M. *The bisected brain.* New York: Appleton-Century-Crofts, 1970.

Geschwind, N., and Kaplan E. A human cerebral deconnection syndrome. *Neurology*, 1962, *12*, 675–685.

MacLean, P. Cerebral evolution and emotional processes. *Annals of the New York Academy of Sciences*, 1972, *193*, 137–149.

Monakow, C. von. Experimentelle und pathologische-anatomische Untersuchungen, etc. *Archiv für Psychiatrie*, 1885, *16*, 151–199.

Rapaport, D. Consciousness: A psychopathological and psychodynamic view. In *Problems of consciousness.* Transactions of Second Conference, New York: Josiah Macy Foundation, 1951.

Sanides, F. Functional architecture of motor and sensory cortices in primates in the light of a new concept of neocortex evolution. In C. Noback and W. Montagna (Eds.), *The primate brain*. New York: Appleton-Century-Crofts, 1970.

Sperry, R. A modified concept of consciousness. *Psychological Review*, 1969, *76*, 532–536.

Stengel, E., and Steele, G. Unawareness of physical disability. *Journal of Mental Science*, 1946, *92*, 379–388.

Teszner, D., Tzavaras, A., Gruner, J., and Hecaen, H. L'asymmetrie droite-gauche du planum temporale. *Revue Neurologique*, 1972, *126*, 444–449.

Wada, J., Clarke, R., and Hamm, A. Cerebral hemispheric asymmetry in humans. *Archives of Neurology*, 1975, *32*, 239–246.

Yakovlev, P. Motility, behavior and the brain. *Journal of Nervous and Mental Disease*, 1948, *107*, 313–335.

5

Robert W. Thatcher and Robert S. April

EVOKED POTENTIAL CORRELATES OF SEMANTIC INFORMATION PROCESSING IN NORMALS AND APHASICS

Of Eric Lenneberg's understanding of language there is one aspect that we consider particularly relevant and which we will emphasize in this chapter. This contribution comes from Lenneberg's belief that neurolinguists must search for a fundamental process that occupies a central position in all higher level cognitive functions. As Lenneberg (1970) states, "No psychobiological model of language can be considered to be adequate unless it comes to grips with the notion of language knowledge and its relationship to knowledge in general" (p. 636). Throughout his writings Lenneberg searched for a single process or a set of central processes which were fundamental to all higher-level operations including perception, language, thought, and knowledge. It was from this background that Lenneberg so forcefully argued that "sensory recognition processes were homologous to language processes" (Lenneberg, 1970). Although Lenneberg never described pre-

Robert W. Thatcher · Brain Research Labs, New York Medical College, New York, New York. *Robert S. April* · Department of Neurology, New York Medical College, Center for Chronic Disease, Roosevelt Island, New York.

cisely what these basic processes were, he nevertheless felt it was important to emphasize that language and logic share the basic property of classification and discrimination (Lenneberg, 1967, 1970). As discussed more completely by Lenneberg (1970), the notions of discrimination and classification were formalized into laws of thought and knowledge by George Boole in 1854. The famous "Boolean algebra" is based on a binary classification scheme which, in essence, creates a formalism of the concepts of "sameness" and "difference." As examined more fully elsewhere (Thatcher, 1976b), the concepts of "sameness" and "difference" are among the most profound known to man. These notions form the basis of order (Bohm, 1969), logic and mathematics (Whitehead and Russell, 1927; McCulloch and Pitts, 1943), and classification in general (Chen, 1973; Sneath and Sokal, 1973). In the context of language and cognition, Lenneberg pointed to the importance of the relational properties of language (Lenneberg, 1974) and emphasized the temporal structure of knowledge where connections are made between succeeding events and the present is compared to the past. Notions of "semantic fields" and "syntactical and semantic structures" involve an elaboration of the concepts of "sameness" and "difference" and the computation of relationships in time (Lenneberg, 1967, 1970).

Physiological Considerations of Language Comprehension

The goal of the present chapter is twofold. One is to introduce procedures that explore the electrophysiological correlates of memory match and mismatch. The procedures involve evoked potential analyses from subjects performing in delayed letter matching and delayed word semantic matching tasks. The evoked potential is particularly relevant since it reflects sensory recognition and cognitive processes held so important by Eric Lenneberg. The second goal is to contrast the electrophysiological results from normal subjects to those obtained from two aphasic patients performing the same tasks. This represents the first efforts by the authors to study evoked potentials and neuropsychological tests of cognitive function in aphasic patients. Evoked potential analyses from such patients may provide a useful measure of cognitive function for studies of language recovery after acquired lesions. In contrast to behavioral examinations the evoked potential reflects only early neurological events—e.g., those that follow stimulus presentation but precede motor output. In this way an electrophysiological correlate of sensory and cognitive function may be examined directly in aphasic patients.

The evoked potential test battery, currently being developed, also includes challenges of auditory and visual information processing. In the present chapter, however, only evoked responses to visual (letter and word) stimuli will be described. Although the results from the aphasic patients are preliminary, they are presented in this chapter in order to emphasize the potential scientific and clinical application of these procedures.

Before describing the electrophysiological procedures a brief theoretical discussion of certain physiological aspects of language processing must be considered. This discussion will necessarily be brief, since no clear neurophysiological models of language comprehension have been developed. Only particular aspects of language comprehension will be considered as they pertain to Lenneberg's views regarding classification and discrimination processes.

Representational Systems

The human scalp evoked potential reflects primarily sensory and cognitive processes and has two major components. The early components reflect the physical attributes of the stimuli, whereas the longer latency components reflect later cognitive processes (Regan, 1972). In terms of linguistic information processing afferent information is transformed by specialized nerve endings into coded impulses which are conducted centrally. The physical features of the sensory stimulus (phonemes in the case of an auditory input and lines, edges, angles, etc., in the case of a visual input) are mapped onto a neural representational system in an, as yet, unknown manner. Various neurophysiological models have been developed to explain the mapping process (Hubel and Wiesel, 1962; Pribram, 1971; Barlow, 1972). Most of these models rely on feature extraction. That is, neural elements respond optimally only to a particular feature of the sensory stimulus. The constellation of neural responses corresponding to the salient features of the stimulus constitute a representational system. Feature extraction models are usually hierarchical (see Barlow, 1972) in which there is a hierarchy of levels of greater complexity both of the feature extraction and the representational systems. There are a few nonfeature extraction models (see Gibson, 1969) in which the anatomy of the brain uniquely determines mappings of the external world onto neutral representational systems. Our concern in this chapter, however, is not with how representational systems are formed but rather with cognitive operations that are performed on representational systems once they have been created. There is reasonable consensus among researchers (see Szentagothai and Arbib, 1974) that, at some stage, both the formation and subsequent operations performed on representational systems involve the active interaction of the present with the past. For example, Szentagothai and Arbib (1974) elegantly presented the commonly expressed view (see Sokolov, 1960; Miller, Galanter, and Pribram, 1960; Pribram, 1971) that models of the external world are continually being created and then refined and updated by matching and mismatching the model with memory as well as successive samples of sensory input. This hypothesis of representational match and mismatch is consistent with many of Lenneberg's views and fits two general hypotheses of linguistic comprehension.

Hypotheses of the Comprehension Process

Currently, there are two general categories of theories of speech perception. One category contains the motor or articulatory theories and the other the sensory theories. The motor theory was proposed first by Halle and Stevens (1962) and elaborated by A. M. Liberman and colleagues at Haskins Laboratories (see Liberman, Cooper, Shakweiler, and Studdert-Kennedy, 1967; Liberman 1970). This theory maintains that the mechanism of speech recognition makes use of internal models of speech production, in which acoustic input is correlated with articulatory patterns necessary to reproduce the input. According to this view phonemes are the basic building blocks for speech and speech perception is presumed to occur in a special "speech mode" which involves unique sensory systems and motor mechanisms. However, there are recent experimental data that challenge the motor theory. For example, Fodor, Bever, and Garrett (1974) failed to observe invariant electromyographic correlates associated with particular phonemes. Also, as noted by Wanner, Taylor, and

Thompson (1976), the phenomenon of "categorical perception" * (Liberman, 1970; Lisker and Abramson, 1970) can be explained strictly in terms of acoustic cues without reference to articulation. Similarly, Ades (1974) and Miller, Weir, Pastore, Kelly, and Dooling, (1974) have shown that categorical perception can be obtained to artificially synthesized sounds which are unrecognizable as speech stimuli. Finally, recent evidence indicates that the syllable and not the phoneme may be the basic perceptual unit for speech (see review by Rubin, 1974). The latter finding is important since a motor theory is not necessary to explain context dependent perception if syllables are the basic units (Wanner *et al.*, 1976).

The purely sensory theories can be divided into two broad categories. The first one is called the transformational hypothesis which evolved from the transformational grammar developed by Chomsky (1957, 1965). The transformational grammar provided a means by which the relation between the structural location of a phrase and its grammatical function could be determined. This was accomplished by introducing an abstract syntactical construct, called the "deep structure," which represents the grammatical functions of a sentence. "Transformational rules" were then developed in order to obtain a description of the order of words or phrases in a sentence, which is called the "surface structure."

The transformational hypothesis evolved from Chomsky's formulations by assuming that the meaning or semantic level of comprehension corresponded to the deep structure and that the physical features of visually or aurally presented words corresponded to the surface structure.

Internal transformational rules determined the relationships between these two representational levels. In the present context one might assert that the surface structure of language corresponds to feature extraction or sensory representational systems, whereas the deep

* "Categorical perception" implies that speech sounds are perceived categorically. That is, discriminable speech sounds are limited to a small number of identifiable categories. For example, syllables such as /ba and /pa differ according to their *voice onset times* or VOT (the delay between the initial sound produced by releasing the lips and the later sound made by vibrating the vocal cords). Sounds with a short VOT (less than about 25 msec) are perceived as /ba, sounds with a longer VOT (greater than about 25 msec) are perceived as /pa. Two sounds which fall on either side of the boundary are easy to discriminate, whereas two sounds which fall on the same side of the boundary are discriminated with slightly better than chance accuracy.

structure corresponds to a long-term memory or semantic representation and the transformational structure reflects a comparator operation involved in matching or mismatching sensory representations at the semantic level (Thatcher, 1976a).

The second dominant view of comprehension can be called the context construction hypothesis. This includes the semantic node hypotheses (Wortman and Greenberg, 1971). However, one of the most promising context hypotheses is believed to be the so-called *augmented transition network* (ATN) developed originally by Thorne, Bratley, and Dewar (1968) and subsequently elaborated by Bobrow and Frazier (1969) and Kaplan (1973). This hypothesis involves a sequential process whereby information at the beginning of a sentence guides the comprehension of later words in the sentence. It is argued that comprehension occurs by formulating hypotheses about the syntactical category of each word, the contextual grouping of words into phrases, and the grammatical function of a phrase. According to this view, sensory input is continually being matched or mismatched with the output of an ongoing hypothesis-refining process.

It is not our purpose to evaluate critically these two hypotheses of the process of comprehension. Suffice it to say that there is experimental evidence favoring both, and conflicts between the two hypotheses are, as yet, unresolved (Wanner, 1974). In the present chapter the sensory theories of comprehension will be emphasized rather than the motoric ones. The evoked potential analyses discussed in this chapter are obtained from widespread scalp regions which include frontal, central (motor), and posterior (sensory) derivations. One might predict that if motor or articulatory processes were involved in letter or word recognition, the principal evoked potential correlates would occur in anterior derivations, rather than posterior ones. However, as will be shown, the largest evoked potential effects observed in our study occurred in occipital, parietal, and posterior temporal derivations. Hence, no evidence for the motoric theory was provided by the evoked potential analysis.

Evoked Potential Correlates of Delayed Letter Matching

Central to the language comprehension hypotheses is the process of representational matching. It is consistent to argue that match–mismatch operations are involved whether surface structure representations are being compared to deep structure representations or whether hypotheses are being confirmed or disconfirmed. This center position of the process of representational matching recently gave rise to experiments designed to obtain evoked potential correlates of memory match and mismatch using linguistic stimuli.

The experiments involve the use of a Background-Information-Probe (or BIP) paradigm (Thatcher, 1974, 1976b). This paradigm permits the evoked potential analysis of background neural excitability changes which precede and follow the presentation of information. The subjects in this paradigm are required to view a series of briefly presented random dot displays, then a letter, then another series of random dot displays, then a second letter. The subjects are asked to make either a match or mismatch choice based on the two successive letter stimuli. This requires remembering the first letter for varying periods (3 to 7 sec) and then matching or mismatching the second with the memory of the first in order to make the correct response. The random dot displays elicit evoked potentials which serve as controls of excitability changes that precede and follow the presentation of the first letter. A major purpose of the experiment was to analyze evoked potentials elicited by physically identical stimuli which differ only in the degree of concordance between the present and the recent past. For example, averaged evoked potentials (AEPs) elicited by the letter *A* preceded several seconds by the letter *A* (match) could be compared to AEPs elicited by the letter *A* preceded several seconds by the letter *B* (mismatch). Figure 1 illustrates the delayed letter matching paradigm in which a series of brief visual displays were presented on an accessory oscilloscope to human subjects. The subjects varied in age from 18 to 32 (one female) and were all either college graduates or college-

Fig. 1. Illustration of trial sequence of computer-generated displays in a delayed letter matching paradigm. There are a variable number of control and ITI displays before and after the first letter (information). All displays are 20 msec in duration and presented at a repetition frequency of 1 Hz. Total luminance and retinal area subtended (1.5°) are the same for all displays. (From Thatcher, 1976a)

bound. These subjects (two left-handed and seven right-handed) had no previous history of neurological dysfunction.

The displays, which were generated by a PDP-12 computer, were 20 msec in duration and presented at a repetition frequency of 1/s. A given trial (Figure 1) involved presenting a variable number (2 to 6) of random dot displays (control) followed by a letter (information display, A, B, or C) followed by another variable number (2 to 6) of random dot displays (intertest interval displays, ITIs) which were followed by a second letter (test) that either matched or mismatched the information stimulus. If the test stimulus was a match, subjects were instructed to delay 1 sec and then move a small lever to the left. If it mismatched, subjects moved the lever to the right. There was a 5-sec delay period between trials, and match and mismatch conditions were equally probable and counterbalanced across a session. There were 24 trials/session and evoked potentials were averaged across four sessions. The direction of lever movement across sessions was counterbalanced and the number of illuminated points and visual angle (1.5°) were the same for all displays. (Further details of the methodology are provided elsewhere: Thatcher, 1976c).

The evoked potentials were recorded from bilateral and midline scalp derivations. The electrodes were applied according to the international 10–20 system (O_1, O_2, P_3, P_4, T_5, T_6, T_3, T_4, F_7, F_8, C_3, C_4, and F_z or C_z) in which the odd numbers refer to left scalp derivations the even to right, and subscript z to the midline (Jasper, 1958). Eye movements were monitored by either F_{p1} and F_{p2} electrodes or by a transorbital bipolar electrode pair. Except when otherwise specified, all recordings were monopolar using linked ear lobes as a reference. The EEG was amplified and band pass filtered (3 db roll-off at .3 Hz and 40 Hz) and evoked potentials were digitized with a PDP-12 computer (5 msec or 6 msec between samples yielding evoked potentials epochs of 512 ms or 640 msec).

An example of one normal subject's AEPs to random dots and letter stimuli is shown in Figure 2. The most common finding was an enhanced late positive component (see horizontal bars, Figure 2) to first letters and also matching second letters. Eight out of the nine subjects showed this enhancement. The mismatch produced significantly less late positivity than the second letter match or first letter AEP. The mean correlation coefficient between first letter AEPs and match AEPs was .72 as compared to .47 for the mean correlation coefficient be-

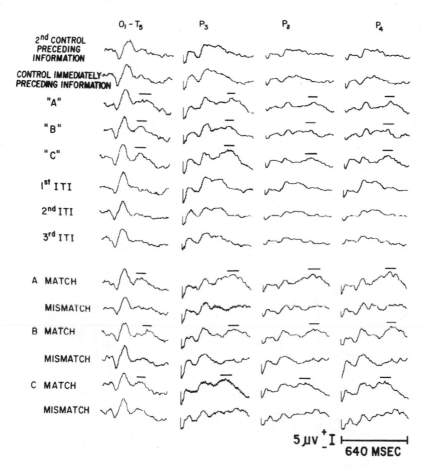

Fig. 2. Examples of AEPs ($N = 24$ for controls and ITIs and 16 for letters) from a subject (J.G.) performing in the letter matching experiment. Bars denote enhanced positivity to first letters and matching second letters. (Positive is up in this and the other figures.) (From Thatcher, 1976a)

tween first letter AEPs and mismatch AEPs. Sign tests showed that first letter AEPs and match AEPs were correlated higher more frequently ($p < .05$) than the first letter and mismatch AEPs. This emphasizes that the mismatch stimulus often results in an attenuated late positive component in comparison to the enhancement observed to both the first letter and the matching test stimuli. It should be noted, however, that a late positive response does occur to the mismatch although it is attenuated with respect to the match. The attenuated late

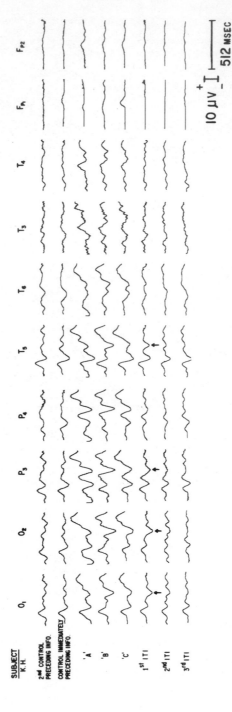

Fig. 3. Examples of AEPs to controls, first letters, and ITIs ($N = 24$ for controls and ITIs and 16 for letters) from a subject (K.H.) performing in the letter match–mismatch experiment. Arrows point to a persistent negative peak to the first ITI following information. Hemispheric asymmetries are evident, particularly in P_3 vs. P_4 and T_5 vs. T_6. Analysis epoch is 512 msec. (From Thatcher, 1976a)

positive component to mismatch stimuli and an enhanced late positive component to the first letter and the match AEP help to explain the results of factor analyses. These demonstrated a shared factor loading between first letter AEPs and match test AEPs (Thatcher, 1974; Thatcher and John, 1975). Another example of late positive component enhancement to first letters in comparison to controls is shown in Figure 3. A clear left–right asymmetry can be seen in this subject, particularly in T_5, T_6 derivations. A persistent AEP change occurred to the first intertest interval display (ITI) which was also asymmetrically distributed (asymmetries emerged in temporal derivations—see arrows). The ITI phenomenon is revealed most clearly in t tests between the AEP immediately preceding the first letter (C_1) and the ITI AEPs which follow the first letter. Figure 4 shows latency histograms of statistically significant ts for the control$_1$ versus the ITI$_1$ through 3 AEPs. It can be seen that most of the significant ts were related to the first ITI, the next most to the second ITI, and the least to the third ITI. The latency band for the most frequent significant ts was between 300 and

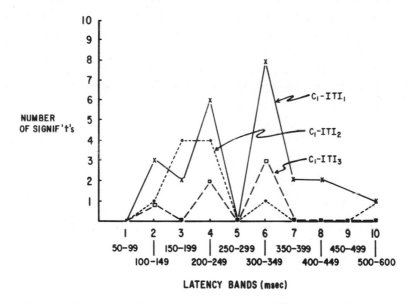

Fig. 4. Latency histograms of significant ts for control$_1$ AEPs versus ITI$_1$, through ITI$_3$ AEPs for normal subjects in the delayed letter matching task. The ordinate represents the number of significant ts and the abscissa represents the latency bin at which significant ts occurred.

349 msec. These data show that AEP amplitude of waveshape changes occur to the first ITI and then decay back to the control condition by the time of the third ITI (or within about 2 sec). As discussed elsewhere (Thatcher, 1976c) such effects may reflect rehearsal processes.

Table 1 shows the total number of significant t tests for the various conditions as a function of derivation. It can be seen that there were only 4 significant ts in the control$_1$ versus control$_2$ AEP tests. In contrast, there was a total of 72 significant ts between control$_1$ AEPs and first letter AEPs. There were also a decreasing number of significant ts between control$_1$ AEPs and the first through the third ITI AEPs (26, 12, and 6). There were nearly twice as many significant ts between control$_1$ AEPs versus match AEPs (84) and control$_1$ AEPs versus mismatch AEPs (47). In addition, there was a total of 31 significant ts between match and mismatch AEPs. Figure 5 shows latency histograms of statistically significant t tests for all of the normal subjects for match and mismatch AEPs and the two control AEPs immediately preceding first letter presentation. It can be seen that significant differences between match and mismatch AEPs occurred primarily at two latency periods (100 to 150 msec and 300 to 400 msec). Table 1 shows that 76% of the significant match–mismatch ts occurred in posterior leads (0_1, 0_2, P_3, P_4, T_5, T_6) white 24% occurred in T_3, T_4, and frontal and central leads.

It is important to ask why there are differences in AEPs elicited by letters that match with the past as compared to identical letters when they mismatch. First, could these effects be due to artifacts of experimental design? This is not likely since the conditions of the experiment were counterbalanced and equally probable. That is, match–mis-

Table 1. Number of Significant ts (3 Successive at $p < .01$) for Normal Subjects in Delayed Letter Matching Task

Condition	$O_1 + O_2$	$P_3 + P_4$	$T_5 + T_6$	$T_3 + T_4$	C_z	$F_7 + F_8 + F_z$	Total
Control$_1$ vs. control$_2$	—	2	2	—	—	—	4
Control$_1$ vs. first letter	16	19	20	10	2	4	71
Control$_1$ vs. ITI$_1$	7	6	6	2	1	4	26
Control$_1$ vs. ITI$_2$	4	—	3	3	—	3	13
Control$_1$ vs. ITI$_3$	2	1	3	—	—	—	6
Control$_1$ vs. match	19	19	27	10	3	6	84
Control$_1$ vs. mismatch	12	9	14	8	1	3	47
Match vs. mismatch	7	10	6	2	3	3	31
Total	67	66	81	35	10	23	

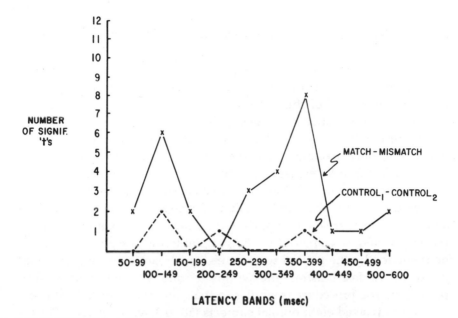

Fig. 5. Latency histograms of significant *t*s for control₁ AEPs versus control₂—AEPs versus mismatch AEPs for the nine subjects in the delayed letter matching task. The ordinate represents the number of significant *t*s and the abscissa represents the latency bin at which the significant *t*s occurred.

match AEP differences cannot be explained by factors such as differential attention, expectancy, arousal, uncertainty resolution, or cognitive acts of decision. Second, can these differences be due to pathway facilitation? According to this view particular pathways are activated by the first letter resulting in an enhanced late positive component to the matching second letter. However, this explanation is inadequate because there was an enhanced evoked response to the first letter. Third, are these differences due to enhanced variance in the latency of the late positive component to mismatch stimuli? This explanation is also inadequate since the evoked potential variance was slightly greater to match stimuli and analyses of single evoked potentials can discriminate between match and mismatch conditioning (Thatcher, 1976c).

The most parsimonious explanation is that the process of representational matching itself contributes to the enhanced late positive component in the evoked potential.

Evoked Potential Correlates of Semantic Match and Mismatch

One might assume that the enhanced late positive component reflects the match of the physical features and not uniquely the linguistic attributes of the letter stimuli. Considerations of this sort gave rise to other experiments designed to test the linguistic nature of the representational match hypothesis. One experiment involved a match–mismatch paradigm using synonyms, antonyms, and neutral words rather than letters (see Thatcher, 1976a). In this paradigm comparisons are made only at the level of semantic, not physical, features. The prediction was that the late positive component to synonyms and antonyms, comparison of which would involve semantic match or pairing, would be enhanced in comparison to the late positive component elicited by the neutral word pairs which lack a semantic fit. Figure 6 and Table 2 illustrate the synonym, antonym, and neutral word paradigm. The procedure is similar to that shown in Figure 1. This experiment involved eight normal subjects (18 to 37 years of age). Thirty-six different first words and 12 different second words were presented in a session. For one-third of the trials the second words were synonyms, for one-third of the trials the second words were antonyms, and for one-third of the trials the second words were neutral (see Figure 6). Thus, physically identical stimuli (the same 12-second words) served as synonyms, antonyms, and neutrals and were presented in a counterbalanced order within a session. Each subject was given two

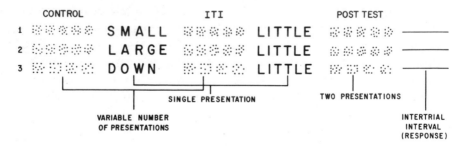

Fig. 6. Illustration of trial sequences and experimental design in the delayed semantic task. Within a session of trials the total number of illuminated dots and the average retinal area subtended was the same for all display conditions. Displays were 20 msec in duration and presented at 1 Hz. (From Thatcher, 1976a)

Table 2. Some Examples of
Counterbalanced First and Second Word
Pairings Used with Normal Subjects

First word	Second word
Help	Hurt (A)
Easy	Far (N)
Break	Crack (S)
Smooth	Rough (A)
Dark	Black (S)
Neat	Crack (N)
Begin	Finish (A)
Early	Black (N)
Harm	Hurt (S)
Mend	Crack (A)
Near	Far (A)
Coarse	Rough (S)
Lift	Finish (N)
Name	Hurt (N)
Remote	Far (S)
End	Finish (S)
Light	Black (A)
Part	Rough (N)

sessions ($\approx$ 12 min/session) with at least a 30-sec rest period between sessions. The subjects moved a lever to the left if the second word was a synonym, to the right if it was an antonym, and both left and right if it was neutral.*

Examples of AEPs from one subject elicited by first words, controls, and synonyms and antonyms are shown in Figure 7. An enhanced late positive component (440 to 460 ms) occurred only to second words (see arrows, Figure 6). Hemispheric asymmetries (see T_5, T_6, T_3, T_4, Figure 6) occurred in the second word condition but not the first word condition. Note that the late positive component to second words was anatomically widely distributed, appearing even in frontal derivations (F_7, F_8) although less in amplitude. AEP differences between the first word condition might be explained by the fact that retrieval of the meaning of the first word and a comparison with the meaning of the second word only occurred in the second word condition. Figure 8 shows examples of AEPs elicited by second words in the three semantic conditions, t tests between synonym and neutral AEPs

---

* The direction of lever movement was counterbalanced across sessions.

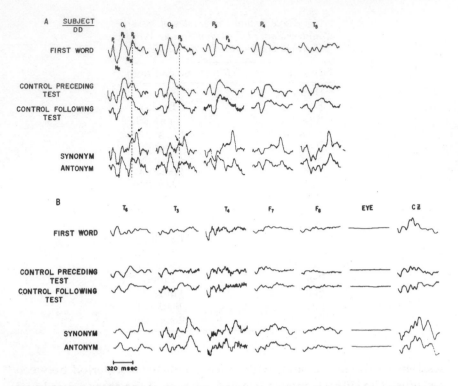

Fig. 7. Averaged evoked potentials ($N = 24$ for synonym and antonym and 48 for the other conditions) to words and random dot controls in one subject. A shows P-300 in occipital regions (dotted line) to both first and second words. Arrows show the P-400 process to synonyms and antonyms which is anatomically and temporally differentiable from the P-300. B, same as A, but showing AEPs from anterior derivations. Note difference between first word and second word responses in T_5, T_6 and T_3, T_4. Note also, asymmetries in the temporal lobe to second words, which are not present in control or first word AEPs.

are shown at the bottom of the figure. The results of this study demonstrated a statistically significant difference ($p < .01$, two-tailed) between synonym or antonym AEPs and neutral AEPs in each of the eight subjects. Significant differences occurred primarily in posterior (O_1, O_2, P_3, P_4, T_5, T_6) derivations with latencies ranging from 405 to 460 ms. In summary, the enhancement of the late positive component to synonyms and antonym AEPs was similar to that seen for letter match AEPs in the first paradigm. The attenuation of the late positive component with neutral word AEPs resembled that for mismatch second letters. This result is consistent with the representational match hypothesis. In terms of the two paradigms an antonym is not analogous to a mismatch. Instead, the words composing an antonym word pair such as *large–little* belong to the same semantic class as the synonym word pair such as *small–little*. The difference is that the antonym and the synonym word pairs represent different ends of the class.

In order to analyze the late positive component (referred to here as the P-4(00)), the absolute amplitude (in μmV) of the maximum late positive peak between 400 and 500 ms was measured with respect to a prestimulus baseline for each condition and each derivation. Using this measure, mean P-4(00) amplitude to random dot displays and words are shown in Figure 9. A repeated measures analysis of variance demonstrated significant differences between synonym and neutral conditions ($F = 80.7$, $df = 1/146$, $p < .001$), as well as between antonym and neutral conditions ($F = 49.3$, df-1/146, $p < .001$). No significant differences in mean P-4(00) amplitude were noted between synonyms and antonyms ($F = .28$, $df = 1/146$, $p = $ n.s.). All of the second word AEP conditions were significantly different from the first word AEP condition ($p < .01$). Also the first word P-4(00) was significantly different from the control ($F = 16.7$, $df = 1/46$, $p < .001$). There were no significant differences between C_1 and ITI ($F = 2.8$, $df = 1/146$, $p = $ n.s.), or between left and right derivations when all leads were averaged

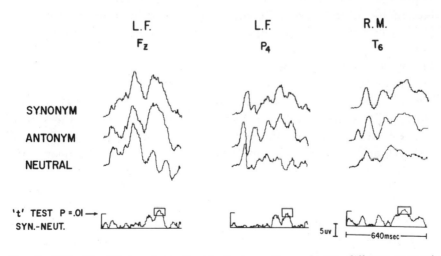

Fig. 8. AEPs ($N = 24$) to physically identical words possessing different semantic relationships. Bottom shows t tests between synonym and neutral AEPs.

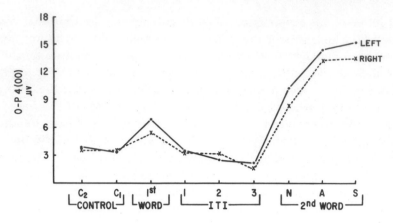

Fig. 9. Mean baseline to P-4(00) amplitude for left and right electrode sites for the various conditions of the experiment. (From Thatcher, 1976a)

together ($F = 3.56$, $df = 1/7$, $p =$ n.s.). However, there was a significant side X derivation interaction ($F = 2.34$, $df = 9/63$, $p < .05$). The latter finding indicates that hemispheric asymmetries, while present, are not uniform across posterior–anterior derivations.

This finding justified additional analyses which showed significant left–right differences ($F = 6.57$, $df = 1/71$, $p < .05$) in posterior derivations ($O_1 + P_3 + T_5$ versus $O_2 + P_4 + T_6$) in the second word condition. No significant left–right differences were noted in anterior derivations ($T_3 + F_7$ versus $T_4 + F_8$) to either the first or second word conditions, nor was a significant difference noted in posterior derivations to the first word condition alone.

Since several workers have reported only rather small AEP symmetries, i.e., 1 to 3 μv (Buchsbaum and Fedio, 1970; Morrell and Salamy, 1971; Wood, Goff, and Day, 1971), a sign test for the side of greatest late positive component amplitude for each subject for control, ITI, and second word conditions was conducted. The results of a binary sign test (Hays, 1963) reveal clear asymmetries in posterior derivations (occipital, parietal, and posterior temporal) during the ITI and first and second word conditions (combined) but not during the control (Thatcher, 1976b). Significant asymmetries always involved left side greater than right (100% of the subjects exhibited left > right in occipital derivations in the word condition). It is interesting that asymmetries are not present to random dot stimuli that precede the first word but emerge to random dot stimuli that follow the first word. This suggests that lateralized operations were active during the ITI or so-called rehearsal period.

In summary, evoked potential analyses from normal subjects performing in delayed letter matching and delayed semantic matching paradigms reveal similar effects, namely, an enhanced late positive component to the match stimuli. Both paradigms demonstrated AEP component and amplitude changes in the random dot display (ITIs) that follow the first word or first letter presentation. Some correlates of hemispheric lateralization were also observed in both paradigms (see Thatcher, 1976b). Also, both paradigms resulted in phenomena that occur largely in posterior derivations (O_1, O_2, P_3, P_4, T_5, T_6) in comparison to anterior regions. These data indicate that motor processes are not responsible for the effects.

Results of Delayed Matching Experiments in Two Aphasic Patients

After the data were acquired from normal subjects, it became possible to examine the performance of some aphasic patients—i.e., those with a localized brain lesion resulting in specific speech–language dysfunction. This approach was felt to be important because it might allow one to examine central representational processes in patients where dysfunction has been described traditionally in terms of specific alterations in input–output functions of language alone (Geschwind, 1972). Since the recovery of function depends on processes in the remaining intact neural substrate (Smith, 1975), observation of task-specific AEPs might give one an opportunity to examine the nature of hemispheric electrical phenomena which parallel the recovery of performance. It is emphasized once again, however, that this method correlates best with the sensory aspect of language and does not give one a measurable correlate of later stage motor processing.

The paradigms used with the aphasic patients were the same as described previously. A complete study with aphasic patients is being planned and only preliminary results from two patients will be presented at this time.

Patient Histories

The two aphasic patients are F.C. (male, right-handed, age 43) and L.F. (male, right-handed, age 25).

F.C. had a sudden onset of aphasia and right hemiparesis in October 1973. A complete diagnostic work-up at the Massachusetts General Hospital revealed the presence of a complete left middle cerebral artery occlusion. The lasting dysfunction consisted of right hemiparesis and nonfluent aphasia.

Language testing at the time of study of the patient's evoked potentials revealed the following. His spontaneous speech was characterized by occasional blocking of complicated sentences, paraphasia, attempts to correct, stammering, and frustration. He was able to read newspapers and books and comprehended both auditory and visual information normally. When given tasks including more than three steps of information, the patient was often confused and had difficulty even repeating manual rhythms tapped by the examiner. He scored 26 on the Symbol Digit Manipulation Test, when the examiner wrote the number that the patient chose on the matching list of symbols. This score represents the mean of score distributions for aphasics tested by Dr. Aaron Smith of the University of Michigan (1973). The patient performed at a high level in the Peabody Picture Vocabulary Test, especially in items involving action pictures. He had no difficulty matching objects, pictures, and words. The functional language problem for this patient consisted principally of going from any input modality to spoken or written output performance. Thus, he was a typical severe Broca's aphasic. A clinical EEG showed very high amplitude intermittent focal delta activity localized at F_{p1}, F_7, F_3, T_3. The patient's clinical neurological course had been complicated by occasional grand mal seizures which were controlled with anticonvulsants.

L.F., a 25-year-old right-handed man, developed headache and the insidious onset of trouble speaking in June 1975. Hospitalization and neurological work-up followed, indicating the presence on cerebral arteriogram of a localized avascular mass in the posterior superior region of the left temporal operculum. On clinical examination there were no abnormalities in cranial nerve function and no lateralizing abnormalities on motor or sensory testing. His spontaneous speech was fluent and there was no paraphasia. When the examiner spoke very rapidly, the patient had difficulty in comprehending the entire meaning of the spoken statement. The patient was unable to follow commands of three-step content. He had difficulty repeating sequences of phonemes (such as, "bee-key-gee") and would say them back erroneously ("pee-key-bee"). More formal language testing revealed errors in phonemic discrimination, but not in reading. WAIS performance IQ was 91. His score on the Raven's Coloured Progressive Matrices was 31/36.* An EEG showed continuous monorhythmic delta activity which was focal at T_3.

The clinical impression was aphasia, Wernicke's type, probably secondary to a left posterior temporal mass lesion, exact nature undetermined.

Task Performance

The scalp electrode locations and recording procedures for F.C. and L.F. were the same as described earlier for the normal subjects. The list of words constituting the delayed semantic task, however, were made much simpler. For example, word pairs such as up–down, high–low, soft–hard, long–short, etc., were used, rather than the pairs in Table 2. F.C. performed above chance on the delayed letter matching task, although his performance was significantly poorer than for normals. For example, only 72% of F.C.'s responses were correct for two sessions as compared to a mean of 98% in normals. F.C.'s performance in the delayed semantic task was even poorer. F.C.'s correct responses were only slightly above chance. However, F.C. clearly understood the instructions for the task and consistently responded correctly to particular word pairs.

A similar performance in the delayed letter matching and delayed semantic matching tasks for F.C. was observed in patient L.F. A primary difference between the two patients, however, was that L.F. was

---

* Recently, Kertesz and McCabe (1975) reported the results of scores on the Raven's Coloured Progressive Matrices in a variety of aphasic patients classified according to taxonomic criteria, based on the Western Aphasia Battery scores. The purpose of the study was to correlate nonverbal intelligence with different kinds of aphasia. Interestingly, global, Wernicke's, and transcortical sensory aphasics performed significantly more poorly than did Broca's and other aphasic types. It is therefore of interest to point out that our patient L.F. scored significantly better on the Raven's than did the 18 Wernicke's aphasics in Kertesz and McCabe's series. In fact, his score was superior to that of any of their patients, including controls. Perhaps this relates to the exquisitely localized nature of his pathology.

unable to grasp the concept of antonym and usually confused the antonym and neutral categories. However, L.F. did appear to understand the concept of synonym and did obtain some consistently correct scores to a few synonym word pairs. L.F. scored 76% correct on the delayed letter matching task and only 22% correct in the delayed semantic matching task.

Evoked Potential Results: F.C.

Figure 10 shows AEPs from bilateral parietal (P_3 and P_4) and bilateral frontal (F_7 and F_8) derivations to controls, first letters, and match and mismatch stimuli in the delayed letter matching experiments in patient F.C. It shows that an enhancement of the late positive component occurred in P_3 and P_4 derivations but was poorly developed in the F_7 derivation. The correlation coefficients between the homologous pairs of AEPs is shown at the side in Figure 10. The most notable finding was a deterioration of interhemispheric symmetry of AEPs in the F_7–F_8 derivations to the match–mismatch stimuli. The poor stability of AEP waveforms from F_7 is further demonstrated by the mean correlation coefficient computed for all possible pairs of AEPs. The correlation values at the bottom of each column of AEPs reflect the replicability of AEP waveforms across condition (i.e., C_1–C_2; info–C_1, info–C_2, match–mismatch, match–info, match–C_1, match–C_2, mismatch–info, mismatch–C_1, mismatch–C_2). The F_7 AEPs exhibit marked variability. Table 3 shows the correlation coefficients between homologous pairs in both the letter matching and semantic matching tasks. It can be seen in Table 3 that in the letter matching task the correlation coefficients are reasonably high to the control stimuli but decrease to the letter stimuli showing a decrement in T_5 vs. T_6 and reaching lowest values in F_7 vs. F_8. A similar deterioration of hemispheric symmetry occurred in T_3 vs. T_4 and F_{61} vs. F_8 derivations in the semantic matching task. Table 4 shows the correlation coefficients between AEPs from F_7 and F_8 and AEPs from all other derivations in the two tasks. The significant finding is that the correlation coefficients between F_7 AEPs and AEPs from other derivations is consistently lower than the correlation coefficients between F_8 AEPs and AEPs from other derivations. These data indicate a marked decoupling of the left frontal (F_7) region from other regions, particularly in anterior leads in the match condition. This contrasts with right frontal (F_8) AEPs, which correlate well with all other AEPs and decouple strongly from left anterior AEPs.

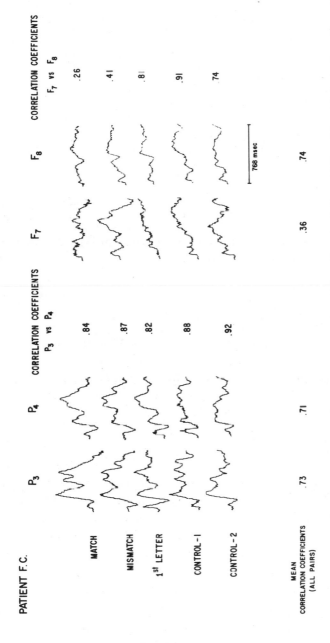

Fig. 10. Average evoked potentials ($N = 24$) from patient F.C. from bilateral parietal (P_3 and P_4) and frontal derivations (F_7 and F_8) to controls, first letters, and match and mismatch stimuli in the delayed letter matching task. Correlation coefficients between homologous derivations is shown at the right of each pair of AEPs. The mean correlation coefficient for a given derivation across conditions (i.e., C_1–C_2, info–C_1, info–C_2, match–mismatch, match–info, match–C_1, match–C_2, mismatch–info, mismatch–C_1, mismatch–C_2) is shown below each column of waves.

Table 3. Correlation Coefficients of AEPs for Homologous Derivations from Patient F.C.

	O_1 vs O_2	P_3 vs P_4	T_5 vs T_6	T_3 vs T_4	F_7 vs F_8
Delayed letter matching					
Control-2	.96	.92	.78	.75	.74
Control-1	.94	.88	.81	.77	.91
1st letter	.95	.82	.65	.88	.81
Mismatch	.93	.87	.58	.54	**.41**
Match	.94	.84	.69	.61	**.26**
Delayed semantic matching					
Control-2	.91	.86	.75	.12	.25
Control-1	.95	.87	.69	.20	.39
First word	.93	.83	.68	.28	.38
Neutral (2nd word)	.95	.89	.70	.40	**.03**
Syn+Ant (2nd word)	.95	.92	.68	.32	**.08**

These data indicate that a functional deficit begins approximately at T_5 and extends forward, reaching a maximum at F_7.

Evoked Potential Results: L.F.

L.F.'s abnormality appears to be much more localized than F.C.'s. Figure 11 shows AEPs from 11 derivations from both tasks. A marked hemispheric asymmetry was noted in the T_5 vs. T_6 derivations (see arrow at top, Figure 10). In these derivations the mean correlation coefficient was .47 as compared to .86 for O_1–O_2, .88 for P_3–P_4 and .68 for T_3–T_4.

A late positive component occurred consistently in both posterior and anterior derivations (except in T_5) in the delayed letter matching task. However, a late positive component enhancement failed to occur in the anterior derivations (particularly C_3, C_4, and F_z) in the delayed semantic matching task (see arrows, Figure 11). The absence of an enhanced late positive component occurred primarily in AEPs to second words. It should be recalled that L.F. was unable to perform the delayed semantic task. These data may reflect L.F.'s performance deficit.* It is interesting that there is a dissociation between the anterior

---

* The absence of a late positive component in the anterior derivations was not due to subject fatigue or habituation. This is known since L.F. subsequently performed in a third task requiring delayed form matching and the late positive components were again present.

and posterior derivations with the posterior derivations exhibiting an enhanced late positive component. A similar dissociation was never observed in normal subjects.

Discussion

Lenneberg was an advocate of simple perspectives although he possessed an enormous capacity to synthesize diverse, complicated facts and to extract the salient invariant relationships. We believe in the importance of Lenneberg's emphasis on the fundamental roles of classification and categorization in the aquisition of language and knowledge. In this chapter and elsewhere (Thatcher, 1976a) it has been

Table 4. Correlation Coefficients of AEPs for Frontal versus All Other Derivations from Patient F.C. [a]

Delayed Letter Matching Left frontal			Right frontal		
	Control	Match		Control	Match
F_7 vs O_1	.46	.43	F_8 vs O_1	.44	.50
F_7 vs O_2	.60	.35	F_8 vs O_2	.60	.60
F_7 vs P_3	.59	.50	F_8 vs P_3	.58	.50
F_7 vs P_4	.72	.25	F_8 vs P_4	.75	.70
F_7 vs T_5	.73	.47	F_8 vs T_5	.75	.47
F_7 vs T_6	.71	.26	F_8 vs T_6	.81	.75
F_7 vs T_3	.81	.62	F_8 vs T_3	.79	.51
F_7 vs T_4	.88	.34	F_8 vs T_4	.95	.84
F_7 vs F_8	.91	.26	F_8 vs F_7	.91	.26

Delayed Semantic Matching Left frontal			Right frontal		
	Control	Syn + ant		Control	Syn + ant
F_7 vs O_1	.14	.32	F_8 vs O_1	.64	.51
F_7 vs O_2	.15	.31	F_8 vs O_2	.62	.66
F_7 vs P_3	.31	.33	F_8 vs P_3	.64	.61
F_7 vs P_4	.18	.34	F_8 vs P_4	.64	.80
F_7 vs T_5	.54	.37	F_8 vs T_5	.56	.40
F_7 vs T_6	.21	.26	F_8 vs T_6	.77	.87
F_7 vs T_3	.77	.58	F_8 vs T_3	.28	.21
F_7 vs T_4	.19	.21	F_8 vs T_4	.90	.96
F_7 vs F_8	.39	.08	F_8 vs F_7	.39	.08

[a] Note more pronounced changes in correlation in left frontal compared to right frontal.

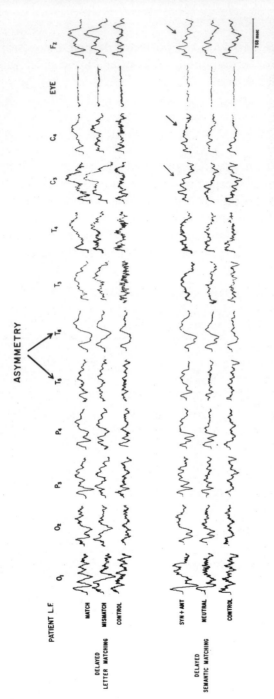

Fig. 11. Average evoked potentials ($N = 24$) from patient F.C. for 12 leads in the delayed letter matching task (top) and the delayed semantic matching task. Arrow above T_5 points to marked asymmetry and attenuated AEPs in the posterior temporal lead. Arrows in delayed semantic task point to an attenuated late positive component in central (C_3, C_4) and frontal (F_z) leads.

emphasized that there is one central concept that underlies the notion of order and classification: namely, the extraction of invariant relations by determining sameness and difference and similarities of such differences. Recently, David Bohm (1969), a quantum mechanist, developed a model of order and information which was based entirely on the extraction of similarities of differences and hierarchies of differences. We argue that one of the fundamental processes for which Lenneberg searched is the perceptual and cognitive operation of determining sameness and difference. This process is believed to be fundamental to logic, language, and mathematics. Classification schemes which arise from the determination of sameness and difference are important not only for semantic categorization and other cognitive functions but also for basic perceptual processes (see Gibson, 1969).

The data presented in this chapter show evoked potential correlates of the match–mismatch process. In normal subjects there are amplitude and waveform asymmetries between evoked potentials elicited by identical physical stimuli that either match or mismatch with stimuli in the past. These effects are observed at different levels of cognitive function—such as, letter feature match–mismatch and word semantic match–mismatch. The match–mismatch AEP asymmetries occurred primarily in the long latency components (300–500 msec), although some differences were also noted between 100 and 149 msec. This major long latency phenomenon indicates that the asymmetries represent processes occurring at the level of memory or semantic representations. That is, the early components of the evoked potential are classically related to the physical attributes of the evoking stimulus and early sensory processing. The late component AEP phenomena related to higher-level processing had a widespread distribution but were maximal in posterior derivations. The strong posterior dominance might be due, in part, to the fact that visual stimuli were used. Future experiments will be designed using both auditory and visual stimuli. Auditory and visual–auditory cross-modal tasks may have more relevance for the study of aphasia.

The paradigms described in this chapter allow precise psychophysical control of the parameters of stimulation. That is, the number of illuminated dots and retinal area subtended were the same for all displays. The paradigm allows the presentation of linguistic or nonlinguistic stimuli (e.g., geometric forms, faces, objects, etc.) and can ascend different levels of complexity and thus challenge specific information processing. In this way a patient with a localized brain lesion might be challenged with tasks which are initially very simple but become successively more complex and can be tailored to the particular domain of neurological deficit. The philosophy behind this approach is that evoked potential diagnosis of functional pathology can be optimized by providing challenges specific to the cognitive deficit as contrasted with classical clinical EEG which lacks cognitive challenges. Not only may the region of pathology be localized more precisely by this method but, perhaps more importantly, specific functional or organizational deficits may appear in brain regions that are normal but which are nonetheless an integral part of a network subserving the probed cognitive function. In this regard there are three findings from the aphasic patients worthy of emphasis.

First, a late positive enhancement failed to occur during semantic processing in patient L.F., who also failed to perform correctly. This gives added support to our hypothesis that late positive enhancement is directly related to correctness of processing rather than to stimulus features themselves.

Second, the enhanced AEP components were bilateral and widespread at many electrodes. Thus, the representational process probed is not limited solely to the traditional language region of the left hemisphere.

Third, we noted striking left–right waveform asymmetries during processing of information loaded stimuli if one of the electrode pairs was situated near the local brain lesion. This points out the value of probing cognitive function with specific stimulus loads in order to uncover maximum lack of regional processing. We refer the reader to Tables 3 and 4, which show that the correlation coefficients were much lower when the stimuli contained information.

More data must be gathered systematically, using a variety of stimulus arrays (geometric form match–mismatch, probes of logic and simple mathematics, cross-modal match–mismatch, etc.). Patients with a variety of local lesions (with and without aphasia) should be chosen. In this way it might be possible to describe systematically central representational processes after cerebral lesions as reflected in components of the AEP.

References

Ades, A. E. Categorical perception and the speech mode. *Cognition*, 1974.

Barlow, H. B. Single units and sensation: A neuron doctrine for perceptual psychology? *Perception*, 1972, *1*, 371–394.

Bobrow, D., and Fraser, B. An augmented state transition network analysis procedure. In D. Walker and L. Norton (Eds.), *Proceedings of the International Joint Conference on Artificial Intelligence*. Washington, D.C., 1969.

Bohm, D. Some remarks on the notion of order. In C. H. Waddington (Ed.), *Towards a theoretical biology*. II. Sketches. Chicago: Aldine, 1969. Pp. 18–58.

Boole, G. *An investigation into the laws of thought*. Cambridge: Cambridge University Press, 1854 (reprinted by Dover Press, New York, 1951).

Buchsbaum, M., and Fedio, P. Hemispheric differences in evoked potentials to verbal and nonverbal stimuli in the left and right visual fields. *Physiology and Behavior*, 1970, *5*, 207–210.

Chen, C. H. *Statistical pattern recognition*. Rochelle Park, New Jersey: Hayden Book Co., 1973.

Chomsky, N. *Syntactic structures*. The Hague: Mouton and Co., 1957.

Chomsky, N. *Aspects of the theory of syntax*. Cambridge: M.I.T. Press, 1965.

Fodor, J. A., Bever, T. G., and Garrett, M. F. *The psychology of language*. New York: McGraw-Hill, 1974.

Geschwind, N. Language and the brain. *Scientific American*, 1972, *4*, 76–83.

Gibson, J. J. *Principles of perceptual learning and development*. New York: Appleton, 1969.

Hays, W. L. *Statistics for psychologists*. New York: Holt, Rinehart & Winston, 1963.

Halle, M., and Stevens, K. Speech recognition: A model and a program for research. *IRE Transactions on Information Theory*. IT-8: 155–159, 1962.

Hubel, D. H., and Wiesel, T. N. Receptive fields, binocular interaction and functional architecture in the cat's visual cortex. *Journal of Physiology* (London), 1962, *160*, 106–154.

Jasper, H. H. The ten–twenty electrode system of the international federation. *Electroencephalography and Clinical Neurophysiology*, 1958, *10*, 371–375.

Kaplan, R. A general syntactic processor. In R. Rustin (Ed.), *Natural language processing*. Englewood Cliffs. New Jersey: Prentice-Hall, 1973.

Kertesz, A., and McCabe, P. Intelligence and aphasia: Performance of aphasics on Raven's coloured progressive matrices. *Brain and Language*, 1975, *2*(October), 387–395.

Lenneberg, E. H. *Biological foundations of language*. Wiley, New York, 1967.

Lenneberg, E. H. Brain correlates of language. In R. O. Schmitt (Ed.), *The neurosciences: Second study program*. New York: Rockefeller University Press, 1970. Pp. 361–371.

Lenneberg, E. H. Language and brain: Developmental aspects. *Neurosciences Research Program Bulletin*, 1974, *12*(4).

Liberman, A. M. The grammars of speech and language. *Cognitive Psychology*, 1970, *1*, 301–323.

Liberman, A. M., Cooper, F. S., Shankweiler, D. P., and Studdert-Kennedy, M. Perception of the speech code. *Psychological Review*, 1967, *74*, 431–461.

Lisker, L., and Abramson, A. S. A cross-language study of voicing in initial stops: Accoustical measurements. *Word*, 1964, *20*, 384–422.

McCulloch, W. S., and Pitts, W. A logical calculus of the ideas immanent in nervous activity. *Bulletin of Mathematical Biophysics*, 1943, *5*, 115–133.

Miller, G. A., Galanter, E., and Pribram, K. F. *Plans and the structure of behavior*. New York: Holt, Rinehart & Winston, 1960.

Miller, J. D., Weir, C. C., Pastore, R. E., Kelly, W. J., and Dooling, R. J. Discrimination and labeling of noise-buzz sequences with various noise-lead times: An example of categorical perception. *Journal of the Acoustical Society of America,* 1974. In press.

Morrell, L. K., and Salamy, J. F. Hemispheric asymmetry of electrocortical responses to speech stimuli. *Science,* 1971, *174,* 164–166.

Pribram, K. H. *Languages of the brain.* Englewood Cliffs, New Jersey: Prentice-Hall, 1971.

Regan, D. *Evoked potentials in psychology, sensory physiology and clinical medicine.* London: Chapman and Hall, Ltd., 1972.

Rubin, D. C. The subjective estimation of relative syllable frequency. *Perception and Psychophysics,* 1974, *16,* 193–196.

Smith, A. Symbol digit modalities test. Manual. Los Angeles: Western Psychological Services, 1973.

Smith, A., and Sugar, O. Development of above normal language and intelligence 21 years after left hemispherectomy. *Neurology.* 1975, *25,* 813–818.

Sneath, P. H. and Sokal, R. A. *Numerical taxonomy.* San Francisco: W. H. Freeman, 1973.

Sokolov, E. M. Neuronal models and the orienting reflex. In M. A. B. Brazier (Ed.), *CNS and behavior* (Vol. 3). New York: Macy Foundation, 1960.

Szentagothai, J., and Arbib, M. A. Conceptual models of neural organization. *Neurosciences Research Program Bulletin,* 1974, *12*(3).

Thatcher, R. W. Evoked potential correlates of human short-term memory. *Proc. Fourth Ann. Neurosci. Conv.,* 1974, p. 450.

Thatcher, R. W. Electrophysiological correlates of animal and human memory. In R. D. Terry and S. Gershon (Eds.), *The neurobiology of aging.* New York: Raven Press, 1976. (a)

Thatcher, R. W. Evoked potential correlates of hemispheric lateralization during semantic information processing. In S. Harnad, L. Goldstein, R. Doty, and J. Jaymes (Eds.), *Lateralization in the nervous system.* New York: Academic Press, 1976. (b). In press.

Thatcher, R. W. Evoked potential correlates of delayed letter matching. *Behavioral Biology,* 1976 (c). In press.

Thatcher, R. W., and John, E. R. Information and mathematical quantification of brain states. In N. Burch and H. L. Altschuler (Eds.), *Behavior and brain electrical activity. New York: Plenum Press, 1975.*

Thorne, J., Bratley, P., and Dewar, H. The syntactic analysis of English by machine. In D. Mitchie (Ed.), *Machine intelligence 3.* New York: American Elsevier Press, 1968.

Wanner, E. *On remembering, forgetting, and understanding sentences: A study of the deep structure hypothesis.* The Hague: Mouton, 1974.

Wanner, E., Taylor, T. J., and Thompson, R. F. The psychobiology of speech and language—an overview. In J. Desmedt (Ed.), *The cerebral evoke potential in man.* London: Oxford University Press, 1976.

Whitehead, A. N., and Russell, B. *Principia mathematica* (Vol. 1, 2nd ed.). Cambridge: University Press, 1927.

Wood, C. C., Goff, W. R., and Day, R. S. Auditory evoked potentials during speech perception. *Science,* 1971, *173,* 1248–1251.

Wortman, P. M., and Greenberg, L. D. Coding, recoding and decoding of hierarchical information in long-term memory. *Journal of Verbal Learning and Verbal Behavior* 1971, *10,* 234–243.

6

Ola A. Selnes and Harry A. Whitaker

MORPHOLOGICAL AND FUNCTIONAL DEVELOPMENT OF THE AUDITORY SYSTEM

There is an extensive body of literature available on both structural and functional properties of the auditory system in adult organisms (Bekesy, 1960; Rasmussen and Windle, 1965; Tobias, 1970–1972; Whitfield, 1967). While most of the anatomical and physiological studies are concerned with subhuman species, particularly the rat, cat, rabbit, and monkey, a few such studies have also been done on humans (Tasker and Organ, 1973). Much less work has been done on the development of the auditory system, at least in humans, and so far, no systematic treatment of morphological and functional characteristics of the developing auditory system is available. Such an undertaking would, needless to say, be of great value both for an understanding of auditory perception in general and for an understanding of more specialized auditory functions, like processing of linguistic stimuli.

While the present chapter will not in any way provide a comprehensive survey of developmental aspects of audition, an attempt will be made to bring together in a systematic fashion data from different lines of investigation (neurophysiology, electrophysiology, audiology, etc.) bearing on the question of onset and functional development of

Ola A. Selnes and *Harry A. Whitaker* · Department of Psychology, University of Rochester, Rochester, New York.

the sense of hearing. The emphasis will be on human studies, but animal studies will also be discussed whenever data from humans are lacking, or when they are otherwise considered to be relevant. We agree with Hecox (1975) that the development of the auditory function cannot be fully appreciated without placing it in its proper anatomical context.

The peripheral auditory apparatus is traditionally divided into the external, middle, and internal ear, and these parts differ in their phylogenetic origin and individual development. The internal ear is by far the oldest part, and contains specialized sensory receptors. These receptors are clearly related to the ones found in the vestibular apparatus, having to do with orientation and movement, but have undergone a special development for the perception of much finer and more rapid movements, namely the successive compressions and rarefactions of particles which constitute sound. The development of hearing in ear-breathing species necessitated the development of special sound-collecting (outer ear) and transmission (middle ear) mechanisms, and these structures are thus phylogenetically much younger, and they also appear much later in ontogenetic development.

Embryogenesis of the Ear

The earliest indication of the developing ear can be found in embryos of about 22 days, and is in the form of a thickening on both sides of the still-open neural plate (Figure 1). During the fourth week, these thickenings, the otic placodes, which represent the primordium of the membraneous labyrinth, rapidly invaginate to form the otocyst (auditory pit). By the end of the fourth week, the surface opening in the otocyst becomes closed, and is then referred to as the otic or auditory vesicle. As the embryo continues to grow, the auditory vesicle changes its form and becomes elongated in the dorsoventral direction. About this time (5 weeks) the more expanded dorsal portion of the auditory vesicle can be identified as the primordium of the vestibular part of the membraneous labyrinth, and the more slender ventral extension as that of the cochlea. The connection between the cochlear portion and the saccule of the vestibule gradually narrows to form the ductus reuniens. The development of the semicircular canals and the

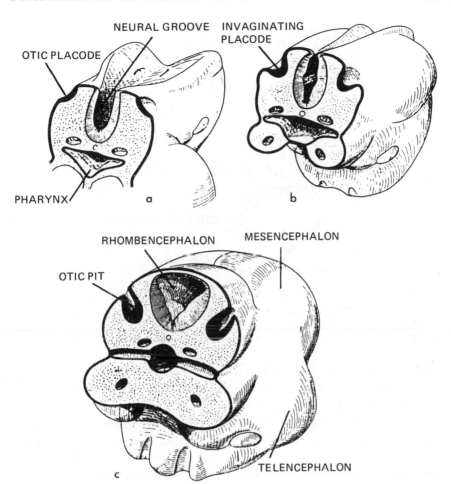

Fig. 1. Schematic of cephalic ends of human embryo, transversely cut, showing formation of the otic pit. A: about 22 days; B: about 24 days; C: about 27 days. (Adapted from Tuchmann-Duplessis, Auroux, and Haegel, 1974.)

endolymphatic duct, which precedes that of the cochlea, is shown in Figure 2.

During formation of the auditory vesicle a small group of cells become detached from its wall and forms the statoacoustic ganglion. Other cells, probably derived from the neural crest, also participate in the formation of this ganglion (Politzer, 1956). Later during develop-

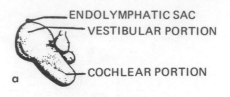

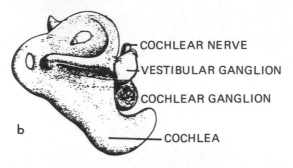

Fig. 2. Development of the membraneous labyrinth in man. A: about 36 days; B: about 42 days; C: about 50 days; D: about 60 days. (Adapted from Tuchmann-Duplessis *et al.*, 1974.)

ment this ganglion divides into a vestibular portion, innervating the saccule, utricle, and semicircular canals, and an acoustic portion, innervating the organ of Corti.

Differentiation of the cochlear portion of the membraneous labyrinth starts during the sixth week with a rapid elongation and forward bending of its distal end. This elongation continues during the seventh and eighth weeks, and the initial bend rapidly develops into a spiral. By the end of the eighth week, 1¾ turns are accomplished. The adult form of the cochlea (about 2¾ turns) is achieved around 10 weeks. Beyond this stage the spiral grows in size, but no further turns are added, and it reaches its maximum growth during midterm, when the vertical height of the spiral measures about 6–7 mm.

Development of the structures within the cochlea starts at the basal end and proceeds gradually toward the apex. The cochlear duct (scala media), which is the only part of the cochlea present up to about 8 weeks, is initially surrounded by a fibrous basement membrane, and a thick cartilaginous shell. The cross-sectional shape of the cochlear duct is at first oval, but around 10 weeks it appears more circular, and there is a notable difference between the flat base with thick epithe-

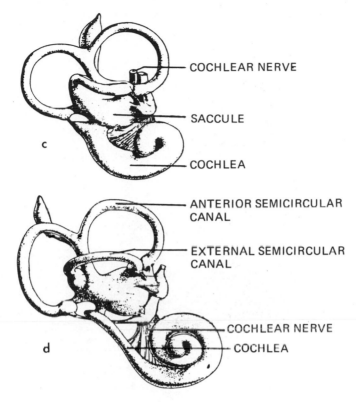

COCHLEAR NERVE

SACCULE

c

COCHLEA

ANTERIOR SEMICIRCULAR
CANAL

EXTERNAL SEMICIRCULAR
CANAL

COCHLEAR NERVE

d   COCHLEA

Fig. 2 (continued).

lium and the single-layered epithelium of the roof. Around the same
time, large openings begin to appear in the cartilaginous shell surrounding the cochlear duct (Figure 3). These are the early signs of the
differentiation of the scala vestibuli and scala tympani. With the
growth of these structures, the cross-sectional shape of the cochlear
duct changes from rounded to triangular. The anterior wall gradually
merges with the wall of the scala vestibuli, forming Reissner's membrane, and the posterior wall fuses with the wall of the scala tympani
to form the basilar membrane.

At around 15 weeks, the epithelial cells at the base of the cochlear
duct have already started to differentiate, forming two ridges. The
larger of the two, close to the center of the cochlea, is the future spiral
limbus. The outer ridge gives rise to the sensory cells proper, one row
of inner and four rows of outer hair cells. The development of the
outer hair cells is somewhat slower than that of the inner ones (Bred-

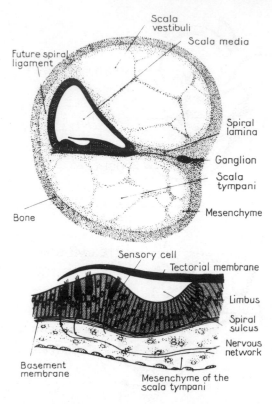

Fig. 3. Differentiation of the cochlear duct. Left: embryo of about 5 months. Right: at term. (From Tuchmann-Duplessis *et al.*, 1974.)

berg, 1968). The apical end of the cochlear duct still remains fairly un-differentiated. The surface of the epithelial cells is covered (initially only in the basal turn) by a gelatinous membrane, the future tectorial membrane. Both stereo- and kinocilia are present at this stage, but in the cochlear duct, unlike the vestibular system, the kinocilia disappear before birth, and the only evidence of their earlier presence is in the form of the remaining basal bodies.

The sensory hair cells do not reach the apical turn of the organ of Corti until about 4 months, and approximately one month later they assume mature shapes, with the stereocilia arranged in a W-pattern. Surface preparations of the organ of Corti reveal that the shape of the W is somewhat more pointed for the outer than for the inner hair cells (Bredberg, 1968). The organ of Corti is not fully developed, however,

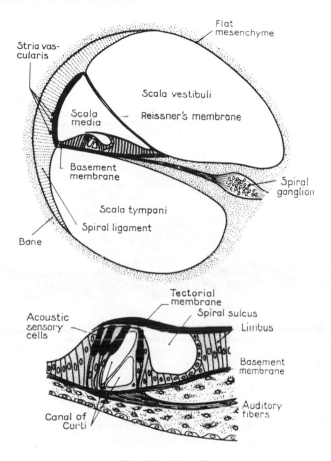

Fig. 3 (continued).

until about 8 months (Figure 4). At this stage, the pattern of sensory as well as supporting cells and the fluid spaces show adult characteristics throughout the entire length of the cochlea.

The question of the onset of functional maturity of the organ of Corti is not entirely clear. Studies of the cat (Lindeman, Ades, Bredberg, and Engström, 1971) have shown that the surface topography of the organ of Corti is not fully developed until about 3–5 weeks after birth. Until this time, the tectorial membrane remains attached at its outer edge to the long microvilli of Deiters' cells, and may thus prevent excitation of the hair cells. The detachment of the tectorial membrane, starting about 10 days postnatally in the basal turn, is the final stage of maturation of cat cochlea. This could explain why cochlear

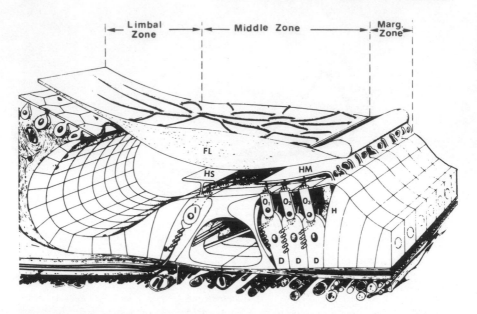

Fig. 4. Diagrammatic representation of the tectorial membrane and its relationship to the organ of Corti. HS (Hensen's stripe) and HM (Hardesty's membrane) are part of the inferior surface of the tectorial membrane. FL: fibrous layer of the tectorial membrane. H: Hensen's cell, D: Deiters' cell, I: inner hair cell, O_1, O_2, O_3: outer hair cells. (Modified from Lim, 1972.)

microphonic potentials have not been found to attain adult values until about 4–5 weeks in kittens, and might suggest that the tectorial membrane "exerts a protective function until hearing is needed" (Wright, 1974).

There is no available information, however, concerning the time at which the tectorial membrane in the human fetus/infant becomes detached. The long-standing debate as to whether or not the tectorial membrane simply rests on top of the stereocilia or whether there is a closer contact between these structures has, on the other hand, been resolved, in that photomicrographs of the inferior surface of the tectorial membrane clearly show imprints of the stereocilia of the outer hair cells, thus suggesting that they are actually embedded in the membrane. Their adhesion is so strong that upon dissecting the tectorial membrane away, some of the stereocilia are frequently broken loose, and remain attached to the membrane. The stereocilia of the inner hair cells do not appear to be in contact with the tectorial membrane, however (Lim, 1972).

The tectorial membrane starts to develop around 10 weeks, and appears initially as a gelatinous layer resting on top of the almost undifferentiated cells of the organ of Corti. About 4 weeks later it becomes attached to the limbus, but it does not yet reach out over the future hair cells. In its adult form, the tectorial membrane is much larger in the apical than in the basal turn, and is made up of 90% water structured by protein into a soft gel.

Some authors have, on the basis of the morphological characteristics of the tectorial membrane, expressed some doubt that it can exert a shearing force relative to the rather stiff stereocilia (Naftalin, Harrison, and Stephens, 1964). Instead, these authors suggest that the acoustic wave energy is responsible for ion exchanges within the tectorial membrane, and causes variations in the electric field which eventually result in hair cell stimulation. Dallos, Billone, Durant, Wang, and Raynor (1972), while agreeing with a mechanoelectrical theory of sensory transduction for the outer hair cells, suggest that the adequate stimulus for excitation of the inner hair cells may be fluid velocity, since the stereocilia of these cells do not make contact with the tectorial membrane.

Development of the Middle and Outer Ear

The middle ear is of entodermal origin and is derived chiefly from the first pharyngeal pouch, which appears in embryos of approximately 4 weeks. The distal portion of the pouch widens and forms the middle ear chamber, while the proximal part remains narrow and forms the Eustachian tube. At around 7 weeks, a number of condensations appear in the mesenchymal cells of the middle ear cavity, which represent the precursors of the ossicles—the malleus, incus, and stapes. Even though the ossicles appear quite early, they remain embedded in mesenchyme until the eighth month, when the surrounding tissue begins to dissolve. When the ossicles are completely free of surrounding mesenchyme, the entodermal epithelium serves to connect them to the walls of the middle ear cavity. Compared to other bones of the body, most of which do not attain full adult length until about 17–20 years, the growth of the ossicles is extremely rapid. The stapes have adult dimensions around 23 weeks, although ossification and erosion of the crura is not complete until about 30 weeks.

The primordia of the tensor tympani and stapedius muscles both appear approximately at the end of the second month of intrauterine life, but the tensor tympani differentiates somewhat earlier than the stapedius (Candiollo and Levi, 1969). The process of differentiation is at first independent, but later becomes closely related to the morphogenetic development of the structures with which the muscles are connected. The middle ear muscles are not fully developed until after birth (Candiollo, cited by Candiollo and Levi, 1969). A unique feature of the middle ear muscles is that they are completely enclosed in bony canals, and only their tendons enter the middle ear cavity. This, according to Bekesy (cited by Zemlin, 1968) may serve to reduce muscular vibrations which might interfere with the transmission of sound. The tensor tympani muscle is innervated by the mandibular branch of the trigeminal nerve and the stapedius by the facial nerve.

The external auditory meatus is derived from the dorsal part of the first pharyngeal groove, which grows medially towards the entodermal lining of the middle ear cavity. It remains separated from the middle ear by a solid core of epithelial cells, the so-called meatal plug. Approximately 2 months before birth, this plug begins to dissolve, but it sometimes persists until birth, resulting in congenital conduction deafness. In the adult, the external auditory meatus measures about 2.7 centimeters, and has a best resonance frequency of about 2.6 KHz, which may contribute as much as a 12 dB increase in sound pressure for this frequency region at the eardrum (Shaw, 1974). The shorter length of the external auditory meatus in children implies that its natural frequency will be somewhat higher. Gilbert (1975), referring to a personal communication with Shaw, discusses the possibility that if all the structures of the middle and outer ear were "scaled down by a constant factor with respect to adult dimensions, then such an hypothesis would lead to the view that the sound pressure transformation from the free field to the eardrum will have the shape and magnitude of the adult curves (Shaw, 1974), *but* shifted up the frequency scale by the appropriate factor." Interestingly enough, this would suggest that the range of frequencies optimally transmitted by the infant ear will be somewhat above the area of the spectrum containing the major acoustic information of speech. However, the assumption that the structures of the external and middle ear all develop at the same rate remains to be verified.

The eardrum (tympanic membrane) consists of three layers: (1) an ectodermal epithelial lining which is continuous with that of the external meatus, (2) an entodermal lining derived from the middle ear cavity, and (3) an intermediate layer of connective tissue (mesoderm). The intermediate fibrous layer is the most complex portion of the tympanic membrane, being made up of two distinct fiber arrangements, one circular and the other radial. The major part of the eardrum is firmly attached to the handle of the malleus and is formed only after the mesenchyme surrounding the ossicles has dissolved.

During the sixth week of development, the primordium of the auricle (pinna) develops from a number of mesenchymal proliferations at the dorsal end of the first and second pharyngeal arches, surrounding the first pharyngeal groove. They gradually begin to fuse, and around 4.5 months the auricle has begun to attain adult shape (Figure 5). Developmental abnormalities of the pinna are not uncommon, due to the fact that the process of fusion of the auricular hillocks is very complex. As an aside, it may be noted that recently there was a debate in a leading medical journal on the question of whether or not special

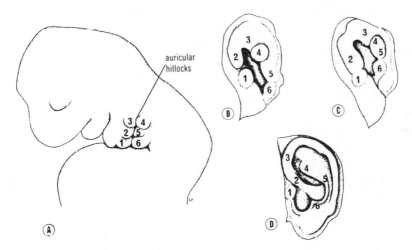

Fig. 5. Development of the auricle (pinna). A: lateral view showing the six auricular hillocks surrounding the future auditory meatus; B, C, and D show the fusion and progressive development of the hillocks into the adult auricle. (From Langman, 1969.)

morphological features of the auricle could be considered indicative of high risk of coronary-artery disease (Frank, 1973; Lichstein, Chadda, Naik, and Gupta, 1974; Scott, 1974; Mehta and Hamby, 1974). Interest in the morphological characteristics of the auricle as possible predictors of disease and mental illness goes back to the end of the 19th century.

The pinna appears to be extremely important for localization of sounds in the median plane (Gardner and Gardner, 1973). Furthermore, measurements with the ear-canal closed (in adults) shows that the concha of the pinna has its best resonance frequency in the region of 4–5 KHz, and may contribute up to a 10 dB gain in sound pressure for these frequencies (Yamaguchi and Sushi, cited by Shaw, 1974; Shaw and Teranishi, cited by Shaw, 1974).

Development of the Auditory Pathways

Very little information is available concerning the structural maturation of the cells and their synaptic connections of the various nuclei of the human auditory pathway. One of the few developmental studies of the human auditory system is Bredberg (1968), but his investigation focused mainly on the innervation of the organ of Corti. The fetuses used in his study were too old (4–5 months) to determine the sequence in which the sensory hair cells are innervated, but earlier investigations (Cajal, cited by Bredberg, 1968; Lorente de No, cited by Bredberg, 1968) indicate that the hair cells in the basal portion of the cochlea are innervated prior to those in the apical end. Each inner hair cell is innervated by one nerve fiber, while the nerve fibers going to the outer hair cells have collateral branches, such that one fiber innervates several adjacent hair cells. The density of the sensory hair cells increases from the base towards the apex, with a maximum density about 2 mm from the apical end. The number of outer hair cells increases by almost 100%, while an increase of about 40% has been found for the inner hair cells.

The first relay station in the auditory pathway, the cochlear nuclei, are highly vascularized and they are extremely vulnerable to anoxia. In humans, the dorsal cochlear nuclei will be more affected than the ventral. Depending on the duration and severity of the anoxia, nerve cell losses from 36 to 66% of the normal population of cells have been observed (Hall, 1964). According to Lierse and Horstmann (1965), the degree of vascularization of the human dorsal cochlear nucleus is exceeded only by that of the cerebellum and putamen.

In the absence of any data on the development of the cochlear nuclei in humans, some of the information available on the maturation of these nuclei in the cat will be reviewed. Kane (1974) has published such data for the dorsal section of the cochlear nucleus. This nucleus contains a large variety of cell types, but Kane's study focused on the development of the fusiform cells. In newborn kittens, the soma of these cells is considerably smaller and less elongated than in the adult cat. The apical and basal dendritic trees are morphologically immature in terms of length, thickness, and appendages. Between 7 and 28 post-natal days several important changes occur: The cell soma becomes elongated and is no longer covered by filopodia, the apical dendritic tree grows peripherally, and both preterminal and terminal growth cones appear in the apical dendritic tree. At around 8 weeks postnatally an unchanging morphology, identical to that of Golgi impregnated fusiform cells from adult cats, is reached (Figure 6).

The fibers from the cochlear nuclei project to the superior olivary complex, of which the medial nucleus of the trapezoid body has been the most thoroughly explored. This nucleus contains some morphologically quite distinct synaptic endings, the so-called calyces of Held, which are probably the largest synaptic endings in the mammalian brain (Morest, 1968). The calcygenic axon migrates from the cochlear nucleus to the contralateral medial trapezoid nucleus through the trapezoid body. The calyx is formed primarily from the branches of a thick axonal tip, or growth cone. The developing calyces pass through three major stages before attaining their mature form: the stage of the migratory growth cone (prior to 8 fetal weeks), the stage of the proto-calyx (prior to 2 postnatal days), and the stage of the young calyx with collateral growth cones. The incidence of mature calyces (exhibiting extensive collaterals) increases gradually in successively older cats: By 94 days of age, nearly all calyces have them. The neurons with which the calyces make synaptic contact, the principal neurons, attain adult morphology at around 2–4 weeks postnatally, which is somewhat later than for the other cell types of the medial trapezoid nucleus, the stellate and elongate neurons (Morest, 1969a, 1969b).

The last relay station in the auditory pathway (Figure 7) is the medial geniculate nucleus, which contains 12 morphologically distinct populations of neurons (Morest, 1965). In the ventral nucleus, how-

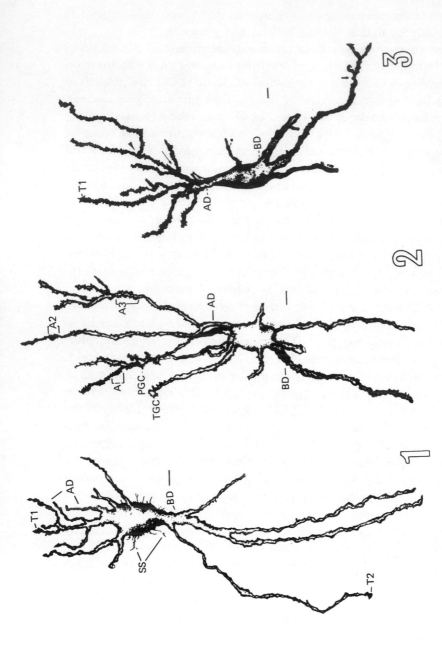

Fig. 6. Developmental sequence of fusiform cells in the dorsal cochlear nucleus of the cat (rapid Golgi impregnation). 1: immature fusiform cells from newborn kitten; 2: intermediate stage of development, 23-day-old cat; 3: mature fusiform cell, 9.5 weeks. SS: long somatic spicules; AD: apical dendrites; BD: basal dendrites; T: terminal dendrites; TGC: terminal growth cone; PGC: preterminal growth cone. Bar length: 10 μ. (From Kane, 1974.)

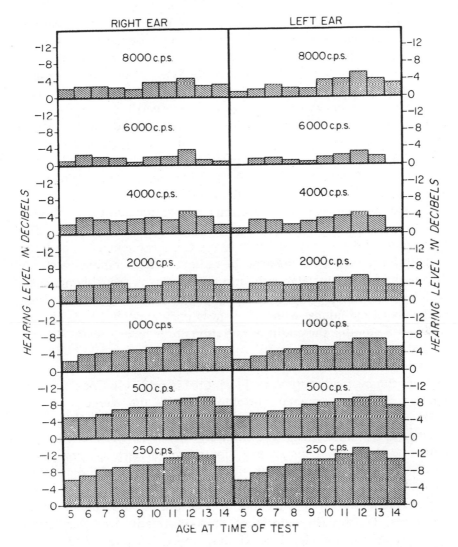

Fig. 7. Mean hearing levels of 2175 otologically normal children (5–14 years), tested between June 1958 and June 1959. Hearing levels in decibels re audiometric zero (American standard). (From Eagles and Wishik, 1961.)

ever, only two categories of neurons may be identified: the principal neurons, the axons of which project to the auditory cortex, and the neurons with short axons (Golgi type II), whose projections generally do not leave the ventral nucleus. The type II neurons account for about 40% of the neuronal population of the ventral portion of the medial geniculate nucleus. Their embryogenesis follows the same pattern as for the development of the type II neurons in the dorsal nucleus in the lateral geniculate nucleus, except that the time of maturation in the medial geniculate occurs about one week later, at 6–7 weeks of age. The principal neurons mature somewhat earlier (Morest, 1969a). It is not clear, however, when the growth of the dendritic endings of the Golgi type II neurons terminate, since a few typical dendritic growth cones with filipodia may still be seen in the young adult cat. It appears, therefore, that some of the developmental processes of the Golgi type II neurons continue long after the nervous system is "mature" and functioning in its adult capacity (Morest, 1971).

Data on myelination of the various parts of the auditory pathways in humans have been provided by Yakovlev and Lecours (1967). The lower parts of the ascending auditory system become myelinated quite early (prior to birth), but the acoustic radiation starts to myelinate only during the first postnatal month, and the process is probably not complete until about 4 years postnatally. Compared with the myelinization of the visual radiations, which also starts postnatally but is completed in about 5 months, the auditory radiations thus have a relatively prolonged period of myelinization.

Concerning the morphological maturation of the auditory cortex in man, the best currently available source is probably Conel's investigation of the postnatal development of the cerebral cortex (1939–1967). He described the regional development of the cortex in newborns, neonates and young children, using some of the following criteria to characterize the state of maturation for each age group: the width of the layers of the cortex, the number and size of the neurons, condition of the chromophil, size and length of axons, state of myelinization, etc. In the 2-year-old child, the neurons of the secondary auditory areas, TA and TB, were found to be more advanced than corresponding cells in the visual association cortex, OA and OB. The cells of the primary acoustic area TC were, however, less advanced than those in the primary visual area OC. In the 4-year-old child, on the other hand, the neurons of area TC were found to be in the same state of development as corresponding cells in area OC, and this stage thus represents one of relative advanced maturity of the primary auditory cortex, although the secondary areas are still not as advanced as the primary areas.

In order to obtain some idea about how data on the morphological development of the auditory system in the cat correlate with functional development, some of the investigations concerned with neurophysiological indices of auditory functioning in this animal will be discussed. As already mentioned, the surface topography of the cat organ of Corti does not achieve mature appearance until several weeks postnatally. The sensory hair cells are structurally mature prior to this stage, but their function probably remains subnormal until the tectorial membrane becomes detached from the microvilli of the Deiters' cells. Despite this limitation, however, the cochlear microphonic (CM) may be recorded as early as two days prenatally (Pujol and Hilding, 1973). The CM is an AC potential which mirrors the acoustic input in a truly microphonic fashion; a 500 Hz tone produces a CM of 500 Hz, with an intensity function which is linear up to about 80–90 dB. It is depressed by anoxia, but persists for about one hour after death. It may be picked up almost anywhere in the cochlea, with low frequencies being recorded best at the apical end and high frequencies at the basal end. The locus of generation of the CM is not entirely agreed on, but most investigators believe it to be somewhere at the cuticular surface of the sensory hair cells. The CM is probably *not* related to the stimulus transduction process, since there are a number of examples of possible dissociations of the CM and the action potential (AP) of the eighth nerve. For example, atropine depresses the AP, but not the CM, and similarly, experimental cooling of the cochlea reduces the AP and increases its latency, but does not affect the CM. Thirdly, stimulation of the crossed olivo-cochlear bundle causes a decrease in the AP, but an augmentation of the CM. Presence of the CM can thus not be taken as evidence that a stimulus is transduced into an action potential, which is consistent with data showing that the earliest recordable eighth nerve potential cannot be reliably elicited until about 2 days after birth (Pujol and Hilding, 1973).

Using cortically evoked potentials, the first responses may be observed in kittens aged 2–3 days (Pujol and Marty, 1968). The most sensitive frequency region is initially about 500–2500 Hz. This region gradually expands, more or less symmetrically, such that at the beginning of the second week responses to tones in the frequency region 150–15000 Hz are recordable. The intensity of the stimulation must initially be quite high (80 dB), but during the first week the threshold is markedly decreased. Even on day 12, the threshold for kittens is still much higher than that for adults cats, and according to

Ellingson and Wilcott (1960), a waveform with typically adult characteristics is not achieved until about 35 days.

Comparing morphological and neurophysiological indices of maturation of the auditory system, there appears to be a certain discrepancy, in that the neurophysiological studies suggest that the auditory system in the cat is functioning at an adult level several weeks prior to maturation of the relay nuclei of the auditory pathway, not to mention the auditory cortex. Assuming that the morphological data are fairly reliable, this discrepancy is most probably due to the fact that the types of auditory stimuli used for the neurophysiological investigations have been too simple (mostly pure tones) to assess the capacities of the auditory system in any detail.

Functional Development of the Auditory System in Humans

Fetal Studies

Considerable efforts have been invested in attempts at determining the earliest stage at which a human fetus will show some physiological or behavioral reaction subsequent to the presentation of an auditory stimulus. While the results of such studies are of both theoretical and practical significance, their interpretation is far from simple. Fetal reactivity to acoustic stimulation was first reported by Peiper (1925). He observed changes of fetal movements in response to intense sound stimulation (generated by a trailer-horn) in a fetus 1 week prior to delivery. His findings were later confirmed by Fleischer (1965) who recorded fetal movements to sound stimulation in mothers during the last month of pregnancy. Murphy and Smith (1962), Johansson, Wedenberg, and Westin, (1964), and Dwornicka, Jasienska, Smolarz, and Waryk (1964) attempted to correlate changes in heart rate with the presentation of an acoustic stimulus. On the basis of these studies, the inference has frequently been made that the auditory system in humans is functional prior to birth. This conclusion is, however, somewhat premature, considering that there is no evidence that the observed changes depended on functional maturity of the fetus's auditory system. The characteristics of the acoustic stimuli used in these studies (low frequency, high intensity sounds) are such that it is entirely possible that other modalities, e.g., the tactile or vestibular, both of which develop prior to the auditory system, could have been stimulated. The role of the mother as a possible "mediating" factor in the elicitation of the fetal response has likewise not been clearly established.

These behavioral studies have more recently been supplemented by investigations of fetal brain potentials using electrophysiological techniques. One of the first studies looking at acoustically evoked responses in the fetus was reported by Barden, Peltzman, and Graham (1968), who used fetal scalp electrodes. They obtained evoked responses presumed to have a temporal relationship with the stimuli in 1 out of 6 subjects, and the waveform of the responses was judged similar to that found for newborns. Scibetta, Rosen, Hochberg, and Chik (1971) also used electrodes attached to the scalp of the fetus, and obtained adequate responses in 21 out of 43 cases. By using the same recording technique in the same subject, fetal and neonatal averaged evoked responses were compared and found to be generally similar. There was, however, considerable variation in the configuration of the response in different subjects, in terms of both latency and polarity of the distinguishable components. The authors attribute this variation partly to variations in electrode placement, but do not provide any specific information about the magnitude of these differences.

Human fetal evoked responses to acoustic stimuli have also been obtained using electrodes attached to the abdominal wall of the mother. Sakabe, Arayamat, and Suzuki (1969) recorded such responses from six subjects in the 32nd to 38th week of pregnancy. The stimuli, 50 ms tone bursts with a frequency of 1000 Hz, were presented one every 4 seconds through a bone vibrator. The latency of the identifiable components ranged from 100 to 800 ms. The authors do not discuss whether or not the obtained responses were similar for all subjects.

These studies indicate that electrical activity, modifiable by externally applied acoustic stimulation, may be recorded from the scalp of the human organism prior to birth. It is not possible, however, as pointed out by Sakabe et al. (1969) to determine whether the response is actually elicited from the fetal cerebral cortex, with the stimulus conducted through the cochlea. These studies are therefore of limited value with respect to inferences about the functional status of the human auditory system prior to birth.

Neonatal Studies

The majority of the studies designed to evaluate the functional status of the auditory system in the neonate have used various behavioral responses as indicators of auditory receptivity. Wertheimer (1961) looked at eye movements in response to the sound made by a "cricket" noisemaker next to the right or left ear. The tests were started 3 minutes after birth, and the stimulus was presented about 8 times per minute. The observers agreed on the direction of the eye movements for 22 out of 55 trials, and of these 18 were in the direction of the click, and 4 in the opposite direction. These findings suggest that reflexive auditory-visual coordination is present at birth, and imply some maturity of the brainstem portion of the auditory system participating in this reflex.

Other investigations of neonatal auditory behavior have used far more dramatic stimuli; sound intensities up to 110–115 dB (re .0002 dyne/cm²) have sometimes been used (Froding, 1960; Wedenberg, 1956). Both of these studies used the auropalpebral reflex as the response measure, and found that this reflex can be elicited in most infants approximately ½ hour after birth. Common to all behavioral investigations of auditory sensitivity in neonates is the all-or-none character of the response measure, and they are therefore of limited usefulness, particularly since it has been demonstrated that absence of the moro- or auropalpebral reflexes, even to the most intense acoustic stimulation, does not necessarily indicate that the neonate is deaf or hearing-impaired (Froding, 1960). Furthermore, it is obvious that these studies cannot provide any useful information about the range of frequencies to which the neonate is sensitive, about thresholds for these frequencies, or about the ability to process acoustic waveform patterns.

A somewhat more promising technique for obtaining norms and quantitative data on neonatal hearing is the use of averaged evoked potentials, sometimes referred to as evoked response neonatal hearing is the use of averaged evoked potentials, sometimes referred to as evoked response audiometry. Several such studies have been performed (reviewed by Graziani and Weitzman, 1972), but only one will be mentioned here. Taguchi, Picton, Orpin, and Goodman, (1969) tested 250 newborns, ranging in age from 6 hours to 12 days, for air-conduction auditory evoked responses, and an additional group of 60 neonates (4 hours to 10 days old) for bone conduction thresholds. All tests were performed with the infants in light or deep sleep. Three different stimulus frequencies were used: 500, 1000, and 2000 Hz, with a duration of 60 ms (fall/rise time: 30 ms). The threshold was found to decrease somewhat with decreasing stimulus frequency, and the infants less than 2 days old had significantly higher thresholds (60 dB) than those over 2 days old (30–40 dB). Concerning the latency of the various components of the evoked responses, it was found that the younger infants had longer latencies for the N2 component, but no significant differences were detected for the mean peak latency of the P2 component. There was also a tendency for the latency to decrease with increase in stimulus intensity. One additional feature which emerged from this study was that the threshold for bone conduction was significantly lower than that for air-conduction in the infants less than 2 days old. These differences (up to 30–40 dB) were generally not found in infants older than 2 days, thus suggesting that the middle ear conduction system need not be completely developed at birth. (According to Elliot and Elliot, 1964, the middle ear is filled with fluid for about a month after birth).

In general, it appears that the auditory evoked responses in neonates and infants differ from those of adults with respect to waveforms; furthermore, the amplitude is lower than in adults, most components of the response tend to be delayed compared with adult latencies, and thresholds are also significantly higher in early infancy. In terms of the reliability of averaged evoked responses as an audiometric procedure, with adult subjects it is not uncommon to obtain an evoked response threshold which is within a few decibels of the subjective threshold. In preschool children, the sensitivity of the test is reduced by a factor of about 10–12 dB, while in the neonatal period this factor may be as large as 40 dB (Beagley, 1972). This decrease in reliability is chiefly due to larger background EEG activity and less stereotyped form of the evoked response in early infancy and childhood. According to Ellingson, Danahy, Nelson, and Lathrop (1974), the P2 component (latency of about 250 ms) is the most consistently detected part of the response, both within and between recording sessions.

Recently, some work has been directed toward exploring the capa-

bilities of young infants to discriminate between linguistically significant sounds (Eimas, Siqueland, Jusczyk, and Vigorito, 1971; Moffitt,
1971; Morse, 1972; Trehub, 1973). All of these studies used habituation
paradigms, and it was found that children as young as 4 weeks
showed evidence of dishabituation to linguistically contrasting elements. Some current reviews of infants' discrimination of acoustic
cues used in speech perception may be found in Eimas (1975) and
Schiefelbusch and Lloyd (1974). While some investigators have viewed
these findings as representing support for the claim that linguistic processing mechanisms in man are innate, recent data suggesting that
some subhuman species are capable of performing similar linguistic
discriminations obviously necessitate a revision of this view. Burdick
and Miller (1974) found that chinchillas can correctly "classify" novel
instances of /i/ and /a/, in spite of variations in talkers, pitch levels, and
intensity, and Kuhl and Miller (1974, 1975) showed that chinchillas can
also reliably differentiate between /t/ and /d/, as well as between /b/ and
/p/, despite variations due to talkers, vowels, and intensity. Comparable findings have been reported by Walker and Halas (1972), using
neurophysiological techniques. Regardless, then, of what the underlying mechanism for the human infant's capacity to make linguistic discriminations might be, it appears that it is based on properties of the
auditory system which are also present in subhuman species. Walker
and Halas's study would furthermore suggest that the locus of this
mechanism could be at the brainstem level.

   Habituation techniques have also recently been used to investigate nonlinguistic auditory processing in neonates. Stratton and
Connolly (1973) used heart-rate responses to determine the ability of a
group of 3- to 15-day-old neonates to discriminate between auditory
stimuli differing in terms of intensity, pitch, and temporal characteristics. While these authors concluded that the human neonate is indeed capable of such discriminations, their technique was not sensitive enough to permit quantification in terms of difference limens.
Wormith, Pankhurst, and Moffitt (1975) studied the ability of
1-month-old infants to discriminate between pure tones of different
frequencies, using nonnutritive sucking as the behavioral response.
Their results show that the infants were able to discriminate between
frequencies of 200 and 500 Hz, a finding which is perhaps not so
surprising in light of the studies of linguistic processing in infants.

Studies with Young Infants and Children

As the infant grows older, a general increase in responsitivity to sounds of different character develops, and the threshold for eliciting a response also decreases markedly. The accuracy with which an infant can localize a sound source also improves, and is well developed by around 25 weeks. Attempts at imitation of sounds starts at around 36 weeks, and at 1 year of age simple linguistic structures are generally understood. Standard audiometric procedures cannot be used with any reliability until the child is about 3 years of age. Large-scale audiometric testing of young children (2–17 years) were performed by Eagles and Wishik (1961). Their data presentation unfortunately does not allow inferences about the performance of the children below 5 years of age, but it is clear from their data (Figure 8) that the hearing level of children older than 5 years is significantly better than audiometric zero (adult reference), particularly for low frequencies. There is a gradual improvement of absolute sensitivity up to about 13 years of age, which probably represents the stage at which human hearing is the most sensitive.

Fior's data (1972) indicate, however, that maximum acuity for the central audiometric frequencies (1, 2, and 4 KHz) is reached about 7 years of age. In addition to pure tone testing, Fior also administered several other tests to his subjects (70 children, aged between 3 and 13 years), including speech intelligibility tests, adaptation tests, fatigue tests, and masking tests. On the speech discrimination tests, 80% of the words were correctly reported in the age group between 5 and 6, 90% in the group under 7 years, and the older subjects made practically no errors. The results of the fatigue test (change in threshold due to exposure to a loud tone) showed that in children under 5 years old, the threshold variation was about +15 dB. In children between 5 and 8 years, there was less change in threshold due to fatigue, the median value being +8 dB. In the children above 8 years, however, the effect was again high, about +20 dB. This is slightly higher than adult values for the stimulus parameters used by Fior. There is no simple explanation for the apparent increase in resistance to poststimulatory auditory fatigue in children between 6 and 8 years, but granted that these data are replicable, they demonstrate very clearly that the auditory system undergoes changes in its functional characteristics even during late childhood.

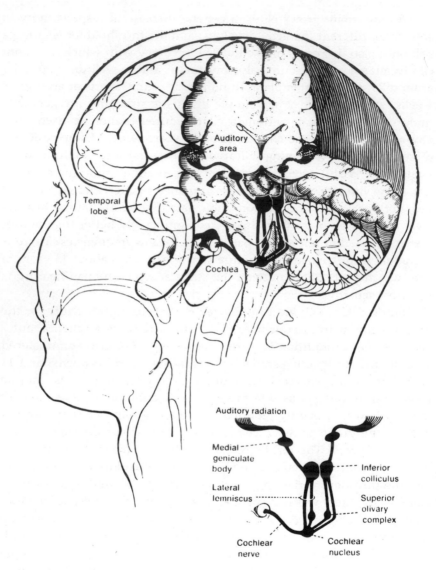

Fig. 8. Schematic representation of the major nuclei of the ascending auditory pathway and its projection to the auditory cortex. (From Grollman, 1974, p. 183.)

Fior also tested the ability of children to detect a pure tone embedded in a 40 dB white noise signal of the same frequency. The youngest subjects could detect the pure tone only when its intensity was above 70 dB, and a median value of 50–60 dB was found up to the age of 8 years. Only the subjects 10 years or older could detect the pure tone at an intensity level similar to that of the masking noise. Whether or not the ability to detect a signal embedded in noise depends on functional maturation of the efferent pathways of the auditory system is not known, but is evidently a function which matures quite late during development.

Additional data supporting the notion that development of certain complex auditory functions is a slow and gradual process come from studies of dichotic listening, delayed auditory feedback, and the verbal transformation effect. Berlin, Hughes, Lowe-Bell, and Berlin (1973) tested children 5 to 13 years old on a dichotic task, and their data show that the ability to identify both the left and right ear stimulus (double correct identification) steadily increases with age. MacKay (1968), in a study of delayed auditory feedback (DAF), found that DAF is more disruptive for young children (4–6 years) than for older children (7–9 years) and adults (20–26 years), regardless of the delay time. The delay time causing maximal disruption of the speech of young children was found to be .5 sec; for older children, .4 sec; and for adults, .2 sec. Warren and Warren (1966) reported that 5-year-old children do not appear to experience so-called verbal transformations—i.e., perceptual changes during listening to a continuously repeated auditory stimulus—while most 6-year-old children do. Furthermore, if the stimulus is a nonsense syllable, the youngest children experiencing the effect tend to report phoneme sequences which do not necessarily obey sequential rules for English phonemes. This was not found to be the case for young adults.

Auditory Deprivation

A large body of behavioral, neurophysiological, and anatomical evidence has recently appeared which demonstrates that early visual deprivation exerts rather profound influences on the developing mammalian visual system. Researchers in the field of audition have in general been more concerned with effects of excessive rather than reduced stimulation (Aleksandrovskaya and Chizenkova, 1973; Nikolov and

Dragwanski, 1973), but a few studies concerned with the effects of deprivation of auditory stimulation have also been performed.

There are obvious practical difficulties involved in rearing animals without exposing them to any sounds, but one way around this is to investigate the auditory system of congenitally deaf animals. Rawitz (1897) found the size of the auditory area in the temporal lobe to be reduced in the deaf white cat. Alexander (1900), on the other hand, found no abnormality of the brain in the same animal. Hudson, Durham, and Rubin (1962) reported that the brain of a deaf Dalmatian was apparently normal, and there were no abnormalities of the auditory tracts of the brainstem. In a deaf human with Waardenburg's syndrome, Fisch (1959) found some degeneration in the acoustic nerve root, but no abnormalities were detected in other parts of the central auditory system. In a more recent study of the deaf white cat, West and Harrison (1973) found reduced cell size in the ventral cochlear nucleus and the superior olivary nucleus. Apart from the reduction in size of these cells, they appeared histologically normal, and the authors state that "nothing in our observations would preclude the possibility of their capacity to function."

Gyllenstein, Malmfors, and Norlin (1966) looked at the development of cells in the auditory cortex of mice that had been reared in darkness from 2 to 4 months, and found hypotrophy of the cells of the auditory cortex (as well as the visual cortex) during the first 2 months. Studying animals that had been reared in the dark for about 4 months, they found that while the hypotrophy of the cells of the visual cortex persisted, the cells of the auditory cortex now showed *hypertrophy* (in terms of internuclear material and nuclear size). Ryugo, Ryugo, Globus, and Killackey (1975) reported an increase in the density of dendritic spines in the auditory cortex of rats, following visual and somatic deafferentation.

Concerning behavioral effects of auditory deprivation, Tees (1967a, 1967b) reported that rats deprived of auditory input from birth to 60 days showed deficits on an auditory pattern discrimination task and a task involving discrimination between the durations of a series of tones.

Batkin, Groth, Watson, and Ansberry (1970) studied evoked potentials to acoustic stimulation in albino rats that had been confined to a highly sound-attenuated environment for 8 months postnatally, and a significant loss of auditory sensitivity was found, but some recovery took place after subsequent exposure to ambient noise.

While the lack of any prominent changes in the auditory nuclei and cortex of congenitally deaf animals and man are somewhat surprising, it may be explained either by assuming that deafness is seldom complete, and thus suggests that even minimal input is sufficient for relatively normal morphological development of the auditory system, or alternatively by assuming that the changes are too subtle to be detected by conventional histological techniques. Since behavioral and electrophysiological studies suggest that auditory deprivation does entail certain deficits, it would be surprising if these were not somehow correlated with morphological alterations.

Summary and Conclusions

The embryogenesis of the ear starts around 22 days with the formation of the otic placodes. The sequence in which the various parts of the ear differentiates in general reflects their phylogenetic development, although there is no absolute correspondence. In terms of gross morphology, the ear is of adult appearance several months prior to birth, but full differentiation of the organ of Corti is not achieved until about 8 months. The precocious development of the ear is obviously of functional significance, since the basis for both frequency and intensity discrimination is the pattern and degree of displacement of the basilar membrane, which in turn depends entirely on the morphological characteristics of the membrane and its surrounding medium. If the inner ear were to function before the basilar membrane had achieved its full length, it would be necessary for the central nervous system structures involved in auditory discrimination to continually adjust or relearn the neural correlates of pitch and intensity as the membrane continued to grow.

Studies of newborn infants have demonstrated a gross ability to discriminate both frequency and pitch, which is consistent with the fact that these functions of the auditory system are more or less built in at the peripheral level. Systematic quantitative data of even the most basic type—e.g., audiograms—are still lacking, however. The studies showing that infants are capable of fine linguistics discriminations are interesting inasmuch as they indicate a fairly high degree of "autonomous" processing at lower levels of the auditory system. Electrophysiological investigations suggest that the auditory cortex is electrically active at birth, but whether or not this implies any cortical auditory processing remains unclear. Despite frequent claims to the effect that the auditory system is functional prior to birth, simple auditory tests have shown that certain functions are acquired only during late childhood (8–10 years), clearly indicating that development of the full range of auditory capacities is a relatively prolonged process, which is also consistent with the fragmentary data on morphological development of the central components of the auditory system.

References

Aleksandrovskaya, M. M., and Chizenkova, R. A. Analysis of changes of Glial cell number in the auditory cortex of the brain during sound stimulation of different intensity. *Fiziologicheskii Zhurnal SSSR*, 1973, *59*, 870–874.

Alexander, G. Zur vergleichenden, pathologischen Anatomie des Gehörorgans und Gehirn einer unvollkommenem Albinotischen weissen Katzen. *Archiv fuer Ohrenheilkund*, 1900, *50*, 159–181.

Barden, T. P., Peltzman, P., and Graham, J. T. Human fetus electroencephalographic responses to acoustic signals. *American Journal of Obstetrics and Gynecology*, 1968, *100*, 1128–1134.

Bast, T. H., and Anson, B. J. *The temporal bone and ear.* Springfield, Illinois: Charles C Thomas, 1949.

Batkin, S., Groth, H., Watson, J. R., and Ansberry, M. Effects of auditory deprivation on the development of auditory sensitivity in the Albino rat. *Electroencephalography and Clinical Neurophysiology*, 1970, *28*, 351–359.

Beagley, H. A. The cortical evoked response in audiometry. *Proceedings of the Royal Society of Medicine*, 1972, *65*, 87.

Bekesy, G. *Experiments in hearing.* New York: McGraw-Hill, 1960.

Berlin, C. I., Hughes, L. F., Lowe-Bell, S. S., and Berlin, H. L. Dichotic right ear advantages in children 5 to 13. *Cortex*, 1973, *9*, 394–402.

Bredberg, G. Cellular pattern and nerve supply of the human organ of Corti. *Acta Otolaryngologica*, 1968, *236* (Suppl.), 1–135.

Burdick, C. K., and Miller, J. D. Discrimination of speech sounds by chinchillas: Steady state /i/ vs. /a/. *Journal of the Acoustical Society of America*, 1974, *56* (Suppl.) S 52, Abstr. Z4.

Candiollo, L., and Levi, A. C. Studies on the morphogenesis of the middle ear muscles in man. *Archivfuer Klinischeund Experimentelle Ohren-Nasen-und Kehlkopfheilkunde*, 1969, *195*, 55–67.

Conel, J. L. *The postnatal development of the human brain.* Cambridge: Harvard University Press, 1939–1967.

Costa, A. Embryogenesis of the ear and its central projection. *Advances in Experimental Medicine and Biology*, 1972, *30*, 291–303.

Dallos, P., Billone, M. C., Durant, J. D., Wang, C., and Raynor, S. Cochlear inner and outer hair cells: Functional difference. *Science*, 1972, *177*, 356–358.

Dwornicka, G., Jasienska, A., Smolarz, W., and Waryk, R. Attempt of determining the fetal reaction to acoustic stimulation. *Acta Otolaryngologica*, 1964, *57*, 571.

Eagles, E., and Wishik, S. A study of hearing in children. *Transactions of the American Academy of Ophthalmology and Oto-laryngology*, 1961, *65*, 261–282.

Elimas, P. D. Speech perception in early infancy. In L. B. Cohen and P. Salapatek (Eds.), *Infant perception*. (Vol. 2). New York: Academic Press, 1975.

Elimas, P. D., Siqueland, E. R., Jusczyk, P., and Vigorito, J. Speech perception in infants. *Science*, 1971, *171*, 303–306.

Ellingson, R. J., and Wilcott, R. C. Development of evoked responses in visual and auditory cortices in kittens. *Journal of Neurophysiology*, 1960, *23*, 363–375.

Ellingson, R. J., Danahy, T., Nelson, B., and Lathrop, G. H. Variability of auditory evoked potentials in human newborns. *Electroencepholography and Clinical Neurophysiology*, 1974, *36*, 155–162.

Elliott, G. B., and Elliott, A. Observations on the constitution of the petrosa. *American Journal of Roentgenology and Radium Therapy*, 1964, *91*, 633–639.

Fior, R. Physiological maturation of auditory function between 3 and 13 years of age. *Audiology*, 1972, *11*, 317–321.

Fisch, L. Deafness as part of a hereditary syndrome. *Journal Laryngology*, 1959, *73*, 355–382.

Fleischer, K. Untersuchungen zur entwicklung der Innerohrfunktion. *Zeitschrift fuer Laryngologie, Rhinologie, Otologie*, 1955, *34*, 733–740.

Frank, S. T. Aural signs of coronary-artery disease. *New England Journal of Medicine*, 1973, *289*, 327–328.

Froding, C. A. Acoustic investigation of newborn infants. *Acta Otolaryngologica*, 1960, *52*, 31–40.

Gardner, M. B., and Gardner, R. S. Problem of Localization in the median plane: Effect of pinnae cavity occlusion. *Journal of the Acoustical Society of America*, 1973, *53*, 400–408.

Gilbert, J. H. V. Speech perception in children. In E. Cohen and S. J. Nootebohm (Eds.), *Dynamic aspects of speech perception*. Berlin: Springer Verlag, 1975.

Graziani, L. J., and Weitzman, E. D. Sensory evoked responses in the neonatal period and their application. *Handbook of Electroencephalography and Clinical Neurophysiology*, 1972, *15B*, 73–88.

Grollman, S. *The human body*. New York: Macmillan, 1974.

Gyllenstein, L., Malmfors, T., and Norlin, M. L. Growth alterations in the auditory cortex of visually deprived mice. *Journal of Comparative Neurology*, 1966, *126*, 463–470.

Hall, J. G. The cochlea and the cochlear nuclei in neonatal asphyxia. *Acta Otolaryngologica*, 1964, *194* (Suppl.), 1–193.

Hardy, J., Dougherty, A., and Hardy, W. Hearing responses and audiologic screening in infants. *Journal of Pediatrics*, 1959, *55*, 382–390.

Hecox, K. Electrophysiological correlates of human auditory development. In L. B. Cohen and P. Salapatek (Eds.), *Infant perception* (Vol. 2). New York: Academic Press, 1975.

Hudson, W. R., Durham, N. C., and Ruben, R. Hereditary deafness in the dalmatian dog. *Archives of Otolaryngology*, 1962, *75*, 213–219.

Johansson, B., Wedenberg, E., and Westin, B. Measurement of tone response by the human fetus: A preliminary report. *Acta Otolaryngologica*, 1964, *57*, 188–192.

Kane, E. C. Synaptic organization in the dorsal cochlear nucleus of the cat: A light and electron microscope study. *Journal of Comparative Neurology*, 1974, *155*, 301–330.

Kuhl, P. K., and Miller, J. D. Discrimination of speech sounds by the chinchilla: /t/ vs. /d/ in CV syllables. *Journal of the Acoustical Society of America,* 1974, *56* (Suppl.), S 52, Abstr. Z5.

Kuhl, P. K., and Miller, J. D. Speech perception by the chinchilla: phonetic boundaries for synthetic VOT stimuli. *Journal of the Acoustical Society of America,* 1975, *57* (Suppl.), S 49, Abstr. X13.

Langman, J. *Medical embryology.* Baltimore: Williams and Wilkins, 1969.

Lichstein, E., Chadda, K. D., Naik, D., and Gupta, P. K. Diagonal ear-lobe crease: Prevalence and implications as a coronary risk factor. *New England Journal of Medicine,* 1974, *290,* 615–616.

Lierse, W., and Horstmann, E. Quantitative anatomy of the cerebral vascular bed with special emphasis on homogeneity and inhomogeneity in small parts of the gray and white matter. *Acta Neurologica Scandinavica,* 1965, *14* (Suppl.), 15–19.

Lim, D. J. Fine morphology of the tectorial membrane, its relationship to the organ of Corti. *Archives of Otolaryngology,* 1972, *96,* 199–215.

Lindeman, H. H., Ades, H. W., Bredberg, G., and Engström, H. The sensory hair cells and the tectorial membrane in the development of the cat's organ of Corti. *Acta Otolaryngologica,* 1971, *72,* 229–242.

MacKay, D. G. Metamorphosis of a critical interval: Age-linked changes in the delay in auditory feedback which causes maximal disruption of speech. *Journal of the Acoustical Society of America,* 1968, *43,* 811–821.

Mehta, J., and Hamby, R. I. Diagonal ear-lobe crease as a coronary risk factor. *New England Journal of Medicine,* 1974, *291,* 260.

Moffitt, A. R. Consonant cue perception by twenty-four-week-old infants. *Child Development,* 1971, *42,* 717–731.

Morest, D. K. The laminar structure of the medial geniculate body of the cat. *Journal of Anatomy,* 1965, *99,* 143–160.

Morest, D. K. The growth of synapses in the human brain: A study of the calyces of the trapezoid body. *Zeitschrift fuer Anatomie und Entwicklungsgeschichte,* 1968, *127,* 201–220.

Morest, D. K. The differentiation of cerebral dendrites: A study of postmigratory neuroblasts in the medial nucleus of the trapezoid body. *Zeitschift fuer Anatomie und Entwicklungsgeschichte,* 1969, *128,* 271–289. (a)

Morest, D. K. The growth of dendrites in the mammalian brain. *Zeitschrift fuer Anatomie und Entwicklungsgeschichte,* 1969, *128,* 290–317. (b)

Morest, D. K. (1971) Dendrodendritic synapses of cells that have axons: The fine structure of the Golgi Type II cells in the medial geniculate body of the cat. Zeitschrift fuer Anatomie und Entwicklungsgeschichte, 1971, *133,* 216–246.

Morse, P. A. The discrimination of speech and nonspeech stimuli in early infancy. *Journal of Experimental Child Psychology,* 1972, *14,* 477–492.

Murphy, K. P., and Smyth, C. N. Responses of fetus to auditory stimulation. *Lancet,* 1962, *1,* 972–973.

Naftalin, L., Harrison, M. S., and Stephens, A. The character of the tectorial membrane. *Journal of Laryngology and Otology,* 1964, *78,* 1061–1078.

Nikolov, T., and Dragwanski, M. Modifications histochemiques du cortex sous l'action du Bruit et des vibrations. *Journal Francais d' O.R.L.,* 1973, *22,* 409–411.

Patten, B. M., and Carlson, B. M. *Foundations of embryology.* New York: McGraw-Hill, 1974.

Peiper, A. Sinnesempfindungen des Kindes vor seiner Geburt. *Monatschrift fuer Kinderheilkunde,* 1925, *29,* 236–241.

Politzer, G. Die Entstehung des Ganglion Acusticum beim Menschen. *Acta Anatomica,* 1956, *26,* 1–13.

Pujol, R., and Hilding, D. Anatomy and physiology of the onset of auditory function. *Acta Otolaryngologica,* 1973, *76,* 1–10.

Pujol, R., and Marty, R. Structural and physiological relationships of the maturing auditory system. In Jilek and Trojan (Eds.), *Ontogenesis of the brain.* Prague: Charles University Press, 1968. Pp. 377–385.

Rasmussen, G. L., and Windle, W. F. *Neural mechanisms of the auditory and vestibular systems.* Springfield, Illinois: Charles C Thomas, 1965.

Rawitz, B. Ueber die Beziehungen zwischen unvollkommenem Albinismus und Taubheit. Archiv fuer Anatomie und Physiologie, Physiologische Abtellung, 1897, *21,* 402–415.

Ryugo, D. K., Ryugo, R., Globus, A., and Killackey, H. P. Increased spine density in auditory cortex following visual or somatic deafferentation. *Brain Research,* 1975, *90,* 143–146.

Sakabe, N., Arayamat, T., and Suzuki, T. Human fetal evoked response to acoustic stimulation. *Acta Otolaryngologica,* 1969, *252* (Suppl.), 29–36.

Schiefelbusch, R. L., and Lloyd, L. L. (Eds.). *Language perspectives—acquisition, retardation, and intervention.* Baltimore: University Park Press, 1974.

Scibetta, J. J., Rosen, M. G., Hochberg, C. J., and Chik, L. Human fetal brain responses to sound during labor. *American Journal of Obstetrics and Gynecology,* 1971, *109,* 82–85.

Scott, M. Ear creases, heart disease and smoking. *New England Journal of Medicine,* 1974, *290,* 1205.

Shaw, E. A. G. The outer ear. In W. D. Keidel and W. D. Neff (Eds.), *Handbook of sensory physiology* (Vol. 5). Berlin: Springer Verlag, 1974.

Stratton, P. M., and Connolly, K. Discrimination by newborns of the intensity, frequency and temporal characteristics of auditory stimuli. *British Journal of Psychology,* 1973, *64,* 219–232.

Taguchi, K., Picton, T. W., Orpin, J. A., and Goodman, W. S. Evoked response audiometry in newborn infants. *Acta Otolaryngologica,* 1969, *252* (Suppl.), 5–17.

Tasker, R. R., and Organ, L. W. Stimulation mapping of the upper human auditory pathway. *Journal of Neurosurgery,* 1973, *38,* 320–325.

Tees, R. C. Effects of early auditory restriction in the rat on adult pattern discrimination. *Journal of Comparative Physiology,* 1967, *63,* 389–393. (a)

Tees, R. C. Duration discrimination in the rat after early auditory deprivation. *Perceptual and Motor Skills,* 1967, *25,* 249–255. (b)

Tobias, J. V. *Foundations of modern auditory theory* (Vols. 1 and 2). New York: Academic Press, 1970–1972.

Trehub, S. E. Infants' sensitivity to vowel and tonal contrasts. *Developmental Psychology,* 1973, *9,* 91–96.

Tuchmann-Duplessis, H., Auroux, M., and Haegel, P. *Illustrated human embryology* (Vol. 3). New York: Springer verlag, 1974.

Walker, J. L., and Halas, E. S. Neuronal coding at subcortical auditory nuclei. *Physiology and Behavior,* 1972, *8,* 1099–1106.

Warren, R. M., and Warren, R. P. A comparison of speech perception in childhood, maturity and old age by means of the verbal transformation effect. *Journal of Verbal Learning and Verbal Behavior,* 1966, *5,* 142–146.

Wedenberg, E. Hörselsbestemning på nyfödda. *Nord. Med.* 1956, *56,* 1022–1024.

Wertheimer, M. Psychomotor coordination of auditory and visual space at birth. *Science,* 1961, *134,* 1692.

West, C. D., and Harrison, J. M. Transneuronal cell atrophy in the congenitally deaf white cat. *Journal of Comparative Neurology,* 1973, *151,* 377–398.

Whitfield, L. C. *The auditory pathway.* New York: Williams and Wilkins, 1967.

Wormith, S. J., Pankhurst, D., and Moffitt, A. R. Frequency discrimination by young
    infants. *Child Development,* 1975, *46,* 272–275.
Wright, I. Hearing and balance. In J. A. Davis and J. Dobbing (Eds.), *Scientific founda-*
    tions of paediatrics. Philadelphia: Saunders, 1974.
Yakolev, P. I., and Lecours, A.-R. The myelogenetic cycles of regional maturation of the
    brain. In A. Minkowski (Ed.), *Regional development of the brain in early life.* Philadel-
    phia: Davis, 1967.
Zemlin, W. R. *Speech and hearing science.* Englewood Cliffs, New Jersey: Prentice-Hall,
    1968.

7

Felix Barroso

HEMISPHERIC ASYMMETRY OF FUNCTION IN CHILDREN

One of the many intriguing characteristics of the human brain is that it functions asymmetrically. This, of course, does not necessarily imply that one side is "dominant"—which, as Ornstein (1972) so keenly points out, is basically a societal distinction—but, instead, that the two hemispheres are not alike with respect to their abilities to handle different cognitive and perceptual functions. It is by now fairly well established that the right hemisphere is involved, primarily, in nonverbal, visuospatial, holistic processing, and the left in sequential, propositional, logical, and verbal—or linguistic—activities. This is a well-documented fact in the pathological literature and there are several excellent sources dealing with it (Mountcastle, 1962; Kinsbourne and Smith, 1974; Dimond and Beaumont, 1974), so this material need not be reviewed here. Additionally, data from work with normals using dichotic listening techniques (Carmon and Nachson, 1973; Bever and Chiarello, 1974; Kimura, 1961), and brief, lateralized visual presentations (Cohen, 1972; Kimura, 1966; Gross, 1972; Geffen, Bradshaw, and Wallace, 1971; Filbey and Gazzaniga, 1969; Durnford and Kimura, 1971) have confirmed and expanded the pathological findings.

The nature of the development of hemispheric specialization,

Felix Barroso · Department of Psychiatry SUNY at Downstate Medical Center, Brooklyn, New York.

however, is still an open question. Data from pathology indicate that one hemisphere may be able to "take over" the functions of the other hemisphere—or that some degree of equipotentiality exists—during early childhood. This is a controversial point since issues of plasticity, of what area takes over what, and of what type of reorganization takes place, tend to obscure the fact that injury to the young brain does result in outcomes not easily predictable, and certainly not as readily classifiable as they are for the adult brain. This is most evident in the problem of aphasia, which the findings with children have primarily dealt with. It seems that the permanent aphasic deficits observed in the adult after injury to the left hemisphere are not generally present if the damage was sustained at a relatively young age.

On the basis of the evidence, Lenneberg (1967) has concluded that children 4 to 10 years of age present the same symptoms as the adults but most of these children recover fully. His conclusions are based on published case reports and on his own work at the Children's Hospital Medical Center of Boston. His review shows that children who sustained the damage prior to age 10 do not show aphasic deficits on follow-up testing some years later. If the damage took place after age 10 or thereabouts, aphasic residues are still present after 2 or more years, and all indications are that these deficits are permanent.

According to Lenneberg, the course of aphasia is different before the age of 10 from that after 10. With unilateral injury occurring prior to age 9 or 10, appropriate cerebral readjustments take place that will leave the individual free from aphasic defects as an adult. The strongest evidence for this physiological readjustment in the young brain comes from findings with patients who have sustained massive lesions at a young age (Basser, 1962).

Prior to speech development, lesions to the right or to the left hemisphere delay speech onset (Basser, 1962). Basser proposes, on the basis of this, that at least in the very young child lateralization of speech functions is absent. If the lesion occurs after speech has been developed, left-sided trauma results in aphasic symptoms (Basser, 1962), most of which disappear in about 2 years' time if the accident took place before puberty. Still, injury to the right hemisphere also results in some speech disturbances but in a smaller percentage of the cases.

Basser (1962) has also reviewed cases in which it has been necessary to remove an entire hemisphere. In some of these patients the hemisphere was removed at puberty or thereabouts. The rest had hemispherectomies later in their adult lives. The important fact to emerge from the study of these cases is that if the original lesion (which led, eventually, to the hemispherectomy) occurred before ages 10 or 11, no permanent aphasias resulted, although it is not clear whether the patients had some more subtle verbal defects. Of 52 left hemispherectomies, with a history of prior damage before age 11, only 3 patients show permanent aphasic disturbances. All of the patients with lesions sustained after puberty showed permanent aphasic deficits. This evidence is sufficiently strong to warrant the conclusion that the right hemisphere took over the functions of the left hemisphere at the time the original injury took place, or that some equipotentiality for speech is operating up to as late as age 10. Additional support for this notion is provided by Boone (1965) who found that any type of unilateral injury to the brain seldom produced a severe or persistent aphasia if the damage took place before the age of 9 or 10. Children older than 10 years of age tend to develop aphasia with left-sided lesions, whereas aphasic children under 9 exhibit an amazingly rapid recovery. In an older report, Sugar (1952) also concluded that temporary aphasias resulting from unilateral injury are usually observed between the ages of 5 and 10.

The picture that emerges from pathology suggests that, prior to age 10, either some functions may be lateralized but not others, or lateralization has not taken place at all, with the hemispheres functioning, essentially, in an equipotential or symmetrical fashion. However, and in contradistinction with the adult groups in which comparable and complimentary pathological and normal data have been obtained, the results with normal children, so far, are not in agreement with what has just been discussed. We now turn to these data.

Kimura (1963) has demonstrated, with the dichotic listening tasks used with adults, a right ear effect for verbal material for children as young as 4 years. In the adults, the dichotic technique of simultaneously presenting two different auditory stimuli to each ear has yielded "ear effects" for the ear contralateral to the hemisphere known to handle the particular type of analysis. In this vein, left ear effects have been shown for nonverbal material (Kimura, 1964) and right ear effects for verbal stimuli (Kimura, 1961), tapping functions of the right and left hemispheres, respectively.

The Kimura findings for children seem to contradict the absence of speech lateralization inferred from the clinical reports. Kimura (1963) argues that her study shows left hemisphere superiority for this task but it does not rule out the participation of the right hemisphere at early ages in the recovery process. The clinicopathological evidence certainly supports this notion.

Another study by Kimura (1967) has confirmed her previous results and has led her to propose the possible lateralization of speech by age 4 but no later than age 6. Knox and Kimura (1967) have replicated the right ear effect with children, using both verbal and nonverbal methods of report. In their study, a left ear effect was found by age 5 for environmental sounds, a nonverbal task which has been found to depend on the integrity of the right hemisphere (Spreen, Benton, and Finchman, 1965; Spinnler and Vignolo, 1966).

These results with normal children provide evidence for lateralization of function at an age earlier than that at which recovery is still possible according to the clinicopathological data. Several objections can be raised, though, as to the feasibility of comparing the results with normal children to the pathological data. One of these objections has to do with the conclusions that can be drawn from the work with normal children. These conclusions must be limited because only auditory (dichotic) tasks have been used. No comparable effects have been reported in other modalities as it is the case for the adult findings for experiments using brief lateralized visual presentations.

Tachistoscopic work with adults, which at times have raised more questions than provided answers (see White, 1969, 1972, for lucid reviews of the issues involved), have, in combination with reaction time arrangements, demonstrated strong and replicable field effects. Generally speaking, the research with adult groups have shown that verbal material fares better in the right visual field (RVF) and nonverbal material in the left visual field (LVF). A parsimonious explanation for these effects is that they reflect the asymmetrical functioning of the hemispheres in the adult: Verbal material should be favored in the RVF because the initial projection of this field is to the left hemisphere; nonverbal stimuli should fare better in the LVF because of its initial projection to the right hemisphere. To explore hemispheric functioning further in normal children, similar visual tasks are needed to test young subjects. This is precisely what we set out to do.

Although innumerable visual tasks have been used with normal adult subjects, no visual task was found that could be used, or adapted for use, with children. The visual tasks necessary for use with children, for obvious reasons, had to be easy enough for even prereading children to perform. It was necessary, then, to design the new tasks described below.

The Right Hemisphere Task

Kimura (1966) used pairs of nonsense figures to try to elicit a left visual field superiority (to demonstrate a right hemisphere involvement in this task) but was unsuccessful, perhaps because she used a vocal response of "same" or "different." The task could have been performed by using a more sensitive response measure (i.e., reaction time) and the LVF superiority might have emerged then.

Gross (1972) did get a LVF superiority for the comparison of two matrices (a task which could be performed more efficiently by comparing the two matrices in a Gestaltist fashion) indicating a right hemispheric superiority for this activity. In both of these experiments the judgment can be performed in some holistic fashion, a visuospatial analysis of the entire display or of parts of their components, for establishing whether they are the same or different. Although the Kimura figures and the Gross figures cannot be easily analyzed in linguistic terms (and in this respect they could be considered "nonverbal" stimuli), it can be argued that their LVF superiority is not entirely due to this. It is possible that for certain kinds of analyses, although coding in verbal terms may be feasible, it may be more efficient, and less cumbersome, to do the task on other bases. It is intuitively obvious that judging whether two figures (e.g., two drawings or two photographs of two objects or of two faces) are the same or different does not necessarily involve naming them. This judgment can be performed on spatial and dimensional characteristics prior to that point in processing in which verbal labels are attached. If indeed this is the case, the comparison of two figures should be performed more efficiently in the LVF because this type of analysis seems to be the province of the right hemisphere.

Another possible reason why the analysis of two figures may be done faster (more efficiently) in the LVF rests on the fact that the right hemisphere excels in coding information—particularly visuospatial information—in a parallel fashion. The faster response to the two figures could be due to the fact that, during brief exposures, simultaneous analysis of this kind of stimuli is perfomed more effectively in the LVF, regardless of whether it can be done verbally at a subsequent step.

In view of all this, it was decided to use pairs of outline drawings of relatively simple realistic figures. These are illustrated in Figure 1. The simplicity of these figures makes them ideal for work with children. The pairs of figures would be presented randomly in the LVF or the RVF. Sometimes the pairs would be of the same figure, sometimes of different figures. The subject had simply to press one button for the different figures and another for the same figures, measuring how long it would take in each case. If the above consideration held, the judgment of pairs of figures should be faster for those figures appearing in the LVF.

The Left Hemisphere Task

As indicated above, if children of different ages were going to be tested, the verbal task could not involve any reading activity on the part of the subject. On the other hand, if a reaction time measure was to be used in a situation similar to the one for the right hemisphere task, a procedure of showing stimuli to the LVF or to the RVF had to be designed so that the subject could perform a judgment comparable to the one used for the right hemisphere task.

The task designed involved presenting one of the members of the pair verbally, followed by the presentation of the other member in figure form to either the left or the right of fixation. As in the right hemisphere task, in some cases the word heard prior to the showing of the picture would be the name of the picture and in some cases it would not. The subject had to respond pressing a button for "same" in the former, and a button for "different" in the latter case. Since this is predominantly a language-related task, latencies should be shorter for the single figure presented in the RVF. Stimuli in this field reach the naming centers of the brain, in the left hemisphere, more directly and the task then should be performed more efficiently and rapidly.

The next step involved testing adults to determine if the tasks designed elicited the predicted visual field differences. Visual field differences in the predicted directions would confirm that the tasks were

Fig. 1. The stimuli.

sensitive to hemispheric asymmetry of function. If the tasks would differentiate between the hemispheres with adult subjects, they would be used to test groups of children.

Method

Stimuli. Two sets of 4 in. × 6 in. white cards were prepared with the drawings illustrated in Figure 1. One set consisted of pairs of drawings pasted on a card one under the other, ½ in. of separation between the two, positioned to appear in the left visual field or in the right visual field. The other set consisted of single drawings positioned on the card to appear in either the left or the right visual field. The distance from fixation (center of the card) to the beginning edge of the widest figure in the right or the left visual field was approximately 2¾ degrees. Each figure was paired with either an identical figure or word (its name) or a different figure or word. The final sets consisted of twenty "same" cards and twenty "different" cards, or 40 cards total for each condition.

Apparatus. The stimuli were presented for 150 msec via a Gerbrands two-field tachistoscope. The preexposure field consisted of a white card with a red dot in its center which coincided with the center of the stimulus card. The subject responded "same" or "different" by pressing one or the other of two keys with the index finger of either their left or right hands. Presentation of the stimulus started a Hunter clock-counter and pressure on either response key stopped the counter.

Subjects. Fourteen male and 14 female undergraduate students participated in the experiment. All were right-handed with no history of familial sinistrality, with normal vision, and none had any previous neurological illness or impairment.

Procedure. Seven male and seven female subjects participated in the right hemisphere (nonverbal) condition. In this condition, two figures were presented to either the left or the right visual field; for half the trials, the figures were identical, for the other half, the pictures were different. The subjects were instructed to respond by pressing one key if the figures were the same and the other key if the figures were different. Seven males and seven females participated in the left hemisphere (verbal) condition. In this condition, the experimenter would say the name of a figure approximately 5 sec prior to the showing of a single figure, which was presented, in random order, either to the right or the left visual field. The subject had been told to press a key for "same" and another key for "different," depending on whether the single figure shown to the left or to the right of the fixation point was the same or different from the word previously heard. All subjects had been instructed to fixate the red dot on the preexposure field, an instruction that was repeated prior to each trial and stressed throughout the experiment. Half of the subjects in each condition responded "same" with their right hands and "different" with their left hands, and the other half responded "same" with their left hands and "different" with their right hands.

Each condition consisted of 120 trials, the 40 cards being repeated three times. There was a short break between the first 40 trials and the last 80 trials. Prior to the start of the second set of trials, a new set of 4 stimulus cards were used to bring back the subject to a reasonably similar level of performance to the one attained prior to the break. The first 40 trials and the 4 prior to the second set of trials were discarded and only the data from the final 80 trials were used in the statistical analysis.

Results

Mean RTs (in msec) for each visual field (right or left) for each type of stimuli ("same" or "different") were computed for each subject for the final 80 trials. These means excluded error trials; however, the mean error rate for the few subjects that made errors in these final 80 trials was very low (.49 for the verbal condition and .71 for the nonverbal condition).

The average of the combined ("same" and "different" stimuli) means for the verbal condition were 637 for the LVF and 589 for the RVF; for the nonverbal condition, 645 for the LVF and 690 for the RVF. An analysis of variance on the means for the verbal and nonverbal conditions was done, with the between-groups variables being sex (males vs. females), condition (verbal vs. nonverbal), hand-group (right hand "same"/left hand "different" vs. right hand "different"/left hand "same"), and the within-groups variables being figures ("same" stimuli vs. "different" stimuli) and field (LVF vs. RVF). Since the verbal and nonverbal conditions were included in the same analysis, field differences would show up as an interaction between Field and Condition, rather than as a simple Field effect. The analysis of variance yielded a significant Field × Condition interaction (F (1,16) = 78.115; $p. < .01$). For the verbal task the RTs were faster for the RVF than for the LVF, and for the nonverbal task, the RTs were faster for the LVF than for the RVF. All of the subjects in the verbal condition showed faster RTs to RVF stimuli; all of the subjects in the nonverbal condition showed faster RTs to LVF stimuli.

No other effects or interactions were significant. Traditional measures of laterality effects have included differences in percent correct report between fields. The low error rates in the present study precluded any analysis of this nature.

The tasks used in this experiment with adults have shown opposite visual field superiorities in reaction time to verbal and nonverbal stimuli. In the light of the knowledge about hemispheric functioning, the tasks are sensitive to the functional asymmetry of the human brain, with nonverbal material in the LVF engaging, more readily, the superiority of the right hemisphere for this type of activity. Faster RTs to verbal stimuli in the RVF, in the same vein, reflect a left hemisphere involvement in language-related tasks. Further discussion of these results will be undertaken later.

The Study with Children

The first step in the study with children was to establish an exposure duration at which young subjects would be able to identify all the figures. The children used in this preliminary procedure were drawn from the pool of subjects available for the main study but these children did not participate in the main study conducted subsequently.

The stimulus cards were presented, at varying durations, to 12 12-year-olds, 8 6-year-olds, and 8 5-year-olds. To achieve 100% recognition in the 5-year-old children, the stimuli had to be exposed for a minimum of 200 msec; for the older children (as for the adults), 150 msec was an adequate exposure duration.

Method

The stimuli and apparatus used were the same as the ones employed for the testing of the adult groups.

Subjects. Participants in the study were 150 children from a Catholic elementary school serving a wide socioeconomic sector in the New York metropolitan area. There were 30 6-year-old children (mean age 6:5); 32 8-year-old children (mean age 8:6); 27 9-year-old children (mean age 9:7); 28 10-year-old children (mean age 10:5), and 33 12-year-old children (mean age 12:6). Approximately half of the children in each group were boys and the other half girls. All of the children tested were right-handed, had normal vision, and had not had any illnesses which could have caused neurological damage. All of this information was obtained from the school's records.

In order to corroborate the handedness of the child, three procedures were employed. First, the child was asked to sign his or her name on the back of the data sheet, which was on a table, with a pencil centered 1 or 2 inches above the sheet. The experimenter noted the hand the child used for picking up the pencil and for writing. All of the children used their right hands for both actions.

The second procedure consisted of asking the child to pick up a ball that had also been placed on the table and throw it inside a box placed on the floor a couple of feet away from the child. In all cases, the children used their right hands to pick up and throw the ball.

The third procedure involved having the child demonstrate to the experimenter "how he would eat ice cream" using a bowl and a teaspoon that were also on the table. All of the children held the bowl in the left hand and used the right hand to pick up the spoon and perform the movements necessary to take the imaginary ice cream to their mouths.

As was the case with the adults, the children were naive as to the purpose of the experiment.

Procedure. A procedure identical to the one used with the adults was followed to test the children with a few minor modifications. One of these was that during the short break each child was invited to share with the experimenter a few pieces of candy placed in a small plastic cup.

The children in each age group were assigned randomly to the conditions and to whether they had to respond "same" with the right hand or with the left. The instructions given the children, except for the minor additions indicated between parentheses, were identical to those given the adult subjects. For the nonverbal condition, the instructions ran:

I am going to show you two pictures on that screen all the way in the back (do you see the screen?). Sometimes the pictures are going to be on one side of the red dot, sometimes on the other side. Sometimes the two pictures are going to be two pictures of the same thing and sometimes two pictures of two different things. When the pictures are the same, I would like you to press this button with the index finger of your right/left hand (E would here take the hand of the child, with the index finger extended, and would place it on the key). When the pictures are different, I want you to press this button with the index finger of your right/left hand (the hand of the child would be taken and placed on the key). Before I show you each pair of pictures I am going to say, "Look at the red dot." (Do you see that little red dot in the center, back there? Good. Now, it is very important, *[name of the child]*, that you look at the red dot when I tell you to because, you see, if you are not looking at the red dot, you will not see the pictures, and you wouldn't want to miss them, would you?) You should immediately look at the red dot when I ask you to because otherwise you may have difficulty in seeing the pictures since they go by very fast. It is very important that you press the button as soon as you can after you see the pictures (because, you see, this is like that game on television and the moment the figures show, this clock here *[demonstrating with the Hunter timer]* starts running and you stop it by pressing the key like this, you see? So you must beat the clock!) It is also very important that you do not make mistakes. Do you understand what you have to do? Good, remember, try to be as fast as you can in pressing the keys. Also, the moment I say, "Look at the red dot," your eyes should immediately look at it, no matter where you were looking before. Also, do your best in trying not to make mistakes (because, you see, if you make mistakes the game is not good. This is a game that we have to play without making mistakes). So, are you ready to start now?

The same instructions were used for the verbal condition except that they were modified to include that the experimenter would say a word, then a picture would appear to the right or to the left of the red dot, and one key had to be pressed if the word was the name of the picture, and another if it was not.

None of the children had any difficulty in understanding these instructions and went through the experimental session eagerly, with a minimum of complaint and with what looked like absolute attention to what they had to do.

Results

Mean RTs (in msec) for each visual field (right or left) for each type of stimuli ("same" or "different") were computed for each subject in each age group for the final 80 trials of each condition. These means excluded error trials, although the mean error rates for the few subjects that made errors in those final 80 trials were very low. The pattern of

Table 1. Averaged Means across Subjects in Each Condition for Children's Groups

Age groups	Verbal			Nonverbal		
	LVF	RVF	Error	LVF	RVF	Error
6-year-olds	1,122	1,122	.60	1,074	1,073	.63
8-year-olds	921	912	.68	867	872	.81
9-year-olds	837	820	.38	837	809	.36
10-year-olds	688	632	.57	690	747	.43
12-year-olds	700	656	.70	695	739	.94

means obtained averaged across subjects, for both conditions, combining "same" and "different" stimuli, are shown in Table 1, which also lists the mean error rates in each age group.

An analysis of variance on the means for each group (verbal and nonverbal conditions together) was performed. The significant main effects and interactions are presented in Table 2. It will be recalled from the discussion of the adult results that visual field differences would show up as an interaction between Field and Condition rather than as a simple Field effect.

For the 10- and 12-year-old children the analyses of variance

Table 2. Significant Effects and Interactions for the Children's Groups

Age group	Effect or interaction	Significance level
6 years	Figures	$p < .01$
	Figures × field × sex	$p < .05$
	Figures × field × hand	$p < .01$
8 years	Figures	$p < .01$
	Field × hand	$p < .01$
	Figures × field × hand	$p < .05$
9 years	Figures	$p < .01$
	Field	$p < .05$
	Field × sex	$p < .05$
	Figures × field × hand	$p < .01$
10 years	Figures	$p < .01$
	Field × condition	$p < .01$
	Field × sex × hand	$p < .05$
12 years	Figures	$p < .05$
	Field × condition	$p < .01$
	Figures × field × sex	$p < .01$

showed that RTs for the verbal task were faster for the RVF than for the LVF, and faster for the LVF than for the RVF for nonverbal task. This was shown in the significant Field × Condition interaction for the 10-year-olds (F (1,20) = 40.274; $p < .01$), and for the 12-year-olds (F (1,24) = 85.562; $p < .01$). Every one of the 10- and 12-year-old subjects in the verbal condition showed faster mean RTs to RVF stimuli than to LVF stimuli; in the nonverbal condition, every one of the 10- and 12-year-old subjects showed faster mean RTs to LVF stimuli than to RVF stimuli. The pattern of means for these 10- and 12-year-old children, then, is the same as that obtained for the adult groups.

For the 6-, 8-, and 9-year-old children, RTs for the verbal task were not faster for the RVF than for the LVF—they were approximately equal for both fields. RTs for the nonverbal task were also approximately equal for both fields. The Field × Condition interaction was not significant for any of these age groups, which shows that these younger children responded at approximately the same rates to stimuli in the RVF or in the LVF, regardless of condition.

The break between the 6-, 8-, and 9-year-old groups and the 10- and 12-year-olds is sharp even when one considers the behavior of individual subjects rather than the group means. For each subject, any difference of less than 15 msec between the RTs for each field was considered to indicate "no difference" between the fields. The distribution of subjects who showed "no difference," differences in the "predicted direction," and differences in the "opposite direction" is shown in Table 3. It can be seen that the 6-, 8-, and 9-year-old children show approximately a 50/50 split, which could be viewed as random fluctuations about a 0 difference between the fields. By contrast, the 10- and 12-year-old groups show the differences in the predicted

Table 3. Number of Children in Each Age Group Showing No Difference, or Differences between Fields in the Predicted or in the Opposite Direction

Age	Verbal			Nonverbal		
	Predicted	Opposite	No difference	Predicted	Opposite	No difference
6	9	6	1	8	6	2
8	9	6	1	5	6	5
9	7	4	2	4	7	3
10	14	0	0	13	0	1 (predicted)
12	16	0	1 (predicted)	16	0	0

Table 4. Means for the Figure × Field × Hand Interaction

| | Left hand different/ Right hand same | | | | Left hand same/ Right hand different | | | |
| | Same | | Different | | Same | | Different | |
Age group	LVF	RVF	LVF	RVF	LVF	RVF	LVF	RVF
6-year-olds	1,041	976	1,097	1,121	1,073	1,150	1,181	1,144
8-year-olds	869	814	928	914	852	908	927	933
9-year-olds	833	785	882	885	775	794	858	796
10-year-olds	655	632	679	691	685	699	739	738
12-year-olds	673	675	702	690	694	698	720	726

direction (although in two instances this difference was less than the 15 msec criterion).

A consistent finding in the 6-, 8-, and 9-year-old children was the third order interaction of Figures × Field × Hand. These younger children responded faster to ("same" or "different") stimuli appearing in the visual field on the same side as the hand responding ("same" or "different"). The overall means for this interaction are given in Table 4. This triple interaction is not significant for the 10- and 12-year-old children.

The judgment of "different" takes longer in all age groups across conditions. As Table 5 shows, the mean RTs for "same" stimuli averaged across tasks are shorter than for "different" stimuli. The differences between these means are significant and appear as Figures effect for all child groups, as shown in Table 2.

A few other significant interactions appeared, as shown in Table 2, but they are not consistent across age groups, nor did they lend themselves to any plausible interpretations. Furthermore, considering the number of possible comparisons involved in each age group, one

Table 5. Mean Reaction Times for "Same" and "Different" Stimuli

Age groups	Same stimuli	Different stimuli	Different–Same
6-year-olds	1,060	1,136	86
8-year-olds	861	926	65
9-year-olds	797	855	58
10-year-olds	667	712	45
12-year-olds	685	709	24

would expect significance—for example, at the .05 chance level—of at least 1½ of these comparisons by chance. It is likely that, since these interactions are not repeated in adjacent age groups, they can be considered random effects.

The main results of this study with children, then, show that only 10- and 12-year-old children showed the adult pattern of faster RTs for the RVF than for the LVF in the verbal condition, and faster RTs for the LVF than for the RVF in the nonverbal condition. The 6-, 8-, and 9-year-old children do not show this pattern.

Discussion

The findings in this study raise several important questions related to hemispheric asymmetry of function, and its development, in children. Before we can turn to these questions, however, it is necessary to discuss the implications of the findings for the adult groups.

The present findings with adults are consistent with the earlier results in the literature. Previous investigations have primarily dealt with right-handed adults since dextrals have consistently shown a pattern of hemispheric asymmetry of function in which the left hemisphere subserves verbal activities and the right hemisphere is involved in visuospatial, holistic processing. An exhaustive and incisive recent review by Levy and her associates (Levy, 1974) has established that 99.67% of dextrals indeed have a left hemispheric dominance for language. All of the adults tested in the present study were right-handed and exhibited the same pattern observed in previous tachistoscopic work with lateralized visual presentations: The verbal task was responded to faster in the RVF than in the LVF, whereas this asymmetry reversed for the nonverbal task. The results of this study, then, support an interpretation based on hemispheric asymmetry of function.

The verbal task used in the present study involved, basically, assessing whether a word heard was the name of a figure subsequently seen (whether the word was the "same" as, or "different" from, the figure). It has been suggested (Paivio, Rogers, and Smythe, 1968) that words are generally coded and stored in verbal form, although object names can also elicit pictorial images (Paivio, 1967). Recently, however, Lutz and Scheirer (1974) have shown that subjects will rarely code words pictorially, even highly concrete words similar to the ones used in this study. It is therefore quite plausible to assume that the comparison of the word and the figure in this study can be performed on verbal, or linguistic, bases. The faster reaction times found for the stimuli in the RVF are then a reflection of the more direct accessibility stimuli in this field have to the language-processing centers, which, in these right-handed subjects, reside in the left hemisphere.

The other task involved comparing two figures for a judgment of whether they were the same or different. For this task, a LVF superiority emerged. The judgment of whether two figures are the same or different can be performed by either comparing the features of one figure with the features of the other or by comparing the shapes or Gestalt created by each figure on the stimulus card. In both cases, the comparison could certainly be performed faster through a simultaneous analysis of the features of the two figures or of the Gestalt created by each figure. The right hemisphere has been found to excel in both the parallel processing of visual stimuli and in Gestaltist, holistic analysis of information (Bogen, 1969; Levy-Agresti and Sperry, 1968). The faster reaction times to the pairs of figures presented in the LVF can be interpreted as resulting from the greater advantage this field has in reaching directly precisely these abilities in the right hemisphere.

The rationale behind the adult study was to investigate hemispheric asymmetry of function, with tasks suitable for children, for the purpose of asking when such asymmetrical functioning appeared in children. The present results indicate that only the 10- and 12-year-old children show asymmetrical functioning of the hemispheres—or lateralization to the left hemisphere and to the right hemisphere of, respectively, the abilities required for the verbal and nonverbal tasks used in this study. Two aspects of the data lend support to this conclusion.

One is the Field × Condition interaction found only for the 10- and 12-year-old children. These older children showed the same response pattern of the adults, i.e., the single figure in the verbal condition was responded to faster in the RVF; the pairs of figures in the nonverbal condition yielded shorter latencies when presented in the LVF. The 6-, 8-, and 9-year-old children do not show this effect: Stimuli were responded to at approximately the same rates, irrespective of field, in the verbal and in the nonverbal conditions. The most plausible interpretation of the similar reaction times for material presented to the right or the left visual fields is that the two hemispheres are functioning symmetrically—each hemisphere can analyze verbal or nonverbal material at the same level of efficiency.

Indirect support for this view can be found in another aspect of the data. The interaction of Figures, Field, and Hand was significant in the 6-, 8-, and 9-year-olds but not in the 10- and 12-year-old groups. This interaction indicates that, generally, faster reaction times appeared for stimuli on the side of the hand responding, for the type of response ("same" or "different") assigned to that hand. That is, when the right hand was responding "same" and the left hand "different," "same" stimuli was responded to faster in the RVF (the side of the hand responding "same") and "different" stimuli was responded to somewhat faster in the LVF (the side of the hand responding "different"). The reverse took place when the right hand was assigned the response of "different" and the left hand the response of "same." This third order interaction was significant regardless of whether the children were responding to verbal or to nonverbal stimuli. One possible interpretation of the interaction is that the shorter reaction times are due to stimulus–response compatibility: It is easier to respond with the hand that is on the same side as the stimulus. From this point of view, the lack of an interaction in the older groups would be due to an overshadowing of the effects of response compatibility by the emerging hemispheric specialization.

The interaction can be interpreted in another, equally plausible way by considering the relation between locus of input analysis and the locus of response initiation. If the hemispheres in these young children are equally competent in analyzing verbal and nonverbal stimuli, a faster response to stimuli in one field may depend on whether the hemisphere originally receiving this input is also initiating the response to it. That is, for stimuli in the RVF, which goes first to the left hemisphere, responding with the right hand may be faster since the left hemisphere also initiates the response of this hand. Conversely, LVF material should be responded to faster by the left hand since both input analysis and response initiation are performed by the same right hemisphere. In this vein, "same" stimuli should be responded to faster in the RVF when the right hand is responding "same" and in the LVF when the left hand is responding "same." Similarly, "different" stimuli should be responded to faster in the RVF when the right hand is responding "different" and in the LVF when the left hand is responding "different." Tables 6 and 7, derived from a

Table 6. Means for Subjects of Different Ages Responding "Same" with the Right Hand and "Different" with the Left Hand

	Same stimuli				Different stimuli			
	Verbal		Nonverbal		Verbal		Nonverbal	
Age	LVF	RVF	LVF	RVF	LVF	RVF	LVF	RVF
6	1,022	984	1,059	969	1,127	1,145	1,067	1,097
8	887	819	852	810	957	919	899	910
9	824	787	842	783	895	897	870	873
10	637	552	672	711	670	628	687	754
12	667	621	680	729	722	667	682	713

further breakdown of the material in Table 4, show that these predictions hold for the 6-, 8-, and 9-year-old children in 22 out of 24 possible combinations.

The Figure × Field × Hand interaction, then, lends support to the proposal that, if the observed visual field differences in the adults and in the 10- and 12-year-olds are indeed a reflection of hemispheric asymmetry of function, the three younger groups do not seem to be processing stimuli differentially as a function of field. The interaction is also important from another point of view. It could be argued that the absence of a field effect in the young children is due to poor fixation that obscures asymmetrical processing. However, an argument based on inconsistent gaze seems implausible when fixation is clearly adequate to elicit a significant relationship between visual field and the hand responding. Similarly, an argument that the long reaction times in the young groups are masking field effects is untenable since the interaction emerges in the three younger groups regardless of the magnitudes of the RTs.

Table 7. Means for Subjects of Different Ages Responding "Different" with the Right Hand and "Same" with the Left Hand

	Same stimuli				Different stimuli			
	Verbal		Nonverbal		Verbal		Nonverbal	
Age	LVF	RVF	LVF	RVF	LVF	RVF	LVF	RVF
6	1,131	1,203	1,015	1,097	1,207	1,158	1,154	1,129
8	877	920	827	896	965	992	890	874
9	769	771	781	816	861	825	855	766
10	681	642	689	755	765	707	713	769
12	684	655	704	742	728	680	712	771

Closer scrutiny of Table 1 brings out another interesting aspect of the data. For the 10- and 12-year-olds (as was also the case for the adults), the field that shows the increase and decrease in reaction time as a function of task is the RVF. This points to the left hemisphere as the one that undergoes major readjustments during the final phases of lateralization. Its gain in efficiency for verbal tasks is mirrored by a similar loss for nonverbal tasks. This does not seem to be the case for the right hemisphere since both verbal and nonverbal tasks yield approximately equal latencies for the LVF. One possible explanation for this is that the verbal task used in this study gives the right hemisphere the opportunity to use whatever linguistic ability it has, enabling it to handle the comparison of a word and a picture as efficiently as it handles the comparison of two pictures. That the right hemisphere is capable of handling a verbal task of the nature of the one used in this study is evident from recent research by Eran Zaidel at the California Institute of Technology.* Zaidel's work with split-brained subjects, using his newly developed "Z lens," indicates that the right hemisphere can handle a wider range of linguistic activities than previously thought. Alternatively, the right hemisphere may perform the verbal task in a nonlinguistic fashion, by translating the word heard into a picture and then effecting the comparison. The possibility that the right hemisphere may resort at times to this type of imaginal mediation has been advanced by Seamon and Gazzaniga (1973). In summary, the evidence for the right hemisphere is equivocal: Compared across tasks, the right hemisphere does not perform more efficiently in the verbal task than in the nonverbal task. Further research is necessary to clarify this point.

One finding that appeared at all the age levels tested was that the comparison of "different" stimuli took significantly longer than the comparison of "same" stimuli. Although this effect was not significant in the adults tested in this investigation, the difference obtained was in the same direction. This finding has been reported by other investigators, with adult subjects, with various kinds of stimuli (Hochberg, 1968; Posner and Mitchell, 1967; Robinson, Brown, and Hayes, 1964; Egeth and Blecker, 1971; Moscovitch and Catlin, 1970; Snodgrass, 1972).

* *New York Times,* July 1, 1975, "Language ability found in right side of the brain"; *Science News,* July 12, 1975, "Talking to the quiet brain."

The Onset of Asymmetrical Functioning

Asymmetrical functioning of the hemispheres for the tasks described here appears much later developmentally than the age at which it has been shown in the dichotic listening studies (Kimura, 1967; Knox and Kimura, 1967). For the visual tasks used in this study, asymmetrical functioning appears around age 10, as opposed to as early as age 4 for both verbal and nonverbal auditory stimuli presented dichotically. The question then arises, given that hemispheric asymmetry of function emerges at one age for some tasks and at a later age for others, as to what may be responsible for this discrepancy.

One obvious possibility is that there is a difference in lateralization as a function of modality, with functions for the auditory modality lateralizing earlier than those for the visual modality. An alternative possibility is that different kinds of cues are important in the dichotic listening tasks and in the tasks used here, and that these cues are lateralized at different ages. For example, phonetic discrimination may be critical, in the dichotic verbal tasks, for determining which of the presented words are perceived, and this discrimination may be processed more efficiently in the left hemisphere at a very early age. By contrast, the visual–verbal task used here must depend on a different kind of selective processing on the part of the left hemisphere, presumably processing that is more semantic in nature. Further investigation of the cues underlying the different tasks is required in order to understand the different ages at which lateralization appears.

The data reported here indicate that hemispheric asymmetry of function for the tasks used in this study is not evident until the child is at least 10 years old. It is interesting to note that, according to the clinicopathological reports, it is precisely around this age that what may be called a "deficit boundary" exists. Insult to the human brain prior to this age is not likely to result in severe, permanent impairments. Prior to this age, reorganization is possible, a reorganization which takes advantage of the lability inherent in symmetricality or equipotentiality. After this age, and probably because of cognitive and perceptual demands requiring other characteristics of brain functioning, the hemispheres cannot effectively deal with the restoration of lost abilities.

The present study provides evidence which is compatible with the pathological data. If damage before age 10 does not lead to the same outcomes as damage after age 10, it is possible to interpret this as reflecting a symmetry in the functioning of the cerebral hemispheres during the first 9 or 10 years of life. The evidence from the present work suggests that this may be the case.

Still, there remains the problem of the dichotic work demonstrating asymmetrical functioning much earlier than the age at which it emerges in the present study. Aside from the possible explanations advanced above to account for this, it must be recognized that, obviously, neither the dichotic studies nor the present findings provide the final answers. Much work remains to be done, with both brain-damaged and normal children, before we can fully understand not only hemispheric asymmetry of function but also other mechanisms of the human brain during ontogeny. What the dichotic studies and the work reported here may indicate is that the asymmetrical functioning of the adult human brain is probably the result of an orderly process involving, conceivably, a progressive and systematic specialization of the hemispheres for different cognitive and perceptual activities.

Acknowledgment

This chapter was based on the author's doctoral dissertation at New York University Department of Psychology. I would like to acknowledge here not only my immense debt of gratitude to Professor Lila Ghent Braine for her guidance, counsel, support, and intellectual nourishment during all phases of this and other projects, but also my deep respect for her scientific integrity and acuity. I am also grateful to Professors Martin D. S. Braine, Annick Mansfield, J. Gay Snodgrass, and Richard Koppenaal for their assistance at different stages of this research.

References

Basser, L. S. Hemiplegia of early onset and the faculty of speech with special reference to the effects of hemispherectomy. *Brain*, 1962, *85*, 427–460.

Bever, T. G., and Chiarello, R. J. Cerebral dominance in musicians and non-musicians. *Science*, 1974, *185*, 537–539.

Bogen, J. E. The other side of the brain: An appositional mind. *Bulletin of the Los Angeles Neurological Societies*, 1969, *34*, 135–162.

Boone, D. R. Laterality dominance and language. *Journal of the Kansas Medical Society*, 1965, *66*, 132–135.

Carmon, A., and Nachson, I. Ear asymmetry in the perception of emotional nonverbal stimuli. *Acta Psychologica,* 1973, *37,* 351–357.

Cohen, G. Hemispheric differences in a letter classification task. *Perception and Psychophysics,* 1972, *11,* 139–142.

Dimond, S. J., and Beaumont, J. G. *Hemispheric function in the human brain.* New York: Halsted Press Book, John Wiley & Sons, 1974.

Durnford, M., and Kimura, D. Right hemisphere specialization for depth perception reflected in visual field differences. *Nature,* 1971, *231,* 394–395.

Egeth, H., and Blecker, D. Differential effects of familiarity on judgments of sameness and difference. *Perception and Psychophysics,* 1971, *9,* 321–322.

Filbey, R. A. & Gazzaniga, M. Splitting the normal brain with reaction time. *Psychonomic Science,* 1969, *17,* 335–336.

Geffen, G., Bradshaw, J. L., and Wallace, G. Interhemispheric effects on reaction time to verbal and nonverbal visual stimuli. *Journal of Experimental Psychology,* 1971, *87,* 415–422.

Gross, M. M. Hemispheric specialization for processing of visually presented verbal and spatial stimuli. *Perception and Psychophysics,* 1972, *12,* 357–363.

Hochberg, J. In the mind's eye. In R. N. Haber (Ed.), *Contemporary theory and research in visual perception.* New York: Holt, Rinehart & Winston, 1968.

Kimura, D. Cerebral dominance and the perception of verbal stimuli. *Canadian Journal of Psychology,* 1961, *15,* 166–171.

Kimura, D. Speech lateralization in young children as determined by an auditory test. *Journal of Comparative and Physiological Psychology,* 1963, *56,* 899–902.

Kimura, D. Left–right differences in the perception of melodies. *Quarterly Journal of Experimental Psychology,* 1964, *14,* 355–358.

Kimura, D. Dual functional asymmetry of the brain in visual perception. *Neuropsychologia,* 1966, *4,* 275–285.

Kimura, D. Functional asymmetry of the brain in dichotic listening. *Cortex,* 1967, *3,* 163–178.

Kinsbourne, M., and Smith, W. L. *Hemispheric disconnection and cerebral function.* Springfield, Illinois: Charles C Thomas, 1974.

Knox, C., and Kimura, D. Cerebral processing of nonverbal sounds in boys and girls. *Neuropsychologia,* 1967, *8,* 227–237.

Lenneberg, E. H. *Biological foundations of language.* New York: John Wiley & Sons, 1967.

Levy, J. *Psychobiological implications of bilateral asymmetry.* In S. J. Dimond and J. G. Beaumont (Eds.), *Hemisphere function in the human brain.* New York: Halsted Press Book. John Wiley & Sons, 1974.

Levy-Agresti, J., and Sperry, R. W. Differential perceptual capacities in major and minor hemispheres. *Proceedings of the United States National Academy of Sciences,* 1968, *61,* 1151.

Lutz, W. J., and Scheirer, C. J. Coding processes for pictures and words. *Journal of Verbal Learning and Verbal Behavior,* 1974, *13,* 316–320.

Moscovitch, M., and Catlin, J. Interhemispheric transmission of information: Measurement in normal man. *Psychonomic Science,* 1970, *18,* 211–213.

Mountcastle, V. B. *Interhemispheric relations and cerebral dominance.* Baltimore: Johns Hopkins Press, 1962.

Ornstein, R. E. *The psychology of consciousness.* San Francisco: W. H. Freeman, 1972.

Paivio, A. Paired-associate learning and free recall of nouns as a function of concreteness, specificity, imagery, and meaningfulness. *Psychological Reports,* 1967, *20,* 239–245.

Paivio, A., Rogers, T. B., and Smythe, P. C. Why are pictures easier to recall than words? *Psychonomic Science*, 1968, *11*, 137–138.

Posner, M. I., and Mitchell, R. F. Chronometric analysis of classification. *Psychological Review*, 1967, *74*, 392–409.

Robinson, J. S., Brown, L. T., and Hayes, W. H. Test of the effect of past visual experience in perception. *Perceptual & Motor Skills*, 1964, *18*, 953–956.

Seamon, J. G., and Gazzaniga, M. S. Coding strategies and cerebral laterality effects. *Cognitive Psychology*, 1973, *5*, 249–256.

Snodgrass, J. G. Matching patterns vs. matching digits: The effect of memory dependence and complexity on "same"-"different" reaction times. *Perception and Psychophysics*, 1972, *11*, 341–349.

Spinnler, H., and Vignolo, L. Impaired recognition of meaningful sounds in aphasia. *Cortex*, 1966, *2*, 337–348.

Spreen, O., Benton, A., and Finchman, R. Auditory agnosia without aphasia. *Archives of Neurology*, 1965, *13*, 84–92.

Sugar, O. Congenital aphasia: An anatomical and physiological approach. *Journal of Speech and Hearing Disabilities*, 1952, *17*, 301–304.

White, M. J. Laterality differences in perception: A review. *Psychological Bulletin*, 1969, *72*, **387**–405.

White, M. J. Hemispheric asymmetries in tachistoscopic information-processing. *British Journal of Psychology*, 1972, *63*, 497–508.

8

Marcel Kinsbourne

THE ONTOGENY OF CEREBRAL DOMINANCE

It has long been known that in most people the language function depends on the activity of the left cerebral hemisphere. It is clear that language develops from a base state of no language. But does language lateralization analogously develop from a base state of no lateralization? It has been generally assumed that this is so. The child at the very beginning of language development is regarded as using both cerebral hemispheres for this purpose. Differences of opinion have related more to the time frame within which lateralization occurs (Lenneberg, 1967; Krashen, 1972) than to the question of whether lateralization develops at all.

Once progressive lateralization in childhood was assumed to occur, further assumptions seemed plausible to many. Two of these were that the rate of lateralization in some way represented the rate of language development and the ultimate extent of lateralization its ultimate level of excellence. It was then assumed that adults who were incompletely or anomalously lateralized for language would be found to be deficient in their verbal skills and, conversely, that children who were slow to develop language would be found to be relatively ill-lateralized for the age (Eustis, 1947; Orton, 1937; Silver and Hagin, 1964; Zangwill, 1960). It was only one more, ostensibly easy, step to the en-

---

Marcel Kinsbourne · Hospital for Sick Children, Toronto, Canada.

terprise of attempting to hasten lateralization in the hope of thereby accelerating the development of language skills.

Thus, on the narrow base of the assumption that lateralization develops *pari passu* with language behavior, there has been built a substantial edifice of further assumptions, culminating in elaborate remedial techniques. It is doubly crucial to determine whether the basic assumption is correct. This is so both for scientific reasons and because, if the basic assumption is incorrect, the great investment of time, effort, and expense in remedial techniques intended to modify lateralization would be better spent in a manner more directly applicable to the interest of children with language disorder.

One might first ask whether the notion of developing lateralization is even plausible on general principles. One can then proceed to scrutinize the evidence that has been adduced in favor of the concept. This consists mainly of (1) an appraisal of the effect of early, lateralized brain damage on language, and (2) an interpretation of the life-span development of perceptual asymmetries for verbal material. We will then be in a position to decide whether the hypothesis of developing lateralization has face validity or whether the null hypothesis of lateralization as a stable and invariant characteristic of language development in the human should be regarded as not disconfirmed.

Two propositions can safely be made that contrast the immature and mature nervous system of any species. One is that the immature nervous system subserves a comparatively restricted behavioral repertoire. The other is that, when damaged in one of its parts, the immature nervous system exhibits a relatively high potential for compensation for that part's actual or potential function by the function of some other residual intact area. There are, then, two reasons why focal damage to the immature nervous system often results in less dramatic change in behavior than does comparable damage inflicted on the nature nervous system: (1) There is less behavioral versatility present to lose, and (2) any function that is lost is more readily compensated by other parts of the system. If one identifies a part of the adult brain that subserves a given function and then shows that destruction of a comparable section of the immature brain fails to disrupt that function, one has not thereby necessarily demonstrated a more widely spread localization for that function. The results could be accounted for by the well-known superior compensatory potential of the immature brain. Indeed, the concept that, in the course of maturation, the area of the brain involved with a given function progressively shrinks is a curious one, for which there is no model whatever in the neurophysiological literature for any species. If, indeed, language representation in children retreats from a bilaterally based to a smaller, lateralized arena in the cerebrum, then this phenomenon is the first recognized of its type.

One source of evidence that has been related to the question under discussion is the difference in effect of lateralized cerebral lesions on language function depending on the time in the life span at which the damage occurs. The general proposition has been well validated; it is that damage to the left hemisphere at or around birth has only a minor effect on the rate and ultimate level of verbal development, whereas comparable damage in the fully mature brain may induce a language disability of great severity (Carlson, Netley, Hendrick, and Prichard, 1968; Kohn and Dennis, 1974; Lansdell, 1969; McFie, 1961; Smith, 1974; Wilson, 1970). There is an intermediary period from the origins of language development to puberty, during which left-hemispheric damage does cause disruption of language behavior but also to a lesser extent and for a shorter period of time than one usually encounters in the adult aphasic (Lenneberg, 1967; Krashen, 1972). There are two obvious ways in which such phenomena can be interpreted. It might be argued that in the child the left hemisphere is only part of a bilaterally distributed language area, and therefore, damage to it deprives the individual of only part of his language substrate. But one could more simply rely on the well-established principles of early plasticity and merely remark that, as might be expected, the opposite hemisphere compensates faster and better for damage to the language-relevant side of the brain the younger the individual when the damage occurs. Because of these two possible explanations, the sole fact that greater damage brings less language loss afterward cannot resolve the question of whether cerebral dominance develops as language develops.

Can we instead draw conclusions based on evidence relevant to the question of whether, as maturation progresses, language disorder is more or less likely to appear after selective injury to the ostensibly irrelevant right hemisphere? Lenneberg (1967) has reviewed some reports in the neurological literature that discuss cases of children who were between the ages of 2 and 5 years at the time of an apparently right-sided brain injury which was said to have impaired some aspect of language function. We must ask ourselves two questions about these reports: Can they be trusted? If so, what can we then conclude?

In order to bear on the question of right-hemisphere language, the clinician who reports the case must show two things: (1) that the right hemisphere was selectively damaged, and (2) that language was thereby affected. Cases in the literature fall short on both these counts. It is at the best of times difficult to establish lateralization of brain damage in the absence of autopsy evidence or at least highly sophisticated neuroradiological or direct neurosurgical evidence. In fact, Lenneberg's reported cases (Alajouanine and Lhermitte, 1965; Basser, 1962; Guttmann, 1942) come nowhere near meeting adequate criteria for drawing such conclusions. With the exception of those in one particular series (Byers and McLean, 1962) the reports of right-hemisphere lesion leave open the question of whether the left hemisphere was concurrently involved by the same pathological agent; such a situation would thereby disrupt language, to no one's surprise. Cases in which, perhaps after some virus infection or immunization, a child has one or more epileptic seizures, perhaps paralysis on one side of the body, and some changes in the EEG, cannot with validity be used to indicate a lesion confined to the hemisphere opposite the paralysis. Thus, the various case reports which in sum suggest an incidence of language problems nearly as great for right-sided as for left-sided disease in children under five (Lenneberg, 1967; Basser, 1962) are, in fact, open to the criticism that in every single case any language deficit could have resulted from extension of the damage to the other side of the brain. Furthermore, in the one series in which evidence for right-sided lateralization of the insult in each case was unequivocal, there was not a single case in which that right-hemispheric damage affected language (Byers and McLean, 1962).

The evidence in the other reports (Alajouanine and Lhermitte, 1965; Basser, 1962; Guttmann, 1942) that language was indeed interrupted is equally fragile. In no case are the results of speech and language testing reported, nor indeed is much heed paid to anything other than speech output. Usually the report amounts to no more than the observation that the child was not speaking to the clinician. There are, of course, a number of possible reasons for this (Geschwind, 1967). A brain-based disorder of language cannot be assumed unless the nature of mistakes in language decoding and encoding can be shown to be consistent with this diagnosis and, if language function recovers, unless at recovery patients go through recognizable stages of decreasing aphasic deficit.

Were the evidence not so worthless, it might have been worthwhile adding that, in any case, it is not valid to contrast the relative frequency of a behavioral effect resulting from lesion A and lesion B on the basis of sporadic reports in the literature that one would assume to be biased toward publication of the less expected event. About one percent of aphasic syndromes in right-handed adults arise from lesions limited to the right hemisphere (Hecaen and Ajuriaguerra, 1964). We must conclude that no acceptable evidence has been adduced for the proposition that the proportion is any different in children at any particular age.

There remains the theoretical question: What type of effect might one expect from unilateral damage to a bilaterally represented language system? The nature of the behavioral change would depend on the manner in which two sides of that language system interact to produce the total language skill. If each hemisphere contributed differently to that behavior, there would be qualitative differences in the aphasia produced by right-sided and left-sided damage. None such have been reported. One would then suppose that in some undefined way each hemisphere contributes some portion of total language facility, and damage to either would somewhat reduce it. Damage on one side would be expected to cause only a partial aphasia, rather than a complete loss of language skill. Suppose, however, one were to find such a case with right-sided damage; there would still be two possible explanations for the fact that the aphasia was partial rather than complete. The reason that language is partially spared might indeed be that the other hemisphere was continuing its normal function, but the reason could equally well be that the undamaged part of the same hemisphere was continuing its work. Thus, one might in fact be seeing not a case of bilateral but of right-hemisphere lateralization of language. In order to be sure that the residual language behavior comes from the other side, one would have to have a case in which the right hemisphere was abruptly totally destroyed, leaving language function *immediately* partially preserved (because merely a more rapid than expected recovery of language would only attest to plasticity of the residual young brain). Such cases have not been reported at any age.

Another type of lead on the question of progressive lateralization comes from observation of behavioral characteristics that appear to relate to lateralization of language in the individual. After all, the whole notion of progressive lateralization quite possibly arose from a very old line of speculation about relationships between left- and/or mixed-handedness and a variety of mental defects. Insofar as right-hand preference seems to indicate a left-hemisphere dominance for language, it has been thought that preference for left or neither hand would indicate some other lateralization or lack of lateralization of that function. In fact, the majority of left-handers are right-lateralized for language. In any case, there is no convincing evidence that anomalous lateralization or incomplete lateralization of language in any way reflects the excellence of verbal skills except when the abnormal cerebral representation was the result of brain damage; in the latter case, the brain damage itself is sufficient cause for the cognitive deficit. Simply, anomalous handedness quite often is one consequence of damage to parts of the brain. Language delay is another consequence of such damage. These propositions do not imply a causal relationship between the hand preference and the state of the language function.

More recently a number of novel indicators in language lateralization have been developed. The earliest and best known of these are the hemifield asymmetry in visual recognition threshold for briefly presented verbal material, and the right-ear advantage for the report of two concurrent messages dichotically presented by earphones to the two ears (Kimura, 1963a). The question has been repeatedly asked, as one tests children at a younger age: "Is the right-ear advantage to be found in dichotic listening, for instance, of dwindling magnitude?" It is assumed that if it were, this would indicate a lesser degree of lateralization in such individuals. In fact, this interpretation is unfounded, since it has never been shown that the degree of an ear advantage reflects the degree of lateralization on any test whatsoever. If anything, more likely it indicates the extent to which the subject found it necessary to enlist his verbal capabilities to solve the problem he has been set. This is not merely a function of the lateralization but of the extent to which he tries to perform on the task and uses a specifically verbal strategy to do so. These variables are not at the moment amenable to measurement. In any case, however, the evidence that asymmetries are less in younger children is equivocal, to say the least. In fact, most dichotic studies have shown no change in ear advantage even down to age 4, (Berlin, Lowe-Bell, Hughes, and Berlin, 1972; Kimura, 1963b) and several studies have shown that children as young as 3 years still as a group favor the right ear (Gefner and Hochberg, 1971; Kinsbourne and Hiscock, 1976; Nagafuchi, 1970). The point has been made in one study (Bryden, 1970) that the younger the child, the more he tends to give primacy in his report to the right ear, whereas the older individual shows right-ear advantage even if directed to report the input to his left ear first. It is not clear what should be concluded from this. First of all, we have no way of knowing to which ear the subject initially attends; we merely know which material the subject in fact first reports. Secondly, it would appear that the fact that attention is biased is itself of fundamental importance (Kinsbourne, 1974, 1975). A bias of attention to the right is a direct consequence of left lateralization of language in the context of a verbal task. With regard to this attentional bias, perhaps the most enormous right-ear asymmetry that has been found occurred in a yet unpublished study by Kinsbourne and Hoch, in which 3-year-old children were asked selectively to report only the message coming into one ear, when a pair of dichotic digits was presented on each trial. Children found it easy to report one or both of the digit names represented at the trial. When asked to report from the right ear only, they did so with a good deal of accuracy. They scored very poorly when reporting from the left ear only, but an analysis of those responses showed that they were not failing to respond or responding with extraneous information. Rather, they were responding with the item that was presented to the right, unasked-for, channel. Their bias in attention to the right was far more extreme than it is in more mature individuals.

On general principles, this comes as no great surprise, because one would be quite ready to believe that any maladaptive or adaptively irrelevant biases in behavior would be less evident in the more versatile and flexible mature than the less subtly engineered immature organism. But for purposes of the present argument, at any rate, it is obvious that with respect to dichotic listening no case can be made for decreased lateralization at least down to age 3 years.

Two other newer techniques have been adapted to 5-year-old children. One is the effect reported by Kinsbourne (1972), that verbal thinking induces momentary gaze shifts to the right in right-handed subjects. Kinsbourne attributed this to the left lateralization both of language and of the cerebral control center of rightward gaze, and a hypothesized intimate connection between the two. In an un-published study by Kinsbourne and Jardno, a comparable finding was obtained for normal 5-year-old children. Another paradigm used on a similar group was derived from a study that showed that, when right-handed subjects engaged in a unimanual performance, then in a con-dition in which they were asked simultaneously to speak, the uniman-ual performance was disrupted with respect to the right hand but not with respect to the left (Kinsbourne and Cook, 1971). Kinsbourne and McMurray (1975) adapted this to children by use of a finger-tapping technique. They found that whereas 5-year-old children could tap, on the whole, more rapidly with their right than left index finger, when they were asked either to recite a nursery rhyme or to repeat the names of four animals, the tapping rate on the right suffered more than that on the left. The right-hand advantage disappeared and in-deed was replaced by a trend in the opposite direction.

The effect is based on a hypothesized interference between the programming of two motor sequences, one for speech and one for hand movement in the same hemisphere. For purposes of the present argument it shows that a clear lateralization, in this case of verbal ex-ecutive function, is easily demonstrable as early as 5 years of age.

The view that asymmetries extend down into infancy is interest-ingly supported by studies in very young babies both at the behav-ioral and the electrophysiological level. Newborn infants tend sponta-neously to look to the right about four times as often as to the left (Siqueland and Lipsitt, 1966; Turkewitz, Gordon, and Birch, 1968). Such a rightward preference of gaze certainly seems to arise earlier than right-hand preference, not to mention left-hemisphere lateraliza-tion of language. However, the generally held view that consistent right-hand preference, like the origins of language, is delayed until the second year of life has now been disconfirmed. Babies as young as 3 months of age maintain hold of a rattle far longer with their right hand than with their left (Caplan and Kinsbourne, 1976). Thus, an asymmetry of hand-use can be shown at a very early age, given that an age-appropriate test procedure is used. Related to this is the report of electrical cortical responses, i.e., that verbal stimuli caused a greater response over the left, and nonverbal stimuli over the right, convexity of the skull in newborns (Molfese, 1973; Entus, 1975) long before any behavioral evidence of language skill appears.

Far from supporting the view that lateralization is a slowly emerg-ing function that lags well behind the origins of language development, evidence suggests that some form of lateralization not only accompanies but even precedes the first traces of verbal behavior. The amount of lateralization as judged on behavioral grounds is no less and quite likely greater than that found in the mature organism. Of course, once one speaks of language-related lateralization that actually precedes language behavior, one needs to recast one's models of what left-hemisphere lateralization of language is all about. It could, on the one hand, be argued that language function is present on the left side of the brain long before this is shown in casually observable behavior. After all, Eimas's observation that very young infants could respond differentially to different phonemes would fit well with such a view. But perhaps the most promising, albeit speculative, interpretation might be one that gives priority in time to attentional biases released by specific materials or, more likely, to specific task orientations which form the substrate for the accumulation of experience on which subsequent language skill is based.

Cerebral dominance for language does not develop; it is there from the start. Thus, one could hardly relate the excellence of language behavior to such a development nor sensibly seek for measures which would accelerate that nonexistent process. It would seem advisable, in view of the evidence as summarized, to discontinue remedial therapies based on procedures that supposedly influence language lateralization in favor of procedures designed to act upon language behavior directly.

With reference to the two main questions set for this volume: (1) The building up and the breakdown of language function takes place against an invariant background of cerebral dominance. However, under conditions of lateral brain damage the nondominant hemisphere can more readily compensate in the younger individual. (2) Rate of lateralization of the cerebral representation of language is not a significant dimension of individual difference, because language is lateralized from the start.

Acknowledgment

This chapter was originally published in D. Aaronson and R. W. Rieber (Eds.), *Development Psycholinguistics and Communication Disorders* (New York: New York Academy of Sciences, 1975).

References

Alajouanine, T., and Lhermitte, F. Acquired aphasia in children. *Brain*, 1965, *88*, 653–662.

Basser, L. Hemiplegia of early onset and the faculty of speech with special reference to the effects of hemispherectomy. *Brain*, 1962, *85*, 427–460.

Berlin, C. I., Lowe-Bell, S. S., Hughes, L. F., and Berlin, H. L. Dichotic right-ear advantage in males and females—ages 5–13. Paper read at the 84th meeting of the Acoustical Society of America, Miami Beach, Florida, 1972

Bryden, M. P. Laterality effect in dichotic listening. Relations with handedness and reading ability in children. *Neuropsychologia*, 1970, *8*, 443–450.

Byers, R. K., and McLean, W. T. Etiology and course of certain hemiplegias with aphasia in childhood. *Pediatrics*, 1962, *129*, 367–383.

Caplan, P., and Kinsbourne, M. Baby drops the rattle. Asymmetry of duration of grasp by infants. *Child Development*, 1976, *47*, 532–536.

Carlson, J., Netley, C., Hendrick, E. B., and Prichard, J. S. A reexamination of intellectual disabilities in hemispherectomized patients. *Transactions of the American Neurological Association*, 1968, *93*, 198–201.

Entus, A., Hemispheric asymmetry in processing of dichotically presented speech and non-speech sounds by infants. Society for Research in Child Development, Denver, Colorado, 1975.

Eustis, R. Specific reading disability: A familial syndrome associated with ambidexterity and speech defects and a frequent cause of problem behavior. *New England Journal of Medicine*, 1947, *237*, 243–249.

Gefner, D. S., and Hochberg, I. Ear laterality preference of children from low and middle socio-economic levels on a verbal dichotic listening task. *Cortex*, 1971, *7*, 193–203.

Geschwind, N. Neurological foundations of language. In H. R. Myklebust (Ed.), *Progress in learning disabilities* (Vol. 1). New York: Grune & Stratton, 1967.

Guttmann, E. Aphasia in children. *Brain*, 1942, *65*, 205–219.

Hecaen, H., and Ajuriaguerra, J. *Left handedness: Manual superiority and cerebral dominance*. New York: Grune & Stratton, 1964.

Kimura, D. Right temporal lobe damage. *Archives of Neurology*, 1963, *8*, 264–271. (a)

Kimura, D. Speech lateralization in young children as determined by an auditory test. *Journal of Comparative Physiology and Psychology*, 1963, *56*, 899–902. (b)

Kinsbourne, M. Eye and head turning indicates cerebral lateralization. *Science*, 1972, *176*, 539–541.

Kinsbourne, M. Mechanisms of hemispheric interaction in man. In M. Kinsbourne and W. L. Smith (Eds.), *Hemispheric disconnection and cerebral function*. Springfield, Illinois: Charles C Thomas, 1974.

Kinsbourne, M. The interaction between cognitive process and the direction of attention. In V. P. M. A. Rabbitt and S. Dornic (Eds.), *Attention and performance*. London: Academic Press, 1975. 5, 81–97.

Kinsbourne, M., and Cook, J. Generalized and lateralized effects of concurrent verbalization on a unimanual skill. *Quarterly Journal of Experimental Psychology*, 1971, *23*, 341–345.

Kinsbourne, M., and Hiscock, M. Does cerebral dominance develop? In S. Segalowitz and F. A. Gruber (Eds.), *Language development and neurological theory*. New York: Academic Press, 1976.

Kinsbourne, M., and McMurray, J. The effect of cerebral dominance on time sharing between speaking and tapping by preschool children. *Child Development*, 1975, *46*, 240–242

Kohn, B., and Dennis, M. Patterns of hemispheric specialization after hemidecortication for infantile hemiplegia. In M. Kinsbourne and W. L. Smith (Eds.), *Hemispheric disconnection and cerebral function.* Springfield, Illinois: Charles C Thomas, 1974. Pp. 39–47.

Krashen, S. Language and the left hemisphere. UCLA working papers in phonetics, 1972, *24*.

Lansdell, H. Verbal and nonverbal factors in right-hemisphere speech: Relation to early neurological history. *Journal of Comparative Physiology and Psychology*, 1969, *69*, 734–738.

Lenneberg, E. *Biological foundations of language.* New York: John Wiley & Sons, 1967.

McFie, J. The effects of hemispherectomy on intellectual functioning in cases of infantile hemiplegia. *Journal of Nurology, Neurosurgery and Psychiatry*, 1961, *24*, 240–249.

Molfese, D. L. Cerebral asymmetry in infants, children and adults: Auditory evoked responses to speech and musical stiumuli. *Journal of the Acoustical Society of America*, 1973, *53*, 363(A).

Nagafuchi, M. Development of dichotic and monaural hearing abilities in young children. Acta Oto-Laryngologica, 1970, *69*, 409–414.

Orton, S. *Reading, writing and speech problems in children.* New York: Norton, 1937.

Silver, A., and Hagin, R. Specific reading disability: Follow-up studies. *American Journal of Orthopsychiatry*, 1964, *34*, 95–102.

Siqueland, E. R., and Lipsitt, L. P. Conditioned head turning in human newborns. *Journal of Experimental Child Psychology*, 1966, *4*, 356–377.

Smith, A. Dominant and nondominant hemispherectomy. In M. Kinsbourne and W. L. Smith (Eds.), *Hemispheric disconnection and cerebral function.* Springfield, Illinois: Charles C Thomas, 1974. Pp. 5–33.

Turkewitz, G., Gordon, B. W., and Birch, M. G. Head turning in the human neonate: Effect of prandial condition and lateral preference. *Journal of Comparative Physiology and Psychology*, 1968, *59*, 189–192.

Wilson, P. J. E. Cerebral hemispherectomy for infantile hemiplegia. *Brain*, 1970, *93*, 147–180.

Zangwill, O. L. *Cerebral dominance and its relation to psychological function.* Edinburgh, Scotland: Oliver & Boyd, 1960.

9

Helen J. Neville

THE FUNCTIONAL SIGNIFICANCE OF CEREBRAL SPECIALIZATION

Eric Lenneberg's studies of the biological foundations of language are classic documentations of the intimate relation between the maturation of the brain and maturation of behavior. Lenneberg carefully followed the development of speech and language skills in the growing child and showed impressive correlations between milestones in the acquisition of language and the attainment of adult values of various parameters of brain maturation. The latter included cell body volume of neurons in the cortex, dendritic arborization, gray-cell coefficient, and the chemical composition of cerebral white matter. Lenneberg (1967) showed that these values of brain maturation, taken together with various indices of cerebral specialization of function, predict the point at which the child first puts words together (70% of adult brain values or around 20 months), and the time when language is quite clearly a part of the child's behavioral repertoire, but not yet fully developed (i.e., around 85% of adult brain values and around 4 years of age). Of these variables indexing the state of maturation of the brain, cerebral specialization is the only one for which there are simple methods of observation in the normal child and adult.

It has often been suggested that the development of cerebral func-

Helen J. Neville · Department of Neurosciences, A-012, University of California at San Diego, La Jolla, California.

tional specialization is closely tied to the development of language. However, language, while it is perhaps the most often investigated, is but one type of behavior included under the general rubric of "man's higher cognitive abilities." The language behavior shown by Lenneberg to correlate with neurological maturation included both the ability to speak and the ability to comprehend spoken speech. Almost every aspect of language (including phonology, syntax, semantics) involves the apprehension of relational principles. Thus, a word is not simply a particular sound pattern which is tagged to a particular object, else the user would not be able to name particular objects which he has not seen before. A word stands for a class of objects (e.g., *table*) or relations (e.g., *under*). Similarly, in human visual perception, behavior is characterized by constancies of size, distance, shape, and brightness: A piece of paper seen in the light is perceived as "the same as" the same piece of paper seen in the dark, although optical parameters have changed.

The organism exhibiting "higher cognitive abilities" may be characterized as showing appropriate equivalence matches. He must know when to act toward two objects or relations as "the same" and when as "different." This ability characterizes human language as well as other, nonlanguage cognitive activities. Eric Lenneberg always believed the use of language to be a human peculiarity which is secondary to and which makes explicit the mental processes of conceptualization. It has often been proposed that the unique ability for speech and language may have been the critical factor which led to the development of man's bilateral asymmetry of cerebral functioning (e.g., Levy, 1974). Alternatively, perhaps the important variable could be thought to be the cognitive substrate necessary for, among other things, the acquisition of language. The question to be addressed here is whether hemispheric specialization of function develops concomitantly with the development of speech and language *per se*, or with the development of the special cognitive capacities which Lenneberg believed to be the underpinnings of, and prior to, our ability to acquire natural language.

Hemispheric specialization of function refers to the fact that the two cerebral hemispheres of man do not contribute equally to cognitive functioning. Most of the research in this field has been designed to determine which of man's higher cognitive functions are more dependent on the integrity of his left cerebral hemisphere and which primarily on his right. We will, therefore, first present a brief review of the different experimental approaches to this question and the corresponding results. We will then go on to consider the rather small amount of evidence concerning comparative aspects and the ontogeny of cerebral specialization, and finally a few studies which bear directly on the relation between behavioral abilities and the development of hemispheric specialization.

Cerebral Specialization in Human Adults: Evidence from Neuropathology

Although many writers in antiquity had observed the concomitant occurrence of aphasia and right hemiplegia (see Benton, 1965; Giannitrapani, 1967 for reviews) it was only the middle of the 19th century when the inference was first drawn that aphasia was specifically related to disease of the left hemisphere. In 1861 Broca reported that lesions of the third frontal convolution of the left hemisphere resulted in aphasia and in 1865 he asserted that "nous parlons avec l'hémisphère gauche." This notion was quickly accepted and confirmed, at least for right-handed people. These developments led to a concept of hemispheric cerebral dominance in which the term suggested an absolute superiority of one hemisphere (usually the left) over the other. It was not long, however, before it became apparent that such an extreme view of functional asymmetry was untenable. In 1874 Hughlings Jackson suggested a shift of emphasis from the concept "dominant" to "dominant for what" and proposed that there may be other functions besides language for which the left hemisphere may be dominant and functions for which the right or nonlanguage hemisphere may be superior. That is, cerebral dominance is defined by the function under consideration. For those who did not eschew Jackson's suggestions this is where the limited notion of cerebral dominance was transcended and the concern with problems of hemispheric functional *specialization* began. Systematic investigation of the latter was not undertaken until about 50 years after Jackson was writing. A survey of the recent literature dealing with brain lesion symptomatologies and neurosurgical evidence from "split-brain" research provides evidence that the cerebral hemispheres function qualitatively differently and supports the general concepts of functional cerebral specialization.

The extensive study of clinical symptomatology in unilateral hemispheric lesions has repeatedly shown the greater dependency of speech on the integrity of the left hemisphere (Luria and Karasseva, 1968; Milner, 1958, 1964; Russo and Vignolo, 1967; Weinstein, 1962) and has indicated several functions, often characterized as non-verbal–perceptual in nature, for which the integrity of the right hemisphere is necessary. The latter include performance on visual, tactile, and auditory spatial tasks and nonverbal visual and auditory memory (De Renzi, 1968; Kimura, 1963; Milner, 1968; Newcombe and Russell, 1969).

A typical clinical lesion study involves, for example, comparing the performance of patients with left-hemisphere lesions (LH group) to a right-hemisphere-lesioned (RH) group on a task thought to require predominantly left-hemisphere functioning. If the LH group performs at a significantly lower level than the RH control group one might conclude that the integrity of the left hemisphere was essential for the activity; that is, that the left hemisphere is "dominant" or specialized for that particular function.

Newcombe and Russell's (1969) project to investigate the differential effects of focal missile injury to the left and right hemispheres was based on the hypothesis of hemispheric asymmetry of function. They investigated the hypothesis that the left hemisphere is specialized for language functions and the right hemisphere for visual perceptual and spatial functions. The experimental groups were men with unilateral lesions of either the left or the right hemisphere. The RH group, although unimpaired in standard intelligent tests and tests of language functions, showed a significant deficit on both a visual closure task and visually guided maze task. In contrast, the LH group was impaired in language tests but matched a normal control in the nonverbal visual tests.

That language functioning is disturbed by injury to the left hemisphere has been recognized for a long time. The functional specialization of the right hemisphere has become equally well established. Milner (1958, 1964) has reported deficits in pattern identification tasks following right temporal lobectomy but not after left temporal lobectomy. Others have found RH group deficits on the trail-making tasks

(Reitan and Tarshes, 1959) and on spatial tasks whether visually or tactually presented (De Renzi, 1968).

De Renzi's (1968) study advanced the hypothesis that LH patients would be impaired when required to remember meaningful patterns which could be verbally identified but not when required to remember meaningless patterns which have no name. A reverse impairment was expected for the RH group. Both hypotheses were confirmed, supporting the notion that left and right hemispheric specialization is related to mnemonic as well as perceptual functioning.

Auditory discrimination and recognition is another area where hemisphere disorders appear to be material-specific. Milner (1962), using the Seashore Measures of Musical Talents, found that RH patients performed poorer than LH patients on tests of time, pitch, loudness, timbre, and tonal memory. These findings are consistent with those of Teuber and Diamond (1956) which indicate that there is greater impairment of sound localization with right than with left hemisphere lesions. On the other hand, Kimura (1961) noticed that with *verbal* auditory material, left-lesioned patients were more impaired in performance.

While providing fertile ground for research into the notions of cerebral specialization, the many reports of patients with unilateral brain lesions must be viewed with caution. There must be an accurate estimate of the site and extent of the lesion, and also of the effects of the injury upon blood supply. Also, of course, it should be remembered that one cannot localize a function to the place which, when damaged, produces a deficit in that function. Nevertheless, the clinical data establish that the symptomatology of left and right hemisphere lesions is different, and suggest that the functional organization of each hemisphere is different.

Research on patients who have had their cerebral hemispheres disconnected is most often viewed as providing supportive evidence for the notions of hemispheric specialization of functions. The surgery, which is performed to relieve intractable epilepsy, typically involves complete transection of the forebrain commissures (including the corpus callosum and anterior commissure). Sperry and his associates began an extensive study of these patients and, initially, at least, reported very dramatic separation of left and right hemisphere functions following surgery. Only one hemisphere (usually the left) in these patients was capable of supporting propositional speech and writing. The commissurotomized patient was able to speak only about perceptual information which reached his verbally dominant hemisphere. For example, because each visual field projects solely to the contralateral hemisphere, the patient could not name or describe objects presented in his right visual field (which projects to the left hemisphere). Nor could the split-brain patient verbally label an object manipulated with his left hand (which connects primarily with his right hemisphere), although he was able to remember and tactually or visually (i.e., nonverbally) select the same object when it was placed with a collection of other items.

Other studies of split-brain patients (Bogen and Gazzaniga, 1965; Levy-Agresti and Sperry, 1968) find that in some tests of visuospatial perceptual functioning (e.g., the reconstruction of Necker cubes; block designs; cross-modal spatial relations) the right hemisphere is superior to the left. On the other hand, the right hemisphere seems definitely inferior in handling numerical calculation problems (Sperry, 1968). In nonverbal tests for calculation, the patients' disconnected right hemisphere was unable to support so simple a task as the subtraction of 2 from numbers under 10.

Other studies have demonstrated that, although the production of *speech* is strongly left-lateralized in these patients, the nonspeech hemisphere possesses some, if modest, language *comprehension* skills. For example, written nouns, some phrases, and simple sentences have been correctly responded to after left visual field projection in commissurotomized patients. Recently, Levy (1974) concluded that while the right hemisphere can perform many tasks of language comprehension and even expression, there is no evidence that it can analyze a spoken input into its phonetic components.

The large amount of research done with the split-brain patients has suggested many different ways of describing the functions for which the left and right hemispheres are differentially specialized. The earliest breakdown was simply verbal/nonverbal; recently it has been suggested that the left hemisphere analyzes over time, notes conceptual similarities, perceives detail, codes sensory input in terms of linguistic descriptions, and possesses a phonological analyzer, whereas the right hemisphere synthesizes over space, notes visual similarities, perceives form, codes sensory input in terms of images, and possesses a "Gestalt Synthesizer" (Levy, 1974).

It must be emphasized, however, that the callosectomy is performed on these subjects only after extremely severe epilepsy, which can leave persistent functional defects and also possibly a rather abnormally organized brain. We cannot be sure to what extent data obtained from these patients bear on considerations of functional hemispheric specialization in normals.

Cerebral Specialization in Normal Human Adults

Behavioral Studies

The study of cerebral asymmetries in normal people became widespread with the employment of the technique known as dichotic stimulation (Broadbent, 1954). Dichotic stimulation consists of the simultaneous presentation to each ear of different stimulus material. With normal right-handed subjects this type of presentation of verbal material consistently results in a greater amount of material accurately recalled from the right ear than from the left. This phenomenon has been labeled the right ear effect (Bryden, 1965; Kimura, 1961, 1967; Satz, Achenbach, Pattishall, and Fennell, et al. 1965). These results are interpreted as support for the notions of hemispheric asymmetry: The contralateral auditory pathways in man are stronger than the ipsilateral pathways, and the left hemisphere plays a greater role than the right in the processing of verbal material. Because the right ear has better connections with the left hemisphere than does the left ear, right ear sounds have the advantage of better access to these "speech centers." Electrophysiological evidence from infrahuman and human studies suggests that the contralateral auditory pathways are indeed stronger (Rosenweig, 1951; Sinha, 1959; Tunturi, 1946; Vaughan and Ritter, 1970). Vaughan and Ritter found that, in man, monaural auditory input affects the two hemispheres unequally, the amplitude of the ipsilateral evoked cortical response being appreciably less than the contralateral one.

Auditory asymmetries in normal subjects have most often been demonstrated with dichotic, and less with monaural presentation. Kimura (1961) and others (e.g., Springer, 1973) have proposed that dichotic presentation is more sensitive to cerebral asymmetries because of the "competition" which is set up between the ears: This competition results in occlusion or suppression by contralateral pathways of impulses arriving along ipsilateral pathways. Thus, Kimura argues, the language-specialized left hemisphere begins with stronger connections with the right ear, and these are enhanced by suppression of ipsilateral (left ear) input, resulting in small, but consistently better perception and recall of verbal information at the right ear. This account of the mechanism for the right ear effect is possibly not correct, however, since recently (Catlin and Neville, 1976) the right ear effect has been obtained with *monaural* presentation of verbal material also. In that study, vocal reaction times were faster for words presented to the right ear whether alone, or with competing noise in the other ear. This suggested to the authors that the functionally dominant pathway for speech is always the contralateral auditory pathways, (so that left ear stimuli go initially to the right hemisphere and then across the cortical commissures to the left hemisphere), and this situation is not dependent upon dichotic competition. This conjecture is supported by the fact that in patients with right hemisphere temporal lobe lesions there is a reduction of intelligibility for verbal material presented monaurally to the left ear (Bocca and Calearo, 1963).

Additional evidence for functional specialization comes from dichotic listening studies of right-handers which report a greater *left* ear efficiency (presumed to indicate right hemisphere specialization) in handling certain *nonverbal* auditory stimuli. Actually, as it will become clear, the data showing differential left or right ear advantages do not always conform to a simple verbal/nonverbal division. In fact, the major problem facing investigators in the field of human behavioral asymmetries appears to be explaining why particular task situations result in particular asymmetries. Kimura (1964) with dichotic presentation found melodic pattern perception to be significantly more accurate for the left ear while the same subjects on a verbal task had higher scores for the right ear. Curry (1967) and Knox and Kimura (1968) also obtained a left ear effect with dichotic presentation of environmental sounds (e.g., dog barking, clock ticking).

Spreen, Spellacy, and Reid, (1970) presented solo violin passages (of 2 sec. duration) dichotically, and after 1, 5, or 12 sec an identification stimulus was presented. Ss were asked if either of the dichotic members was identical to the recognition stimulus. Their results support a left ear superiority for these musical stimuli when the interval between the dichotic pair and the identification is short. At 12 seconds waiting time there was no significant difference between the ears in accuracy. Spellacy (1970) used the same paradigm with pipe organ tones and also found a significant left ear advantage at short waiting intervals, but not at long ones. This phenomenon has led some to conclude that the left ear effect reflects primarily perceptual differences, as apart from memory differences (Berlin, 1971). This notion should be investigated further, especially in view of the evidence from lesion studies, presented above, which does suggest hemispheric asymmetries on mnemonic tasks.

Kimura (quoted in Dimond, 1972) reported that speech, when chopped into segments of 200 msec or less, no longer produces a superior response on the right ear, but instead shows superior response in the left ear. Kimura suggests that in sections of this brevity speech is no longer registered as such and remains undifferentiated by the brain from other types of noise. Curiously enough, Kimura and Folb (1968) reported that when sounds produced by reverse playback of recorded speech were presented dichotically, the sounds arriving at the right ear were more accurately identified than those arriving at the left. The same authors concluded that these sounds must have retained their speech characteristics, by virtue of the fact that they produced the right ear effect.

Cerebral specialization of function is also thought to be reflected in the many lateral asymmetries reported in studies of *visual* perception in normal adults. With unilateral visual field presentation, linguistic material (e.g., letters, digits, words) is reported more quickly and accurately after right visual field (rvf) presentation than after left visual field (lvf) presentation. Since the rvf projects directly to the left hemisphere, these studies are taken as support for the notions of left hemisphere superiority in the process of language material (Mishkin and Forgays, 1952; Orbach, 1967; Bryden, 1965; Hines, Satz, Schell, and Schmidlin, 1969; Zurif and Bryden, 1969; Moscovitch, 1972). This appears to be as robust a phenomenon as the right ear effect for speech sounds.

With the presentation of different words to the two hemifields simultaneously, early studies reported a lvf advantage (see White, 1969, for a review) but this has subsequently been found to result from English-speaking subjects' habit of reading from left to right. With careful control of eye fixation an rvf advantage is also found with bilateral presentation of words (McKeever and Huling, 1971).

Many visual stimuli have been shown to result in a *left* visual field (right hemisphere) superiority, and, as with the auditory studies, attempts have been made to classify these stimuli according to the quality which results in a right hemisphere superiority. Different classifications include these stimuli as nonverbal, nonverbal spatial, gestaltlike, and diffuse (as opposed to "focal").

Powell (1962) and Kimura (1963) reported that enumeration of dots is more accurate after left than right visual field presentation. Kimura (1966) again reported enumeration of nonsense figures and dots to be more accurate when these appear in the lvf. These results appear inconsistent with Sperry's result (1968, mentioned above) suggesting that the right hemisphere is inferior to the left in tasks involving calculation. Perhaps the apparent inconsistencies in the literature arise from the difficulty in knowing how best to describe the abilities which are called for in many of the tasks employed in studies of behavioral asymmetries.

Many investigators have studied the recognition of faces in normal adults, the impetus for which came from clinical studies showing greater impairment of physiognomic perception after right hemisphere lesions. Rizzolatti, Umittà, and Berlucci (1971) found a lvf superiority in the recognition of faces for which the subject had no name. In a pilot study, these authors had employed photographs of well-known movie stars, and had obtained a rvf superiority. They conjectured that the Ss were applying a verbal label to the photographs (i.e., the name of the person), thus rendering the task a verbal one. Indeed, the subsequent experiment with "nameless faces" reversed the field effect. Geffen, Bradshaw, and Wallace (1971) also report a lvf superiority for the recognition of unfamiliar faces.

In support of the notion that the task conditions (verbal vs. nonverbal) differentially affect the field superiority, Tibensky and Moscovitch (1975) report that recognition of an identical visual figure can be more accurate in the lvf or rvf depending on specific training. They trained English-speaking Ss who did not read Chinese, to associate each of several ideograms with a name or a face; recognition of the ideograms was superior in the rvf for those Ss who associated the ideograms with a name, and in the lvf for those who had associated the ideograms with a face.

Umiltà, Rizzolatti, Marzi, Zamboni, Franzini, Camarda, and Berlucci (1973) reported a left visual superiority in the perception of orientation of lines which were not readily verbalizable. Fontenot and Benton (1972) also report a left visual field superiority for perception of line orientation. Benton (1975), however, in considering these data, noted that the left visual field effects obtained in normal subjects are often rather weak in terms of the number of subjects who show them. White (1969) also makes the point that right hemisphere effects are uniformly smaller and less robust than left hemisphere effects. This may be because many putative "right hemisphere" tasks can be performed with more than one strategy, including strategies which are, in varying degrees, verbal. We may do well to ask subjects for descriptions of their approaches to various tasks. This would also avoid the tendency of describing the task as "verbal" or "nonverbal" on the basis of the lateral asymmetry which resulted.

In a most interesting paper Klein, Moskovitch, and Vigna (1976) investigated Kinsbourne's view that attentional factors are operating in lateral asymmetries. Kinsbourne assumes that the left hemisphere is specialized for language, and the right hemisphere for nonverbal, spatial material, and hypothesizes that activation of a hemisphere directs a S's attention to the sensory field contralateral to that activated hemisphere. Thus, for example, if S is engaged in a verbal task, the right ear or right visual field advantage is produced, not by the physical path of the input, but by the side of space from which the material seems to come. A hemisphere actively selects for prior processing the message which seems to come from contralateral space (Kinsbourne 1970, 1974 b). Klein et al. tested Kinsbourne's (1970) claim that the manipulation of hemispheric control of attention may diminish or reverse perceptual asymmetries. Specifically, they "primed" or "activated" the left hemisphere by giving the S a verbal task first, and thereby activating the rvf. This was hypothesized to diminish the lvf superiority in a face-recognition task. They found that Ss who had a verbal task first (which produced a rvf effect) showed no field effect on a subsequent face-recognition task; those Ss who had the face recognition task first, showed a strong lvf effect, but the subsequent verbal task resulted in a diminished rvf effect. They discuss the possibility that many experimental situations reinstate a verbal cognitive set which produces an attentional bias toward the right sensory field.

A review of even a majority of the studies designed to explore the perceptual asymmetries of the normal human adult would be a formidable task. It should suffice to say that many of these studies have been designed to see which hemisphere is specialized for the experimenter's particular choice of material. Some attempts have been made at classifying the results along various lines, but most would agree that this has been largely unsuccessful. Nevertheless, these studies show that hemispheric specialization is a phenomenon which can be studied in the normal human adult with these simple behavioral techniques.

Evoked Potential Studies

The considerable functional asymmetries of man's two cerebral hemispheres suggest that electrophysiological measures might also show evidence of asymmetries relating to function. In 1962, O'Leary remarked that the question had not typically been investigated: Electrical recordings were most frequently taken from the vertex, or from one hemisphere only, with the assumption that activity on the other side was identical.

Since 1969, however, several studies have appeared which report averaged evoked potential (EP) correlates of hemispheric specialization. Buchsbaum and Fedio (1969, 1970) visually presented words and geometric figures, and found that left hemisphere EP were more dissimilar to the words and figures than were the right hemisphere EP. They recorded from the left and right occiputs. They interpret their results as consistent with current notions of hemispheric specialization since the left hemisphere differentiated the verbal and nonverbal stimuli more than the right hemisphere.

Wood, Goff, and Day (1971) reported EP differences to the same stimuli which were dependent upon the task in which the subject was engaged at the time of recording. The task was either "linguistic" (differentiation of stop consonants), or nonlinguistic (differentiation of fundamental frequency). They pooled their data across 10 subjects and found statistically significant higher amplitude in EP components during the linguistic task than during the nonlinguistic task. These differences were found only on the left hemisphere. The authors concluded that their data supported the theory of left hemisphere linguistic "decoding." Wood (1975) has replicated and extended these results.

Morrell and Salamy (1971) found larger EP responses over left than right temporoparietal electrodes to acoustically presented nonsense words. The assumption that these nonsense words were perceived as language may be questioned, however, and moreover, they did not employ control (i.e., nonlanguage) stimuli.

Matsumiya, Tagliasco, Lombroso, and Goodglass (1972) reported that the "meaningfulness" (defined by the task; the use made of the stimuli) of both real speech and environmental sound stimuli affected the magnitude of a bipolar response peaking at 100 msec. "Meaningful" stimuli resulted in a waveform greater over the left hemisphere than the right, which suggested to the authors that the significance of the stimuli to the subject, and not the verbal or nonverbal nature of the stimuli, was important in the production of electrographic asymmetry. With bipolar recordings and a different reference for each hemisphere, however, the direction of the asymmetry is obscured and could conceivably have been different for words and sounds.

There are many more issues of controversy in this field than can adequately be dealt with here. The interested reader may wish to consult Friedman, Simson, Ritter, and Rapin (1975), who have carefully reviewed many of the studies of hemispheric asymmetries They criticize most of this research on counts of inaccuracies in design, interpretation, and the statistics employed. In their own study (Friedman et al., 1975) in which EPs from the two hemispheres were compared when the subject either performed a task (lift finger to one of five words) or listened passively to real speech sounds, certain EP components from the left hemisphere were larger than from the right in the task condition only. Although these authors conservatively concluded that their results were marginal, the EP asymmetries are among the largest and most consistent yet reported. Perhaps the use of real speech, in contrast to the synthesized CV syllables which are often employed, was a factor in obtaining the EP asymmetries. The fact that these asymmetries appeared only in the task condition seems especially significant. In view of the fact that behavioral asymmetries are more readily obtained when the task is difficult (Bakker, 1970), perhaps the use of difficult language tasks would also be more conducive to eliciting EP asymmetries. It would also seem probable that more robust EP asymmetries would obtain in situations where the subject is performing a task which results in behavioral asymmetries (e.g., a dichotic listening task). One study of this design (Neville, 1974) suggests such a possibility, although that study also had certain methodological shortcomings.

In any case, the search for EP correlates of hemispheric specialization of function has just begun, and we can anticipate new approaches and results in the near future.

The data from clinical neuropathology constitute perhaps the most compelling evidence for cerebral specialization of function. No one doubts that a lesion of the left hemisphere will in most instances be more likely to disrupt language than a comparable lesion of the right hemisphere. The data from behavioral and electrographic studies of normal adults tend to confirm the notions derived from the clinical data, but the asymmetries, especially of nonlanguage functioning, are small, when obtained, and are often elusive. This may be due, in part, to the wide variety of subject samples, experimental designs, instructions to subjects, stimulus types, nature of response, modes of analyzing the data, etc., variables which apparently cannot be ignored with impunity. However, the small effects also emphasize the extent to which the two cerebral hemispheres are functionally integrated in the normal adult. Taken together, the data from the clinic and from behavioral and EP studies of normal adults at once discourage a precise, structural model of cerebral localization of function, and reinforce the search for a model which will handle both the integration and specialization of the two cerebral hemispheres. This is also clear from the literature concerning the ontogeny of cerebral specialization, which will be considered after a review of comparative studies of cerebral asymmetries.

Comparative Aspects of Cerebral Specialization

Consideration of the unique occurrence of language in the human species and the apparent restriction of cerebral specialization of function to the human species has led to the proposition that the latter developed somehow in aid of the former. For example, many investigators note the advantages of having unilateral motoric control of a midline organ: Left hemisphere specialization for speech avoids the possibility of two different competing commands to the organs of articulation (Semmes, 1968; Levy, 1969; Marler, 1970; Liberman, 1974). There is some evidence, however, for cerebral specialization in other species, which weakens the suggestion that speech and language are the causal factors.

The study of cerebral functioning in infrahumans has often been approached via the split-brain paradigm. If the commissures between the two hemispheres are missing, learning which takes place in one cerebral hemisphere (e.g., by confining the training to one eye after chiasma section, or by training one hand) is usually not evident upon testing of the other (i.e., by testing the other eye, other hand). This is seen to mean (Sperry 1968) that in the intact anmimal the commissures function to allow the two hemispheres to share what was learned. This can be achieved either by transfer of the learned task from the directly trained to the other hemisphere at the time the learning takes place, or by providing the means for access to what was learned at a later time. In the first case the learned task is somehow present both in the directly trained hemisphere and in the other hemisphere. In the other case, the learned task is confined to the directly trained hemisphere, but is normally available to the other by way of the commissures. (Human verbal speech is thought to be an example of the second case, where, normally, e.g., a verbal label can be elicited after left visual field presentation of a word, but after section of the corpus callosum this has been reported to be unlikely.) By cutting the neocortical commissures after learning and before testing for transfer of learning, it is possible to determine the extent to which learning is bilateral (duplicated) or unilateral (specialized) in different situations and species. Most of this sort of work has been done with cats and monkeys.

Myers (1965) transected the crossing retinal fibers at the optic chiasma of cats and covered one eye with a mask, thereby restricting visual input to the hemisphere ipsilateral to the open eye. The cats recalled immediately through one eye pattern discrimination tasks initially learned through the other. If subsequently the corpus callosum and anterior commissures were sectioned, sometimes the cats *failed* to recall through one eye the tasks learned with the other eye. The interesting fact emerged that the ability to transfer in chiasma- and commissure-sectioned cats seemed to depend on the nature of the task. When brightness discrimination or flicker frequency discrimination tasks were used, transfer of training between the eyes (hemispheres) did occur. Also, when an easy (i.e., fewer trials to criterion) pattern discrimination task was learned (e.g., vertical line vs. horizontal line) the task transferred. But when the pattern discrimination task was difficult (more trials to criterion), the "learning" or information did not transfer to the untrained eye. Myers (1965) and Meikle and Sechzer

(1960) suggest that brainstem mechanisms may be adequate for across-the-midline transfer of the brightness and flicker frequency tasks. It is more difficult, however, to explain the transfer of a visual pattern discrimination which took relatively few trials to learn (320), and the failure of one which took relatively many (850).

A similar phenomenon has been reported in primates by three different investigators (Black and Myers 1965; Trevarthen 1965; Downer 1962). Black and Myers (1965) trained chiasma- and callosal-sectioned chimpanzees on various tasks requiring eye–hand control and tested for interhemispheric transfer. They found that "pursuit" tasks, involving ability to track and grasp moving objects with restricted visual input, transferred virtually perfectly from the initially trained eye–hand combination to all other eye–hand combinations. The "latch-box solving tasks," however, which required considerable dexterity in addition to eye–hand coordination, frequently failed to transfer from one hemisphere (eye–hand combination) to the other. Black and Myers propose "that simple eye–hand coordination, such as pursuit, may be consummated largely at subcortical levels. Complex tasks, such as latch-box solving, on the other hand, may be supported to a greater extent at the cortical level and appear to employ the great cerebral commissure for interchange of information between the two brain halves" (1965, p. 57). They refer to a report by Klüver in 1941 suggesting that the discrimination of patterns and colors requires intact cortical mechanisms, while subcortical centers support only discriminations in brightness, and suggest that their latch-box problem was analogous to the former, their visual pursuit to the latter.

Trevarthen (1965), however, found interhemispheric transfer of an easy visual pattern discrimination task (cross vs. circle) but failure to transfer of a difficult task (five- vs. six-sided star). Both of these tasks were surely complex enough (after Klüver, at least) that cortical mechanisms were involved in the training situation. Further, Downer (1962) also reported that easy visual pattern discrimination tasks transferred (e.g., cross vs. circle) while difficult tasks (e.g., square vs. triangle) did not.

These data suggest that cerebral specialization occurs when an animal must learn a complex or difficult task. That is, only the trained hemisphere is able to successfully perform the task. With less difficult tasks, the original training is *not* confined to the directly trained hemisphere, but is duplicated in the sense that after commissurotomy *either* hemisphere is successful on the task.

These studies suggest cerebral specialization under certain circumstances but they do not address the question of a possible analog to the human form of asymmetry, where one hemisphere appears specialized for a particular type of task. There are a few studies, however, which bear on the problem of hemispheric asymmetry from this point of view.

Webster (1972) studied hemispheric functional asymmetries in cats, as related to paw preference. Although the proportion of cats with preference for using the right paw is about the same as those prefering the left, individual cats generally prefer to use one paw more frequently than the other and this preference has been noted to be fairly stable across different testing situations (Cole 1955; Warren 1958). Webster tested each hemisphere of eight split-brain cats for retention of a series of preoperatively learned visual discrimination problems which differed in terms of their perceptual and/or response requirements. The paw preference of the subjects was assessed during pre- and postoperative testing. The postoperative performance of the hemisphere contralateral to the preferred paw (called the "dominant hemisphere") was compared with that of the hemisphere ipsilateral to the preferred paw (called "nondominant"). The results showed that on the Go–No-Go discrimination problem the *nondominant* hemisphere performed significantly better than did the dominant hemisphere in terms of both withheld responses and response latencies. Better performance by the nondominant hemisphere was observed in seven of eight subjects, and all seven comparisons were significant. The nondominant hemisphere also performed significantly better on a pattern discrimination problem (one large circle vs. three small circles), and on a form discrimination problem. Webster suggests that these asymmetries reflect nondominant specialization of an ability related to the perception of space and spatial relationships, and he notes that this would be in agreement with the data on human functional specialization.

In an early experiment of similar design to Webster's, Gazzaniga (1963) tested monkeys' performance on a two choice visual pattern discrimination before and after split brain surgery. Those results also showed better reacquisition (or retention) of the discrimination by the hemisphere ipsilateral to the preferred hand (i.e., by the nondominant hemisphere as in Webster's experiments).

Hamilton and Lund (1970) studied the acquisition of four discrimination problems in rhesus monkeys. They reported left hemisphere superiority on these tasks, which involved the apprehension of spatial orientation. (e.g., discriminating between directions of movement of a field of dots). Trevarthen briefly reports (1974) evidence of cerebral asymmetry of function in the baboon: The "psychological schema" for a complex bilateral manipulative skill required to open a problem box was lateralized more to the left hemisphere than to the right. Also, Hamilton, Tieman, and Farrell (1974) recently reported left hemisphere superiority in the acquisition of a task involving spatial discrimination. Split-brain monkeys took significantly fewer trials with the left than with the right hemisphere to learn to discriminate two fields of lines oriented in different directions. Hamilton et al. (1974) also studied the discrimination of other monkey's faces. They did not find an effect of cerebral specialization which was consistent across monkeys. However, five of seven subjects showed fairly strong asymmetries in this task, some showing left and some showing right hemisphere superiority. In two of these monkeys the asymmetry was significant. The authors suggest the possibility that different monkeys approach this task with different strategies, as has been reported in human split-brain patients (Levy, Trevarthen, and Sperry, 1972).

In view of the interest in anatomical asymmetries of the two cerebral hemispheres of man (e.g., Geshwind and Levitsky, 1968), the recent study of Lemay and Geshwind (1975) showing morphological differences between the two hemispheres of great apes is relevant here. These authors report that in 10 of 12 organgutan brains the Sylvian point (i.e., the posterior end of the Sylvian fissure) is higher on the right than on the left hemisphere. No asymmetries were noted in the brains of lesser apes, Old World monkeys, or New World monkeys. Earlier studies showed that in 86% of right-handed *humans*, but only 17% of left-handers, the Sylvian point was also higher on the right than left (Lemay and Culebras, 1972). Furthermore, the same asymmetry was observed by these authors in the endocranial cast of the fossil of a Neanderthal man (the La Chapellaux-Saints skull). The significance of anatomical hemispheric asymmetries for functional hemispheric asymmetries is, of course, quite unknown. In view of the suggestion, however, that the former may be a substrate for the latter, further studies of the great apes may shed some light on the phylogeny of cerebral specialization.

These few studies point to the possibility that the cerebral hemispheres of certain infrahuman mammals may be functionally asymmetrical rather than symmetrical as they have often been assumed to be (e.g., Jung, 1962; Dimond, 1972). The data from the infrahuman split-brain studies suggest that the circumstances under which cerebral specialization occurs include increased complexity or difficulty of the task to be performed.

Finally, it remains to mention the most closely similar development to that of the lateralized cerebral functions in humans. This is the lateralization of neural control for bird song which has been reported by Nottebohm (1970, 1974) and Marler (1970). The avian syrinx is symmetrical as far as one can see, but the hypoglossal nerves which innervate the syrinx are functionally asymmetrical. Nottebohm has demonstrated in 40 birds, including canaries, chaffinches, and white-crowned sparrows, that the left hypoglossal nerve is dominant in the production of song: If the right is cut in an adult, only one small part of the song drops out. If the left hypoglossal nerve is cut, only one small part of the song is left intact with the remainder being unmodulated bursts of song. Recently (1975) Nottebohm and his co-workers have extended the observations of functional asymmetry to the canary *brain*: Certain lesions of the left hemisphere result in greater song deficits than lesions to the same area of the right hemisphere. Another remarkable parallel with the specialization for human language concerns the differential effects of cutting the hypoglossal nerve depending on the *age* of the bird. If the nerve on the left is cut in a young male who has not yet come into full song, such a bird can develop a complete pattern of song.

Marler suggests that neural lateralization is particularly adaptive when a midline organ such as the human larynx and avian syrinx performs complex and precisely timed motor acts. It may be more efficient for one side of the brain to take a leading role rather than provide the opportunity for the two sides to compete for control. This point is reinforced by noting that other bilateral structures which cooperate closely in generating complex motor outputs show lateral dominance, most notably our own and other primates' hands (Brinkman and Kuypers, 1972; Gazzaniga, 1970).

The rather small amount of evidence from infrahuman animals

seems to suggest two circumstances under which lateral cerebral specialization occurs: (1) with increasing difficulty and/or complexity of the cognitive task and (2) for motor control of complex temporal sequences. These data alone, if taken as evidence to bear on the circumstances in which cerebral specialization develops in man, could be construed as supporting either the notion that hemispheric specialization occurs with increasing cognitive abilities, or the notion that hemispheric specialization occurs with the acquisition of speech. Thus, the question stated at the beginning of this chapter is unresolved.

Ontogeny of Cerebral Specialization

There is strong evidence which suggests that the functional cerebral specialization seen in the human adult is preceded in ontogeny by a period of hemispheric equipotentiality. These data come largely from observations of the effects of cerebral lesions which have quite different consequences in childhood as compared to comparable lesions in adulthood. Lenneberg (1967) gathered evidence to show that cerebral trauma which occur after the beginnings of language acquisition (20–36 months) result in the loss of whatever language development had occurred, and, in recovery, the stages of language acquisition are passed through again. The interesting point is that cerebral traumata to *either* hemisphere appear at this age to have equal effects. Basser (1962) reported data which showed that brain lesions sustained during the first two years of life result in mild language disturbances: in about half of Basser's sample (about 30 children), the onset of speech was delayed, while the other children ($N = 37$) began to speak at the normal time. Again, the distribution of these effects was irrespective of lateral side of lesion.*

Boone (1965) also reports that a severe and persistent aphasia rarely occurs from unilateral cerebral damage of any type before the age of 9 or 10 years. Children under 9 with aphasia show a very rapid

---

* Kinsbourne (1975a) recently has claimed that this and similar evidence presented in favor of early hemispheric equipotentiality is lacking in methodological expertise, and that the available evidence suggests that asymmetry is a property of the brain from infancy onward.

recovery. Kinsbourne (1975b) asserts that after the age of 5, right hemisphere lesions no longer disrupt speech. He notes that this does not necessarily imply that at age 5 the left hemisphere is indispensable for language, especially in view of Lenneberg's compilation of data showing that the right hemisphere can compensate for left hemisphere deficits up until around puberty.

Finally, it is well accepted now that even left hemispherectomy if it occurs early enough does not preclude the patient from acquiring language skills in normal developmental sequence. Kohn and Dennis (1974) reported that there is no difference in verbal intelligence quotients between left and right hemispherectomy patients, if the surgery was performed in infancy. There are other data, however, suggesting that left hemispherectomized patients, and other people presumed to have developed right hemisphere or bilateral specialization for language, have decreased *nonverbal* intelligence quotients (Levy, 1969; Nebes, 1971; Landsdell, 1969; Miller, 1971). These data are interpreted to show that "relocation" or nonrestriction to the left hemisphere of verbal skills compromises the abilities for which the right hemisphere is normally specialized. Recently, however, Smith and Sugar (1975) report a patient who, 21 years after left hemispherectomy at the age of 5½, had superior language skills and normal or above-normal nonverbal skills.

The remarkable recovery of verbal function after early left hemispherectomy is paralleled by recovery after early right hemispherectomy of nonverbal or "performance" skills. For example, Griffith and Davidson (1966) report such a case whose intractable seizures began when he was 10 years of age. Fifteen years after the surgery, which was performed when the patient was 19, this patient showed a WAIS verbal IQ of 121 and a performance IQ of 91.

The data showing extensive recovery for some period early in life are reminiscent of many other data in biology showing the regulatory capacity of the immature brain. Lenneberg (1974) in a compelling discussion, suggested that the compensatory powers of the infantile human brain with respect to language is another example of what is called regulation in embryogenesis. In biology the regulatory phase comes to a close with determination or specialization of tissue. This is surely what we are observing in studies of lesions in children: The cerebral hemispheres are functionally equipotential at birth (though there may be an early *anlage* which, when not disturbed, predisposes for asymmetry), and this situation is gradually superceded by relative differentiation or specialization of the left and right hemispheres.

In this connection it is interesting to note the different consequences of splitting the corpus callosum in adulthood, from the consequences of *agenesis* of the corpus callosum. The reader will recall the rather dramatic effects of adult commissurotomy, reported earlier. In contrast to those results Sperry (1970, 1974), Saul and Sperry (1968), and Zaidel and Sperry (1972) described a patient with agenesis of the corpus callosum who failed to show the disconnection syndrome, and who was in fact normal in every respect. Kinsbourne and Fisher (1971) report data which suggest that not only motor control but also language abilities are bilateral in cases of callosal agenesis. Furthermore, Saul and Gott (1973) have directly showed the two hemispheres to be equipotential for language in one agenesis case, by use of intracarotid amytal.

The ontogeny of hemispheric specialization has also been studied using the dichotic listening and hemifield presentation techniques mentioned earlier in the discussion of normal adults. Kimura (1963) first reported in right-handed children, a right ear advantage in the recall of dichotically presented digits. The effect was comparable to that seen in adults, and was present even in 4-year-olds. Knox and Kimura (1968) presented spoken digits and nonverbal environmental sounds to boys and girls between the ages of 5 and 8 years and found that the right ear was superior in the recall of verbal material, the left for the nonverbal material. Nagafuchi (1970) studied 80 children from 3 to 6 years of age, and found that 6-year-old children and young adults achieved almost identical right-ear effects. Geffner and Hochberg (1971) also found a right ear advantage in children, and this occurred in their youngest Ss, aged 3 years, as well as in the older Ss. Berlin, Hughes, Lowe-Bell, and Berlin (1973) found the right-ear advantage present, and to the same degree, in children aged 5 to 13 years. The data from all of the aforementioned authors are interpreted by Krashen and Harshman (1972) to show no significant change from 5 to 10 years in degree of right ear advantage (and, by implication, no significant change from 5 to 10 years in left hemispheric specialization for language).

In contrast, Bryden (1970), Bryden and Allard (1973), Satz (1973), and Bakker, Satz, Goebel, and Van der Vlugt (1973) also tested young children with dichotic presentation of verbal material and all interpret their data to show that the magnitude of the right ear advantage, and presumably left-hemisphere specialization for language, *does* increase from 5 to 12 years of age.

Porter and Berlin (1974) astutely point out that the studies which find an increase in right ear advantage with age and those that do not differ in the stimulus materials they employ. The former group use dichotic digits presented at the rate of three or four pairs per trial—a rather difficult task, and one with clear mnemonic demands—whereas the latter group use single dichotic nonsense syllables (CVs or CVCs) differing only in a single stop consonant. Following Studdert-Kennedy (1970), these latter tasks can be construed as testing auditory and phonetic processing abilities, and these may develop earlier in children, and, as such, show earlier hemispheric specialization. The digit recall task may be seen as testing quite different abilities, and these may be construed as more language-related inasmuch as they require the S to respond to words. Seen in this light, the data from dichotic listening studies are consistent with the clinical data showing developmental increases in the functional specialization of the two hemispheres.

Buffery (1970) asked children to draw simultaneously, and with eyes closed, a square with one hand and a circle with the other. This task, called the Conflict Drawing Test (CDT) is thought to be a measure of hemispheric asymmetry of function, because under such conditions the proprioceptive feedback from each hand tends to be largely from the contralateral hemisphere. Most right handed-adults draw better figures with their left hand on this task (Lukianowicz, 1970), presumably reflecting right-hemisphere specialization for this sort of skill. Buffery measured the actual drawn square's deviation from an ideal square, constructed in relation to the first line drawn of the actual square, and found nonpreferred, *left* hand superiority on this task, and this asymmetry increased from 3 years of age to 11 years of age.

The evidence is fairly unequivocal that the specialization of function, which typically lateralizes language to the left hemisphere and certain nonlanguage functions to the right hemisphere, occurs rather late in development. Beyond this, little is known about the ontogeny of functional specialization. In order to ascertain the significance of general cognitive abilities or human language (or both) in the development of human cerebral asymmetries, one would like to study this development in, for example, Down's syndrome patients who do have some speech and language but who are intellectually retarded, and in deaf children without normal speech but with normal intellectual abilities.

Down's children, and other intellectually retarded persons, are as likely to be right-handed as left-handed, or to show no determined handedness (Lenneberg 1967). While most of these children do show a certain degree of linguistic accomplishment, they are, of course, retarded in most cognitive abilities. It is especially interesting therefore, that Dustman and Beck (1974), who reported EP asymmetries to flashes of light in normal children, found that Down's children *failed* to show any of these normal asymmetries. Richlin, Weisinger, Weinstein, Giannini, and Morganstern (1971) studied normal children and a mixed group of retarded children (diagnosed as having "minimal brain damage") and again found a larger right- than left-hemisphere EP response to flashes in normal children, but no asymmetries in the retarded group. Rhodes, Dustman, and Beck (1969) studied high-IQ (120–140) children and low-IQ (70–90) normal children, and found that flash-evoked responses were larger from the right hemisphere than the left in 19 of 20 high-IQ children, while not one low-IQ subject showed this asymmetry. They do not report correlations as such, but conclude that the brighter the child, the stronger the hemispheric asymmetries. Both of these groups of children are presumed to have normal language. These data suggest that the presence of hemispheric asymmetries is not correlated with language *per se*, but is correlated with the acquisition of general cognitive skills.

Suggesting some relation between cerebral specialization and language though, are the virtually countless articles from 1937 (Orton) to 1974 (Marcel, Katz, and Smith) suggesting that slowness in learning to read may be associated with abnormal development of hemispheric specialization. Olson (1973) found a strong right visual field (i.e., left hemisphere) superiority for recognition of words in normal children, but not in dyslexic children. Similarly, Marcel *et al.* (1974) found poor readers showed significantly weaker hemispheric asymmetries than good readers in letter recognition (here also the measure was right visual field superiority in tachistoscopic perception).

Also related to language development and cerebral specialization is the suggestion by Travis and Lindsley (1933) that stuttering develops more often in children who fail to show normal lateral dominance—especially as regards hand preference.

Bever (1970, 1974) has made specific predictions about the relation of cerebral specialization (as demonstrated by ear dominance in dichotic tasks) and stage of development in language acquisition. The assertion is that one can be predicted from the other, although he does not state directionality of causal relationship. In the 1970 paper he studied various perceptual strategies in the linguistic behavior of the normal adult. For example, we tend to assume that any noun-verb-noun (NVN) sequence corresponds to actor-action-object. This is presumed to explain the relative difficulty in understanding passive, as opposed to active, sentence constructions. Bever studied the gradual development of this linguistic strategy in children and simultaneously studied the development of the right ear advantage for verbal material in children. He found that children showing the right ear advantage tend, more than children who show *no* ear advantage, to utilize the NVN strategy. He cautiously suggested that there might be a direct association between the development of the NVN strategy and cerebral specialization. Bever notes, however, that the correlation between these two may simply be a function of age: As children get older they pass through a period in which they reverse reversible passive sentences, and they also (perhaps quite independently) develop an ear preference in dichotic listening tasks. Nonetheless, Bever concluded, "Thus, the functional dominance we are studying in speech is a matter of the initial localization of acquired perceptual habits."

More recently (1974) Bever reported studies of bilingual children, whose first language is Spanish and are in the process of learning English as a second language. In Spanish these children already use the NVN strategy, whereas in English they do not. Preliminary results (though these data are not presented) suggest to Bever that these children show a right ear preference in Spanish tests of dichotic listening, but not in English. These are very interesting suggestions indeed.

Many investigators have studied congenitally deaf children, who usually have no spoken speech or speech comprehension, to see how severe language retardation affects other cognitive abilities. Oléron (1957) and Furth (1966) report that deaf children acquire elementary logical operations—as tested by Piaget-type tasks—with only a very slight, or with no retardation as compared to normal children. Furth found the deaf to perform less well than normal on a "logical symbol discovery" task, but they performed equally well on the use of symbols in a structured task. Oléron (1957) found deaf children's performance on seriation slightly poorer than that of normal children, but spatial operations were normal and classifications possessed the same general structures and appeared at the same age as in normals.

Lenneberg (1967) conjectured that congenitally deaf children would show normal cerebral specialization even though their language is abnormal, in view of his own (1967) and other's studies showing their normal nonverbal cognitive development. In support of this notion he noted that deaf children at age 7 years show a normal incidence of right-handedness which seems to emerge at the usual time. Lenneberg noted, however, that hand preference is not an unfailing guide in predicting cerebral specialization.

To investigate this question the present author (1975) studied evoked potential and behavioral cerebral asymmetries in normal children and in congenitally deaf children of normal nonverbal IQs (mean WISC performance IQ= 110; range 93–140). None of the deaf children could speak. They attended a school for the deaf which emphasized oral training and discouraged the use of sign language. The deaf children had all been diagnosed as hereditarily deaf and none had any other neurological abnormality. Both the hearing ($N = 16$) and the deaf children ($N = 15$) ranged in age from 9 to 13 years.

The stimuli were slides of line drawings of common objects, projected to the left or right visual field for 10 milliseconds. Two seconds after each picture was presented the child was shown a card containing five pictures and chose, by pointing, the picture which he thought was a picture of the same thing he had just seen on the screen. This was not a physical match. These stimuli were chosen because Olson (1973) found a left visual field (i.e., right hemisphere) superiority in recognition of these pictures in normal children.

Evoked potentials (EPs) were recorded to each slide presentation. Monopolar EPs were recorded from the left and right posterior temporal regions (T5 and T6 in the 10–20 System; Jasper 1958) and were referred to linked earlobes. Also, recordings were taken from a point between the eyebrows to observe any possible contamination of EPs from eye movements.

Neither the deaf nor the normal children showed significant behavioral asymmetries. There was a small, nonsignificant left visual field advantage for both groups.

The normal children showed strong EP asymmetries, however. The right hemisphere EPs were significantly larger than left hemisphere EPs, and the latencies of the EP peaks occurred earlier in the right than the left hemisphere. These asymmetries were found in 12 of 16 normal children, and were replicated in a second experimental session. These data suggest that the right hemisphere of the normal children was more involved in the perception of these line drawings than the left hemisphere.

The deaf children did not show these asymmetries. The EPs from the left and right hemispheres were very similar in amplitude and latency. These unexpected results suggested that perhaps cerebral asymmetries do not develop in the absence of speech acquisition.

Further analyses were undertaken after each deaf child was asked how, when at home, he communicated with his parents. Eight children indicated that they communicated in sign with their parents and seven indicated that they communicated by way of gesture and pantomime. Analyses with the deaf children broken into these two groups showed that the Signers had significant EP hemispheric asymmetries while the Nonsigners did not. More puzzling, the EP amplitude asymmetries of the Signers were in the opposite direction to the normal children's asymmetries: The EPs from the left hemisphere were larger than EPs from the right hemisphere. Consistent with the EP data is in the fact that the Signing children tended to show a right visual field superiority in recognition of the line drawings.

These results are difficult to interpret and should be taken as evidence of the necessity for more research on cerebral specialization in the deaf. They do, nonetheless, generate a number of speculations. The result suggesting left hemispheric specialization for the perception of line drawings in the Signers may be interpreted in at least two ways. Possibly these children acquire their sign language with left hemisphere specialization playing a role. Since sign language has a large visuospatial component, perhaps other visuospatial tasks (e.g., the one in this study) are also specialized for by the left hemisphere. Alternatively, perhaps sign language is acquired with right hemisphere specialization (owing to its visuospatial nature) leaving the left hemisphere specialized for other, nonlanguage tasks. In support of this notion is the evidence of right hemisphere specialization for language involving haptic–spatial perception: Reading of Braille by blind and sighted children is better with fingers of the left hand (Harris, Wagner, and Wilkinson, 1975).

Clearly, what is needed now are studies of hemispheric asymmetry in signing deaf, where the stimuli are actual signs. These studies are currently under way.

The question remains as to why the nonsigning deaf children did not show cerebral asymmetries. Perhaps the acquisition of some formal language, whether verbal or sign language, is an important variable in predicting the presence of human cerebral specialization. In view of the fact that these nonsigning children had normal nonverbal skills, the importance of general cognitive abilities in the development of cerebral specialization is diminished. Militating against any strong conclusion on this, however, is the fact that the Signers tended to be children of congenitally deaf parents, while the nonsigners were children of hearing parents. One is more certain of the diagnosis of hereditary deafness in the former group. In any event the two groups may have had rather different developmental histories given the different experiences of their parents. One would like to see more research done with nonsigning deaf subjects. For example, a study of cerebral specialization in deaf before and after the acquisition of sign language may be illuminating.

Also, to further explore the possible separability of language and general cognitive skills as they relate to cerebral specialization, further studies of children with Down's syndrome who have some speech and language seem warranted. To date, it appears that the only relevant studies have employed light flashes as stimuli. Further studies with more standard language and nonlanguage stimuli would be of great interest.

Conclusion

Lenneberg proposed that lateralization of cerebral function is one neurological correlate of man's ability to acquire speech and language, and, as such, is also a neurological correlate of more fundamental cognitive abilities. We have reviewed comparative and developmental studies to see whether cerebral specialization develops concomitantly with speech and language or with more general intellectual skills. The available evidence does not permit a conclusion on this point. The paucity of studies designed to investigate the ontogeny and phylogeny of cerebral asymmetries is remarkable. Perhaps some insights into the functional significance of cerebral specialization will be provided (1) by the study of behavioral abilities in humans and other animals who do not show lateral asymmetries, and (2) by the further study of lateral asymmetries in humans with abnormal language or intellectual development.

Acknowledgment

I am indebted to Dr. Philip I. Kaushall for many valuable suggestions made on an earlier draft of this chapter.

References

Bakker, D. Left–right differences in auditory perception of verbal and nonverbal material by children. *Quarterly Journal of Experimental Psychology*, 1967, *19*, 334–336.

Bakker, D. J. Ear asymmetry with monaural stimulation: Relations to lateral dominance and lateral awareness. *Neuropsychologia*, 1970, *8*, 103–117.

Bakker, D. J., Satz, P., Goebel, R. and van der Vlugt, H. Developmental parameters of the ear asymmetry: A multivariate approach to cerebral dominance. Presented to the 1st Meeting, International Neuropsychological Society. New Orleans, 1973.

Basser, L. S. Hemiplegia of early onset and the faculty of speech with special reference to the effects of hemispherectomy. *Brain*, 1962, *85*, 427–460.

Benton, A. L. The problem of cerebral dominance. *Canadian Psychologist*, 1965, *6a* (4), 332–348.

Benton, A. L. Hemispheric cerebral dominance and visual perception. *Neurologia Medico*, 1975, *2*, 143–161.

Berlin, C. I. Review of binaural effects. *American Academy of Ophthalmology and Otolaryngology Mono.* 1970, Reviews of the Literature, 1971, 7–28.

Berlin, C. I., Hughes, L. F., Lowe-Bell, S., and Berlin, H. L. Dichotic right ear advantages in children aged five to thirteen. *Cortex*, 1973, *9*, 393–401.

Bever, T. G. The nature of cerebral dominance in speech behavior of the child and adult. In Huxley and Ingram (Eds.), *Mechanisms of language development*. New York: Academic Press, 1970.

Bever, T. G. The relation of language development to cognitive development. In E. H Lenneberg (Ed.), *Language and brain: Developmental aspects*. Neurosciences Research Program Bulletin 12: No. 4, 1974.

Black, P., and Myers, R. A neurological investigation of eye-hand control in the chimpanzee. In G. Ettlinger (Ed.), *Functions of the corpus callosum*. Boston: Little, Brown, 1965.

Bocca, E., and Calearo, C. Central hearing processes. In J. Jerger (Ed.), *Modern Developments in Audiology*. New York: Academic Press, 1963. Pp. 337–370.

Bogen, J. E., and Gazzaniga, M. S. Cerebral commissurotomy in man: Minor hemisphere dominance for certain visuo-spatial functions. *Journal of Neurosurgery*, 1965, *23*, 394–399.

Boone, D. R. Laterality dominance and language. *Journal of the Kansas Medical Society*, 1965, *66*, 132–135.

Brinkman, J., and Kuypers, H. G. J. M. Split-brain monkeys: Cerebral control of ipsilateral and contralateral arm, hand and finger movements. *Science*, 1972, *176*, 536–538.

Broadbent, D. E. The role of auditory localization and attention in memory span. *Journal of Experimental Psychology*, 1954, *47*, 191–196.

Bryden, M. P. Tachistoscopic recognition, handedness and cerebral dominance. *Neuropsychologia*, 1965, *3*, 1–8.

Bryden, M. P. Laterality effects in dichotic listening: Relations with handedness and reading ability in children. *Neuropsychologia*, 1970, *8*, 443–445.

Bryden, M. P., and Allard, F. Dichotic listening and the development of linguistic processes. Paper read to International Neuropsychological Society, New Orleans, 1973.

Buchsbaum, M., and Fedio, P. Visual information and evoked responses from the left and right hemispheres. *Electroencepholography and Clinical Neurophysiology*, 1969, *26*, 266–272.

Buchsbaum, M., and Fedio, P. Hemispheric differences in evoked potentials to verbal and non-verbal stimuli in the left and right visual fields. *Physiology and Behavior*, 1970, *5*, 207–210.

Buffery, A. W. H. Sex differences in the development of hand preference; cerebral dominance for speech and cognitive skill. *Bulletin of the British Psychological Society*, 1970, *23*(80), 233.

Catlin, J., and Neville, H. The laterality effect in reaction time to speech stimuli. *Neuropsychologia*, 1976, *14*, 141–143.

Cole, J. Paw preferences in cats related to hand preference in animals and man. *Journal of Comparative Physiology and Psychology*, 1955, *48*, 137–140.

Curry, F. A comparison of left handed and right handed subjects on verbal and nonverbal dichotic listening task. *Cortex*, 1967, *3*, 343–352.

DeRenzi, E. Nonverbal memory and hemispheric side of lesion. *Neuropsychologia*, 1968, *6*, 181–189.

Dimond, S. *The double brain*. London: Churchill Livingstone, 1972.

Downer, J. Interhemispheric integration in the visual system. In V. B. Mountcastle (Ed.), *Interhemispheric relations and cerebral dominance*. Baltimore: Johns Hopkins Press, 1962.

Dustman, R. E., and Beck, E. C. The evoked response: Its use in evaluating brain function of children and young adults. Preprint, 1974.

Fontenot, D. J., and Benton, A. L. Perception of direction in the right and left visual fields. *Neuropsychologia*, 1972, *10*, 447.

Friedman, D., Simson, R., Ritter, W., and Rapin, I. Cortical evoked potentials elicited by real speech words and human sounds. *Electroencephalography and Clinical Neurophysiology*, 1975, *38*, 13–19.

Furth, H. G. *Thinking without language*. New York: Free Press, 1961.

Gazzaniga, M. S. Effects of commissurotomy on a preoperatively learned visual discrimination. *Experimental Neurology*, 1963, *8*, 14–19.

Gazzaniga, M. S. *The bisected brain*. Appleton-Century-Crofts, 1970.

Geffen, G., Bradshow, J. L., and Wallace, G. Interhemispheric effects on reaction time to verbal and nonverbal visual stimuli. *Journal of Experimental Psychology*, 1971, *87*, 415–422.

Geffner, O. S., and Hochberg, I. Ear laterality performance of children from low and middle socioeconomic levels on a verbal dichotic listening task. *Cortex*, 1971, *7*, 193–203.

Geshwind, N., and Levitsky, W. Human brain: Left-right asymmetries in temporal speech region. *Science*, 1968, *161*, 186–187.

Giannitrapani, D. Developing concepts of lateralization of cerebral functions. *Cortex*, 1967, *3*, 353–370.

Griffith, H., and Davidson, M. Long-term changes in intellect and behavior after hemispherectomy. *Journal of Neurology, Neurosurgery, and Psychiatry*, 1966, *29*, 571–576.

Hamilton, C., and Lund, J. Visual discrimination of movement: Midbrain or forebrain? *Science, N.Y.*, 1970, *170*, 1428–1430.

Hamilton, C. R., Tieman, S. B., and Farrell, W. S. Cerebral dominance in monkeys? *Neurophyschologia*, 1974, *12*, 193–197.

Harris, L. J., Wagner, N., and Wilkinson, J. Hand differences in braille discrimination by blind and sighted subjects. Presented to the 4th Meeting, International Neuropsychology Society, Toronto, 1976.

Hines, D., Satz, P., Schell, B., and Schmidlin, S. Differential recall of digits in the left and right visual half-fields under free and fixed order of recall. *Neuropsychologia*, 1969, *7*, 13–22.

Jasper, H. The ten twenty electrode system of the International Federation. *Electroencephalography and Clinical Neurophysiology*, 1958, *10*, 371–375.

Jung, R. Summary of the conference. In V. B. Mountcastle (Ed.), *Interhemispheric relations and cerebral dominance*. Baltimore: Johns Hopkins Press, 1962.

Kimura, D. Some effects of temporal lobe damage on auditory perception. *Canadian Journal of Psychology*, 1961, *15*, 156–165.

Kimura, D. Speech lateralization in young children as determined by an auditory test. *Journal of Comparative and Physiological Psychology*, 1963, *56*, 899–902.

Kimura, D. Left-right differences in the perception of melodies. *Quarterly Journal of Experimental Psychology*, 1964, *14*, 355–358.

Kimura, D. Dual functional asymmetry of the brain in visual perception. *Neuropsychologia*, 1966, *4*, 275–285.

Kimura, D. Functional asymmetry of the brain in dichotic listening. *Cortex*, 1967, *3*, 163–178.

Kimura, D., and Folb, S. Neural processing of backwards speech sounds. *Science*, 1968, *161*, 395–396.

Kinsbourne, M. Cerebral basis of asymmetries in attention. *Acta Psychologia*, 1970, *33*, 193–201.

Kinsbourne, M. Lateral interactions in the brain. In M. Kinsbourne and W. Smith (Eds.), *Hemispheric disconnection and cerebral function*. Springfield, Illinois: Charles C Thomas, 1974.(a)

Kinsbourne, M. Mechanisms of hemispheric interaction in man. In M. Kinsbourne and W. L. Smith (Eds.), *Hemispheric disconnection and cerebral function*. Springfield, Illinois: Charles C Thomas, 1974.(b)

Kinsbourne, M. The ontogeny of cerebral dominance. Paper presented to New York Academy of Science Conference on Developmental Psycholinguistics and Communication Disorders, New York, 1975.(a)

Kinsbourne, M. Minor hemisphere language and cerebral maturation. In E. Lenneberg and E. Lenneberg (Eds.), *Foundations of language development: A mutidisciplinary approach*. Paris: UNESCO; New York: Academic Press, 1975.(b)

Kinsbourne, M., and Fisher, M. Latency of uncrossed and crossed reaction time in callosal agenesis. *Neuropsychologia*, 1971, 9, 471–472.

Klein, D., Moscovitch, M., and Vigna, R. Attentional mechanisms and asymmetries in tachistoscopic recognition of words and faces. *Neuropsychologia*, 1976, 14, 55–66.

Knox, C., and Kimura, D. Cerebral processing of nonverbal sounds in boys and girls. *Neuropsychologia*, 1968, 6, 1–11.

Kohn, B., and Dennis, M. Patterns of hemispheric specialization after hemideconnection for infantile hemiplegia. In M. Kinsbourne and W. L. Smith (Eds.), *Hemispheric disconnection and cerebral function*. Springfield, Illinois: Charles C Thomas, 1974.

Krashen, S., and Harshman, R. Lateralization and the critical period. Working papers in phonetics (UCLA), 1972, 23, 13–21.

Landsdell, H. Verbal and non-verbal factors in right-hemisphere speech: Relations to early neurological history. *Journal of Comparative and Physiological Psychology*, 1969, 69, 734–738.

LeMay, M., and Culebras, A. Human brain—morphologic differences in the hemispheres demonstrable by carotid arteriography. *New England Journal of Medicine*, 1972, 287, 168–170.

LeMay, M., and Geshwind, N. Hemispheric differences in the brains of great apes. *Brain Behavior and Evolution*, 1975, 11, 48–52.

Lenneberg, E. *Biological foundations of language*. New York: John Wiley and Sons, 1967.

Lenneberg, E. Language and brain: Developmental aspects. *Neurosciences Research Program Bulletin*, 1974, 12, No. 4.

Levy, J. Possible basis for the evolution of lateral specialization in the human brain. *Nature*, 1969, 224, 614–615.

Levy, J. Psychobiological implications of bilateral asymmetry. In S. J. Dimond and J. G. Beaumont (Eds.), *Hemisphere function in the brain*. New York: John Wiley and Sons, 1974.

Levy, J., Trevarthen, C., and Sperry, R. W. Perception of bilateral chimeric figures following hemispheric deconnexion. *Brain*, 1972, 95, 61–78.

Levy-Agresti, J., and Sperry, R. W. Differential perceptual capacities in major and minor hemispheres. *Proceedings of the National Academy of Sciences of the United States*, 1968, 61, 1151.

Liberman, A. M. The specialization of the language hemisphere. In F. O. Schmitt and F. G. Worden (Eds.), *The neurosciences third study program*. Cambridge, Massachusetts: M.I.T. Press, 1974.

Lukianowicz, M. S. *Temporary regression in the development of some cognitive and linguistic skills*. Unpublished manuscript, 1974.

Luria, A. R., and Karasseva, T. A. Disturbances of auditory-speech memory in focal lesions of the deep regions of the left temporal lobe. *Neuropsychologia*, 1968, 6, 97–104.

Marcel, T., Katz, L., and Smith, M. Laterality and reading proficience. *Neuropsychologia*, 1974, 12, 131–139.

Marler, P. Birdsong and speech development: Could there be parallels? *American Scientist*, 1970, 58, 669–673.

Matsumiya, Y., Tagliasco, V., Lombroso, C.T., and Goodglass, H. Auditory evoked response: Meaningfulness of stimulus and interhemispheric asymmetry. *Science*, 1972, 175, 790–792.

McKeever, W. F., and Huling, M. P. Lateral dominance and tachistoscopic word recognition performance obtained with simultaneous bilateral input. *Neuropsychologia*, 1971, 9, 15–20.

Meikle, T. H., and Sechzer, J. A. Interocular transfer of brightness discrimination in split-brain cats. *Science*, 1960, 132, 734–735.

Miller, E. Handedness and the pattern of human ability. *British Journal of Psychology*, 1971, *62*, 111–112.

Milner, B. Psychological defects produced by temporal lobe excision. Research Publication, *Assn. for Research on Nervous and Mental Disease*, 1958, *36*, 244–257.

Milner, B. Laterality effects in audition. In V. B. Mountcastle (Ed.), *Interhemispheric relations and cerebral dominance*. Baltimore: Johns Hopkins Press, 1962.

Milner, B. Some effects of frontal lobectomy in man. In J. M. Warren and K. Akert (Eds.), *The frontal granular cortex and behavior*. New York: McGraw-Hill, 1964.

Milner, B. Visual recognition and recall after right temporal lobe excision in man. *Neuropsychologia*, 1968, *7*, 191–209.

Mishkin, M., and Forgays, D. Word recognition as a function of retinal locus. *Journal of Experimental Psychology*, 1952, *43*, 43–48.

Morrell, L., and Salamy, J. Hemispheric asymmetry of electrocortical responses to speech stimuli. *Science*, 1971, *174*, 164–166.

Moscovitch, M. A choice reaction time study assessing the verbal behavior of the minor hemisphere in normal, adult humans. *Journal of Comparative and Physiological Psychology*, 1972, *80*, 66–74.

Myers, R. E. The neocortical commissures and interhemispheric transmission of information. In G. Ettlinger (Ed.), *Functions of the corpus callosum*. Boston: Little, Brown, 1965.

Nagafuchi, M. Development of dichotic and monaural hearing abilities in young children. *Acta Otolaryngologica*, 1970, *69*, 409–414.

Nebes, R. D. Handedness and the perception of part–whole relationships. *Cortex*, 1971, *7*, 350–356.

Neville, H.J. Electrographic correlates of lateral asymmetry in the processing of verbal and nonverbal auditory stimuli. *Journal of Psycholinguistic Research*, 1974, *3*, No. 2.

Neville, H. J. *The development of cerebral specialization in normal and congenitally deaf children: An evoked potential and behavioral study*. Unpublished doctoral dissertation, Cornell University, 1975.

Newcombe, F., and Russell, W. Dissociated visual perceptual and spatial deficits in focal lesions of the right hemisphere. *Journals of Neurology, Neurosurgery and Psychiatry*, 1969, *32*, 73–81.

Nottebohm, F. Ontogeny of bird song. *Science*, 1970, *167*, 950–956.

Nottebohm, F. Cerebral lateralization in birds. In E. Lenneberg (Ed.), *Language and brain: Developmental aspects*. NRP Bulletin 12: No. 4, 1974.

Nottebohm, F., Stokes, T. M., and Leonard, C. M. Central control of song in the canary, *Serinus Canaria Neuroscience Abstracts*, Volume 1. Fifth Annual Meeting Society for Neuroscience, New York City, 1975. P. 556.

O'Leary, J. Discussion. In V. Mountcastle (Ed.), *Interhemispheric relation and cerebral dominance*. Baltimore: Johns Hopkins Press, 1962. P. 39.

Oléron, P. *Recherches sur le development mental des sourds-muets*. Paris: Centre National de Recherche Scientifique, 1957.

Olson, Madelyn N. Laterality differences in tachistoscopic word recognition in normal and delayed readers in elementary school. *Neuropsychologia*, 1973, *11*, 343–350.

Orbach, J. Differential recognition of Hebrew and English words in right and left visual fields as function of cerebral dominance and reading habits. *Neuropsychologia*, 1967, *5*, 127–134.

Orton, S. *Reading, writing and speech problems in children*. London: Chapman and Hall, 1937.

Porter, R. J., and Berlin, C. I. On interpreting developmental changes in the dichotic right-ear advantage. *Brain and Language*, 1974, *1*, No. 3.

Powell, C. A. *Tachistoscopic recognition of unfamiliar visual material.* Unpublished thesis, McGill University, 1962.

Reitan, R. M., and Tarshes, E. L. Differential effects of lateralized brain lesions on the trail making task. *Journal of Nervous and Mental Diseases,* 1959, *129,* 257–262.

Rhodes, L. E., Dustman, R. E., and Beck, E. C. The visual evoked response; a comparison of bright and dull children. *Electroencepholography and Clinical Neurophysiology,* 1969, *27,* 364–372.

Richlin, M., Weisinger, M., Weinstein, S., Giannini, M., and Morganstern, M. Interhemispheric asymmetries of evoked cortical responses in retarded and normal children. *Cortex,* 1971, *7,* 98–105.

Rizzolatti, G., Umiltà, C., and Berlucci, G. Opposite superiorities of the right and left cerebral hemispheres in discriminative reaction time to physiognomical and alphabetical material. *Brain,* 1971, *94,* 431–442.

Rosenweig, M. R. Representations of the two ears at the auditory cortex. *American Journal of Physiology,* 1951, *167,* 147–158.

Russo, M., and Vignolo, L. A. Visual figure-ground discrimination in patients with unilateral cerebral disease. *Cortex,* 1967, *3,* 113–127.

Satz, P. Developmental dyslexia: An evaluation of a theory, In P. Sata and J. Ross (Eds.), *The disabled learner: Early detection and intervention.* Rotterdam University Press, 1973.

Satz, P., Achenbach, U., Pattishall, E., and Fennell, E. Order of report, ear asymmetry and handedness in dichotic listening. *Cortex,* 1965, *1,* 377–396.

Saul R. E., and Gott, P. S. Compensatory mechanisms in agensis of the corpus callosum. Paper presented to the 25th Annual Meeting of the American Academy of Neurology, Boston, 1973.

Saul, R. E., and Sperry, R. W. Absence of commissurotomy symptoms with agenesis of the corpus callosum. *Neurology,* 1968, *18,* 307.

Semmes, J. Hemispheric specialization: A possible clue to mechanism. *Neuropsychologia,* 1968, *6,* 11–27.

Sinha, S. P. *The role of the temporal lobe in hearing.* Master's thesis, McGill University, 1959.

Smith, A., and Sugar, O. Development of above normal language and intelligence 21 years after left hemispherectomy. *Neurology,* 1975, *25* (9), 813–818.

Spellacy, F. J. Lateral preferences in the identification of patterned stimuli. *Journal of the Acoustical Society of America,* 1970, *47,* 574–578.

Sperry, R. *Mental unity following surgical disconnection of the cerebral hemispheres.* The Harvey Lectures, Series 62. New York: Academic Press, 1968.

Sperry, R. W. Perception in the absence of the neocortical commissures. *Research Publications, Association for Research in Nervous and Mental Disease,* 1970, *48,* 123–138.

Sperry, R. W. Lateral specialization in the surgically separated hemispheres. In F. O. Schmitt and F. G. Worden (Eds.), *The neurosciences: Third study program.* Cambridge, Mass.: M.I.T. Press, 1974.

Spreen, O., Spellacy, F. J., and Reid, J. R. The effect of interstimulus interval and intensity on ear asymmetry for nonverbal stimuli in dichotic listening. *Neuropsychologia,* 1970, *8,* 245–250.

Springer, S. P. Hemispheric specialization for speech opposed by contralateral noise. *Perception and Psychophysics,* 1973, *13,* 391–393.

Studdert-Kennedy, M. The perception of speech. In T. A. Sebeok (Ed.), *Current trends in linguistics* (Vol. 12). The Hague: Mouton, 1970.

Teuber, H., and Diamond, S. Effects of brain injury in man on binaural localization of sounds. Paper read at 27th Annual Meeting of the Eastern Psychological Association, Atlantic City, 1956.

Tibensky and Moscovitch. Unpublished manuscript reported in preprint of Klein *et al*, 1976.

Travis, L. E., and Lindsley, D. B. Action current. Study of handedness in relation to stuttering. *Journal of Experimental Psychology*, 1933, *16*, 258–270.

Trevarthen, C. Functional interactions between the cerebral hemispheres of the split brain monkey. In E. Ettlinger (Ed.), *Functions of the corpus callosum*. Boston: Little, Brown, 1965.

Trevarthen, C. Functional relations of disconnected hemispheres with the brains—and with each other: Monkey and man. In M. Kinsbourne, and W. L. Smith (Eds.), *Hemispheric disconnection and cerebral function*. Springfield, Illinois: Charles C Thomas, 1974.

Tunturi, A. R. A study on the pathway from the medial geniculate body to the acoustic cortex in the dog. *American Journal of Physiology*, 1946, *147*, 313–319.

Umiltà, C., Rizzolatti, G., Marzi, C. A., Zamboni, G., Franzini, C., Camarda, R., and Berlucchi, G. Hemispheric differences in normal human subjects: Further evidence from study of reaction time to lateralized visual stimuli. *Brain Research*, 1973, *49*, 499–500.

Vaughn, H., and Ritter, W. The sources of auditory evoked responses recorded from the human scalp. *Electroencephalography and Clinical Neurophysiology*, 1970, *28*, 360–367.

Warren, J. M. The development of paw preference in cats and monkeys. *Journal of General Psychology*, 1958, *93*, 229–236.

Webster, W. G. Functional asymmetry between the cerebral hemispheres of the cat. *Neuropsychologia*, 1972, *10*, 75–87.

Weinstein, S. Differences in effects of brain wounds implicating right or left hemispheres. In V. B. Mountcastle (Ed.), *Interhemispheric relations and cerebral dominance*. Baltimore: Johns Hopkins Press, 1962.

White, M. J. Laterality differences in perception: A review. *Psychological Bulletin*, 1969, *72*, 387–405.

Wood, C. C. Auditory and phonetic levels of processing in speech perception: Neurophysiological and information processing analyses. *Journal of Experimental Psychology: Human Perception and Performance*, 1975, *10*, 3–20.

Wood, C. C., Goff, W. R., and Day, R. S. Auditory evoked potentials during speech perception. *Science*, 1971, *173*, 1248–1251.

Zaidel, D., and Sperry, R. W. Functional reorganization following commissurotomy in man. In *Biology annual report*, 1972.

Zurif, E., and Bryden, M. P. Familial handedness and left right differences in auditory and visual perception. *Neuropsychologia*, 1969, *1*, 179–187.

INDEX